The Use and Design of Questionnaires

The Use and Design of Questionnaires

ELAINE MCCOLL AND ROGER THOMAS

Published by
The Royal College of General Practitioners
2000

The Royal College of General Practitioners
was founded in 1952 with this object:

"To encourage, foster and maintain the highest possible standards in general practice and for that purpose to take or join with others in taking steps consistent with the charitable nature of that object
which may assist towards the same."

Among its responsibilities under its Royal Charter
the College is entitled to:

"Encourage the publication by general medical practitioners of research into medical or scientific subjects with a view to the improvement of general medical practice in any field and to undertake or assist
others in undertaking such research.

Diffuse information on all matters affecting general practice and establish, print, publish, issue and cir-
culate such papers, journals, magazines, books, periodicals, and publications and hold such meetings,
conferences, seminars and instructional courses as may assist the object of the College."

First impression 2000

Published by the Royal College of General Practitioners
14 Princes Gate
Hyde Park
London, SW7 1PU

Printed and bound by BSC Print Ltd, Wimbledon

ISBN 0 85084 247 6

CONTENTS

· 1 ·

QUANTITATIVE SURVEY RESEARCH

WHAT IS QUANTITATIVE SURVEY RESEARCH?

The quantitative survey method may be defined as 'a set of scientific procedures for collecting information and making quantitative inferences about populations'. One principal tool used by the quantitative survey researcher to achieve this objective is scientific sampling of populations. The other principal tool is the survey questionnaire. This has been defined as:

> 'an instrument consisting of a series of questions and/or attitude-opinion statements designed to elicit responses which can be converted into measures of the variable under investigation'. *(Franklin and Osborne, 1971)*

Quantitative surveys aim to convert the information they collect to *meaningful numbers* by *classifying, counting and scoring*, followed at the analysis stage by *summarising and estimating*. The central challenge is to devise classifications and scoring systems that, on the one hand, are practical in terms of the data collection process and, on the other hand, satisfy the requirements of data analysis and the making of population estimates. For example, sample units/respondents can be *classified and counted*, on the basis of their questionnaire responses, according to attributes such as their age, their diagnosis, their occupation, their socio-economic class etc. Or they can be *scored* according to the amount of something they do, the frequency of their symptoms, their quality of life measured by a set of questions, the direction and strength of their opinion on a topic, their expressed level of satisfaction etc.

Taken together, counts (which in turn can be converted to rates, percentages and so on) and scores provide summary measures of the sample as a whole. From these sample values, *estimates* of these parameters in the underlying population can be made, using appropriate statistical techniques. Parameters of interest may include age distribution, what proportion have engaged in some form of behaviour, the average rate of performing some behaviour, what proportion are satisfied with a service received and so on.

TYPES OF INFORMATION THAT MAY BE GATHERED IN A SURVEY

Depending on the objectives of the data collection exercise, questionnaire surveys may be used to gather one or more of the following types of information (based on Dillman, 1978; p80):

- *Attributes* – according to Dillman, 'what people are' (for example, personal characteristics, such as age, gender, marital status, personal and familial medical history etc.). Attributes may be seen as something that are an intrinsic and relatively stable part of the respondent, as opposed to something s/he does. Attributes are generally regarded as facts, but of course the *reporting* of facts in surveys may be subject to distortions.

- *Behaviour* and *events* – 'what people do' (for example, frequency of engaging in potentially risky behaviour such as smoking or alcohol consumption) or 'what has happened in people's lives' (for example, having a particular acute disease, suffering a bereavement). Questions about behaviour may refer to past, current or (intended) future behaviour; questions about events usually refer to the past.

- *Beliefs / knowledge* – 'what people think is true' (for instance, beliefs and understanding regarding the causes of illness). Assessing beliefs means assessing what respondents believe to be true or false, correct or incorrect. There is no implied value judgement about what is 'good' or 'bad'. Belief questions include those which test a respondent's knowledge of facts, as well as those which tap into issues for which there is no agreed 'correct' answer.

- *Attitudes / opinions / reasons for doing things etc* – 'what people say they want', 'how people feel about something' (for example, satisfaction with health care services). Attitudes and opinions are essentially evaluative, reflecting respondents' value judgements about what is good or bad, effective or ineffective, desirable or undesirable and so on. Measuring attitudes involves making assumptions about how people structure their perceptual world. For example, it is no use asking questions to elicit people's attitudes to 'this Health Trust' if they have no concept of 'this Health Trust'. Sometimes, questions may be posed in such a way that they tap a mixture of attitudes and beliefs, but the distinction is still usefully made (Fishbein, 1967; Dillman, 1978).

It is important to bear these distinctions in mind when designing questionnaires and determining question wording. Unless the researcher is clear about what s/he is trying to measure, the information yielded by the question may not be what is actually required.

EXERCISE 1

For each of the questions listed below, indicate which category of information – attribute / fact; behaviour; knowledge / belief; attitude / opinion – it is capturing. Give reasons for your choice.

1. Do you take a daily dose of aspirin?

2. What is the address of your nearest dispensing chemist?

3. Are you currently married?

4. Have you ever had an abortion?

5. Should all people who have had a heart attack take a daily dose of aspirin?

6. Should aspirin be available free of charge to anyone who has had a heart attack?

7. Are you planning a pregnancy within the next two years?

8. Why did you decide against having a blood transfusion?

For answers, see Appendix 1.

APPLICATIONS OF QUANTITATIVE SURVEY RESEARCH

In the health field, quantitative surveys are used in the following areas:

- *epidemiology* (for example, health needs assessments, health and lifestyle surveys, surveys of specific disease groups)

- *health services research* (for example, in the context of trials of health care interventions and in health technology assessment, as well as in assessments of health-related behaviour and quality of life)

- *audit* and other *quality assurance* initiatives (for example, in patient satisfaction surveys).

Sometimes surveys are carried out not for these instrumental reasons but to expand basic scientific knowledge; and data collection using questionnaires may also be used in the context of other research designs. For example, in randomised controlled trials of health care interventions, it is increasingly common to gather information on patient outcomes using self-completion questionnaires.

STAGES IN THE SURVEY PROCESS

The key stages in carrying out a survey are summarised in Box 1. In this workbook, the main focus is on steps 6 to 10. For further details on other aspects of the survey research process, see one of the many comprehensive texts available (for example, Moser and Kalton, 1971; Abramson, 1990; Oppenheim, 1992; Fink, 1995; Crombie and Davies, 1996. Bowling, 1997a; Øvretveit, 1998).

BOX 1

Steps in a survey (after Oppenheim, 1992)

1. Define the **aims of the study**

2. **Review current state of knowledge** on the topic

3. **Conceptualise** the study (carefully define the concepts you wish to measure)

4. Determine **appropriate study design** and assess feasibility within resource constraints

5. Decide upon **hypotheses** to be investigated, determine and operationalise **data requirements**

6. **Choose** most appropriate **method of data collection**

7. **Design** or adapt **data collection instruments**

8. Conduct **pilot work** and refine methods and instruments

9. Design and select **sample**

10. Conduct **data collection** (often termed 'field work')

11. **Process** data

12. **Analyse** data

13. **Report** findings

· 2 ·

VALIDITY AND RELIABILITY IN SURVEY RESEARCH

From a scientific viewpoint, survey research is concerned with **measuring** the attributes, behaviour etc of human beings or other entities. Typically, the objective is to collect information from patients, health professionals or members of the general public on personal circumstances, behaviour, attitudes, expectations etc. The aim is then to collect information that is **valid** (in other words, to measure the quantity or concept that is supposed to be measured) and **reliable** (in other words, to measure the quantity or concept in a consistent or reproducible manner). The risk of collecting information that fails either or both of these tests is ever-present.

One reason for this is that survey respondents, wishing to be polite, will often produce an answer even if they do not fully understand the question, or are unable or unwilling to answer it adequately and correctly. Thus, for example, asking people whether they have ever suffered from 'hyperchoriasis' will produce many answers of 'No' and probably a few 'Yes' answers, but all must be **invalid** since this is an invented disease name. On the other hand, a single question asking respondents whether they have recently been depressed may produce answers that are valid (in so far as the respondents understand what 'depressed' means and are prepared to reveal the information), but are **unreliable**, since the wording is vague and their current mood tends to affect what they say. Moreover, procedures or instruments that are **reliable** are not always or necessarily **valid** for their purpose. The question about 'hyperchoriasis' might well provide quite stable and reliable responses over time, particularly when aggregated across a set of respondents, even though quite meaningless.

ASPECTS OF VALIDITY

As already noted, **validity** refers to whether the question is really measuring the construct or concept of interest. As a somewhat extreme example, a question about use of analgesics would not be a particularly valid measure of a person's experience of pain, since factors other than the incidence and severity of pain influence consumption of analgesics. In assessing whether a question or questionnaire is valid, a number of different aspects of validity need to be taken into account.

- *Face validity* – whether 'on the face of it', the question(s) are measuring what they are supposed to measure. Face validity is generally assessed informally, by having non-expert and untrained 'judges' (for example, colleagues, family or friends) examine the questionnaire to see whether the items look all right to them. For example, such judges might feel that the question 'Have you been feeling low-spirited recently?' was valid as a measure of depression. This opinion is worth having, since it indicates that ordinary people can comprehend a term such a 'low-spirited' – perhaps better than the term 'depressed'. However, it is not a sufficient test of the validity of the question.

- *Content validity* – whether the choice of items and the relative importance given to each is appropriate in the eyes of those who have some knowledge of the topic area. This is best achieved by having the questionnaire critiqued by a panel of people knowledgeable about the topic, including members of the target population. This critique involves assessing whether the questionnaire covers everything it should and does not include extraneous matter. For example, the clinical concept of 'depression' covers other symptoms besides feeling low-spirited. However, favourable assessments of content validity do not in themselves *guarantee* that the measure will produce valid information.

- *Construct validity* – whether the results obtained using the questionnaire confirm expected statistical relationships, the expectations being derived from underlying theory. In drafting questions we all make theoretical assumptions about how concepts are related to one another and we should test these assumptions. One of the most common ways of assessing construct validity is through *known-group validity*. This involves making comparisons across groups who would *a priori* be expected to yield different results. For example, if a questionnaire was designed to assess health status, one would expect people with diagnosed, chronic disease to have poorer scores than those with no known current illnesses. Another way of establishing construct validity is through *multi-trait multi-method analysis*

(Campbell and Fiske, 1959). This is most appropriate in the assessment of the validity of measures of health status / well-being. It involves administering more than one instrument which purport to measure similar domains of health (for example, SF-36 and Nottingham Health Profile) and examining the correlation between scores on the various instruments. Higher correlations between scores on domains measuring similar concepts, either within the one instrument or across instruments, and weaker correlations between domains measuring dissimilar traits are indicative of construct validity.

- *Criterion validity* – whether the question / questionnaire yields results which correspond with those obtained by another, 'gold-standard' method, applied simultaneously (*concurrent validity*) or which forecast a criterion value (*predictive validity*). For example, declared smoking status could be validated by a measurement of cotinine in the saliva. Like construct validity, criterion validity is assessed formally, using statistical techniques such as correlation. A major problem with assessing criterion validity is a lack of appropriate 'gold-standard' measures.

- *Freedom from absolute or relative bias* – whether the question / questionnaire yields results which fairly reflect the distribution of some target variable in the population and in sub-populations. An example of *absolute* bias would be where a question or set of questions which may be valid in some senses as a measure of 'disability', is still open to objection because it gives too high or too low an estimate of the prevalence of disability, or a distorted distribution of severity of disability, in the population. An example of *relative* bias would be where the questions obtained responses from elderly people which made them seem less disabled than younger people with similar objective incapacities. (Bias can also arise from faulty sampling methods or from non-response, but in this section we are talking about *measurement* or *response bias*.)

For a more detailed discussion of this topic, see Litwin (1995); Streiner and Norman (1989); Tulsky (1990).

ASPECTS OF RELIABILITY

As already noted, **reliability** refers to whether the question or questionnaire is measuring things in a consistent or reproducible way. As with validity, there are a number of different approaches to measuring reliability:

- *Test-retest reliability* – this is the most logically straightforward measure of reliability. It involves checking whether the same answer is obtained if the question is asked of the same individual at two

points in time, during which period no real change has occurred in that individual in relevant respects. It is important to choose an interval between the two measurements that is long enough that respondents are not simply recalling and repeating their initial answer, but is not so long that real change may have taken place. In practice it is often difficult to apply a satisfactory test-retest check because of the difficulty of simultaneously satisfying both the 'no recall bias' and the 'no real change' conditions.

- *Internal consistency* – whether responses to questions measuring the same or a related concept are consistent with each other. The idea here is that all questions suffer from some degree of response unreliability, but that the degree of logical and conceptual consistency found between responses to questions designed to capture the same property of a subject (for example, satisfaction with doctors' inter-personal skills) provides an indication of the reliability of those responses. Using a carefully designed *set of questions* to measure a given concept also enables us to construct a more reliable measure. This is done by combining responses to the set of questions to produce a composite scale score. This procedure 'distils out' the consistent common strand of meaning, because of the tendency for random errors to cancel each other out. The internal consistency of the scale as a measuring instrument is then assessed using statistical measures based on how well the constituent items are correlated with each other.

- *Within-rater* (within-observer, within-interviewer) *reliability* and *between-rater* (between-observer, between-interviewer) reliability are special cases of test-retest reliability. The first refers to whether the same data collector or assessor (usually an interviewer in the context of questionnaire surveys, but in other contexts it could be a diagnostician) obtains the same responses from a given individual on two occasions, given that no real change has occurred in the meantime. The second refers to whether two (or more) different interviewers obtain the same responses from a given individual, given no real change.

The idea which links the 'test-retest' and the 'internal consistency' conceptions of reliability is *random measurement error*. If a method of measuring some attribute is subject to much random error, the results of applying it on separate occasions will tend to diverge (in a random way). Similarly, if two measures of the same attribute are each subject to random error, they will also produce results which diverge in a random way.

For a more detailed discussion of this topic, see Litwin (1995); Streiner and Norman (1989); Tulsky (1990).

BIAS

Bias can be defined as 'any process at any stage of inference which tends to produce results or conclusions that differ systematically from the truth' (Sackett, 1979). Throughout the survey process there is the potential for bias to be introduced. It is possible for a survey measure to be reasonably *valid* (measuring the right thing) and reasonably *reliable* (free of random error), but still subject to serious *bias* (producing 'readings' that are systematically too high or too low). Notice that 'bias' is a property of methods or procedures, not a property of individual data sets. Survey data sets which are produced using unbiased methods will still not, in general, exactly reflect the population from which they are drawn because of the random variance that is inherent in sampling or measurement procedures.

OTHER POTENTIAL SOURCES OF ERROR

Having introduced the ideas of *(in)validity*, *(un)reliability* and *bias*, we next consider in more detail the ways in which they can arise in quantitative surveys. Key sources of potential error in survey research (some may also occur in other study designs) are listed below. Some are likely to give rise to systematic error (bias); others are more likely to cause random error or 'noise'.

- *Faulty problem definition* – this arises from looking at the 'wrong' problem or issue, or only looking at part of the issue. For example, low uptake of cervical screening may prompt a survey into women's beliefs about and attitudes to smear tests. But health beliefs and attitudes may be only part of the picture – low uptake may also reflect difficulties of access, relating to the time and location of clinics and therefore requiring collection of data on behaviour (for example, how people travel to the clinic) and attributes (for example, car ownership, employment status, working hours).

- *Surrogate information error* – this is caused by a mis-match between the information really required to address the research aims and the information sought by the researcher for reasons of practicality or convenience. For example, it can arise where past behaviour is used as a surrogate for future behaviour, or where information on behavioural intentions is used as a surrogate for evidence on actual behaviour.

- *Defective definition of the study population* – this occurs when the study population is not clearly defined in terms of the research aims and objectives. For example, if the aim is to measure access to a general practice surgery, the population of interest is all patients registered with that practice. A questionnaire survey administered on practice premises to those attending for appointments would miss an important section of this population, and would almost certainly be biased in favour of those with fewer access problems (but more health problems).

- *Sampling frame not representative of population* – if the frame or list from which the sample is drawn is not an adequate representation of the underlying population, sampling frame bias will occur. For example, electoral registers are typically biased against students and other 'floating citizens' who have not registered to vote, or who are ineligible to vote (for example, the homeless, foreign nationals etc).

- *Selection error* – this may arise where a non-probability method of sampling (i.e. a method which does not give each member of the underlying population a known chance of being included) is used. For example, 'invited' samples, such as reader surveys carried out by a journal, are typically non-representative; the readership of even a professional journal is unlikely to be truly representative of all members of that profession.

- *Non-response error* – this is one of the most significant sources of error in survey research, since few, if any, surveys achieve a true response rate that is close to 100%. Surveys with a low response rate have low precision because the sample size is then lower than intended, so that the confidence intervals around any estimates of population parameters (for example, mean age or percentage holding a particular opinion) are widened. Poor response rates are also likely to be a source of bias, since non-respondents tend to differ from respondents in systematic ways that are relevant to the purpose of the enquiry. For example, people who are too busy to take part in a survey are likely to differ in terms of life-cycle stage and in many aspects of their behaviour and attitudes from people who have plenty of time to spare.

- *Auspices / sponsorship bias* – while it is generally considered sound ethical practice to declare who is responsible for commissioning and conducting a survey, respondents' behaviour, both in terms of decisions of whether or not to respond and in respect of the answers given, may be coloured by knowledge of the sponsors. For example, the wish to be polite and not appear ungrateful, or concerns about the repercussions for their treatment, may lead patients to rate their satisfaction with health care more highly when a survey is being conducted by their doctors than they would if it were being carried out by independent researchers.

- *Interviewer effects* – in surveys administered by interviewers, either face-to-face with respondents or over the telephone, the interaction between interviewer and respondent may affect the quantity and quality of response; in surveys with multiple interviewers, observed differences in response patterns may be an artefact of the survey being administered by different interviewers (i.e. poor between-rater reliability) rather than a reflection of true underlying differences between respondents. Different interviewers may pose questions in subtly different ways or may prompt, probe or record responses to a greater or lesser extent. More fundamentally, interviewer characteristics and behaviour may affect response rates, which in turn affects the characteristics of the sub-samples actually interviewed by different interviewers. These two interviewer effects combined may be particularly damaging where each interviewer works in his/her own area, so that what appear to be differences between areas are actually due partly to differences in interviewer performance.

- *Measurement error* – a poorly worded question and/or set of response categories may produce a distorted version of the variable that the researcher intends to measure (a version of invalidity – see above). As we have seen above, it is important to be clear about what type of information is to be gathered and to pose the question appropriately.

- *Response bias* – the content and wording of questions may lead to distortion and bias in respondents' answers. Potential problems include:

  - *recall bias* – in questions involving memory, errors of omission and of telescoping (misplacing an event in time) may occur

  - *estimation bias* – particularly under pressure, many individuals have difficulties in estimating, calculating and extrapolating quantitative information (for example, in working out annual or monthly consumption patterns)

  - *social desirability bias* – in questions on behaviour and attitudes in particular, the desire to appear in a good light may cause respondents to distort their answers, for example to under-report socially undesirable behaviour such as excessive alcohol consumption.

Response bias is particularly likely to arise where respondents are asked questions that are vague or call for information that they do not have readily available. In such cases they tend to look for clues as to what they are 'supposed to say' in the wording of the question and any predetermined response categories.

- *Data recording and processing error* – at each stage in recording, coding, entering and validating data, errors may arise; responses may be incorrectly recorded (for example, a word descriptor circled instead of the corresponding code number) or figures may be transposed in recording or entering data (for example, 213 instead of 231).

- *Data analysis error* – errors may occur both in the transformation of data (for example, in combining responses to two or more questions to yield an aggregate measure of behaviour, belief or attitude) and in applying statistical techniques (for example, choosing tests that are inappropriate to the data).

- *Interpretation error* – as with data analysis, an imperfect understanding of the statistical techniques may lead to the findings being misinterpreted. In particular, in non-experimental study designs, it is extremely dangerous to infer causal relationships from observed associations (correlation between variables) without developing and testing a theory leading to explicit hypotheses as to what associations should (and should not) be expected.

In the real world of survey research, total elimination of error and bias is impossible. Fortunately, in most applications a limited amount of estimation error can be tolerated, particularly if the limits of error can themselves be estimated. However, the survey researcher must be aware of the potential for error and, at each step in the survey process, must take steps to minimise the threat. In the sections that follow, methods for reducing bias and error are discussed in greater detail.

· 3 ·

CHOOSING THE METHOD OF DATA COLLECTION

In quantitative survey research, the most versatile and commonly used modes of data collection are self-completion questionnaires, face-to-face (sometimes termed 'field') interviews and telephone interviews. These can be used in various combinations. Self-completion methods are very popular, largely because they are cheaper and require less specialised resources than interviewing. Postal administration is probably the most common method of administering self-completion questionnaires, but they can also be administered directly to 'captive audiences', for example patients in a waiting room; this approach allows for some supervision and assistance of respondents.

No one mode of data collection has been shown to be superior in all respects, as can be seen from Table 1. Rather, the most appropriate method is likely to depend on the study population, survey topic, and nature and complexity of data to be collected. Resource constraints will also influence the choice of method. In particular, given the statistical need in quantitative survey work to accumulate relatively large samples, interview approaches are likely to be too resource-intensive and expensive for many primary care surveys. In this workbook, therefore, we concentrate on postal and other self-completion surveys.

Further reading
See Articles 1 and 2

Table 1
Advantages and disadvantages of modes of questionnaire administration
(adapted from De Vaus, 1991, after Dillman, 1978)

	Face-to-face interviews	Telephone interviews	Postal questionnaires
Response rates			
General population samples	Usually best	Usually lower than face-to-face	Poor to good
Special population samples	Usually good	Satisfactory to best	Satisfactory to good
Representative samples			
Avoidance of refusal bias	Depends on good interviewer technique	Depends on good interviewer technique	Poor
Control over who completes the questionnaire	Good	Moderate	Poor to good
Gaining access to a named selected person	Good	Good for those with telephones	Poor to good
Locating the named selected person	Good	Good	Good
Ability to handle:			
Long questionnaires	Good	Moderate	Satisfactory to poor
Complex questions	Good	Moderate	Moderate to poor
Boring questions	Good	Moderate	Poor
Item non-response	Good	Good	Moderate
Filter questions	Good	Good	Moderate to poor
Question sequence control	Good	Good	Poor
Open-ended questions	Good	Good	Poor
Quality of answers			
Minimise social desirability responses	Poor	Moderate	Satisfactory
Ability to avoid distortion due to:			
Interviewer characteristics	Poor	Moderate	Good
Interviewer's opinions	Moderate	Moderate	Good
Influence of other people	Moderate	Good	Poor
Allows opportunities to consult	Moderate	Poor	Good
Implementing the survey			
Ease of finding suitable staff	Poor	Moderate	Good
Speed	Poor	Good	Poor
Cost	Poor	Moderate	Good

MINIMISING SURVEY ERROR TO ACHIEVE HIGH QUALITY DATA

As identified above, the aim of the survey researcher is to collect high quality data – in other words, data that are valid, reliable, sufficiently sensitive for their purpose, and free from mistakes, with systematic bias and inherent random error due to sampling and measurement kept to a minimum. But, as we have already seen, at each stage in the survey process threats to data quality occur.

For example, if non-probability methods of sampling are used, sampling method bias is likely – the person drawing the sample may consciously or subconsciously select 'interesting', easy to find or 'likely to co-operate' cases, rather than picking a sample that is truly representative of the underlying population. Response bias may occur in answering the questions; respondents may deliberately lie to portray themselves in a better light, especially when questions involve value judgements; in questions involving recall, they may omit events or misplace them in time. To ensure high quality data, the survey researcher must pay due attention to the design and conduct of all stages in the survey, as summarised in Box 2.

The aim should be 'to identify each aspect of the survey process that may influence either the quality or quantity of response and to shape each one of them in such a way that the best possible responses are obtained' (Dillman, 1978, p12). But the survey researcher will be faced with scarcity of resources: money, time and personnel. As Lynn (1996) states, surveys must be 'value for money' – the value of the information yielded must exceed the cost of obtaining that information. In some cases, compromises between quality and cost will be necessary. For example, a trade-off between, on the one hand, the increased precision and reduced non-response bias of a larger achieved sample following a third reminder and, on the other hand, the cost of sending that reminder.

BOX 2

Ensuring high quality data in survey research

Survey design and sampling
- Correct and appropriate design specification
- Adequate sampling frames and procedures
- Clear view of what population the results are intended to represent
- Freedom from sampling method bias

Survey measurement
- Measuring the target concept (validity)
- Freedom from measurement bias
- Control of random measurement variability (reliability)
- Adequate measurement sensitivity

Stimulating response behaviour
- Maximising rate of response
- Minimising non-response bias

Good survey management and quality control
- Timeliness
- Robust practicality
- Cost-effectiveness

Excellent **execution** cannot save a survey if the design does not fit the aims; for example, the actual population sampled does not match the target population; confounding effects are not properly controlled for (experimentally or statistically); the study design cannot support desired comparisons or conclusions; there is an inadequate sample size, causing insufficient precision in drawing conclusions about the population of interest; key measures (including key classificatory variables) are omitted; the questions and procedures used do not adequately capture the variables they are intended to measure. Similarly, excellent **design** cannot save a survey if: funding is inadequate; human and other resources are inadequate; time allowed is inadequate; and project management and quality control are inadequate.

Further reading
See Article 3

· 4 ·
IDENTIFYING THE VARIABLES FOR SURVEY RESEARCH

APPROACHES TO DETERMINING QUESTIONNAIRE CONTENT

We have already emphasised the need to ensure that we are indeed measuring what we intend to measure, and that the information we collect should be determined by our research aims and objectives. There is no single way of identifying data requirements. Rather, a combination of the following is likely to be required:

- *Literature review* – we need to determine the current state of knowledge on the topic of interest, and to be aware of existing theories and previous empirical findings. For example, for a survey of patient satisfaction, the knowledge that other researchers have found a positive correlation between age and level of satisfaction would suggest that we need to collect data on age to test whether this observed relationship holds true in our population and whether any differences in satisfaction that we find, compared with other studies, could be explained by age differences.

- *Brainstorming* – a 'brainstorming' session by the research team and others interested in the topic can be a useful source of ideas for items that might be included in the questionnaire. However, it is important to guard against including items or questions on the grounds that 'it might be interesting to know…'; there should be a clear picture of where each piece of data fits into the overall plan of analysis, and contributes to addressing the research aims and objectives.

- *Qualitative research* – particularly in researching 'new' topics or populations, qualitative research, in the form of unstructured interviews or focus groups with members of the target population, can be a very fruitful way of identifying relevant issues and concepts and of ensuring adequate face and content validity. In developing measures of health status and quality of life, it is only by asking people with the condition in question about the impact it has on their lives that we can be sure that we are measuring what is important to them, rather than to health professionals. Talking to members of the target audience also allows the researcher to

become familiar with the typical vocabulary of the subjects of the survey, thereby allowing the questions to be worded in an appropriate way. Also refer to the first workbook in this series, *An Introduction to Qualitative Methods for Health Professionals*.

- *Review of concepts and attributes to be measured* – the usefulness of results depends not only on successfully measuring outcome variables (for example, 'quality of life' or 'satisfaction with services'), but also on being able to compare key sub-groups and to provide classificatory detail about sample members which is likely to affect outcomes. We must ensure that appropriate questions are included to measure not only all the relevant outcomes, but also the concepts and variables needed to classify sample members in relevant ways.

DETERMINING THE VARIABLES TO BE INCLUDED

As a very crude rule, there is an inverse relationship between the quantity of data collected in a survey and the quality of those data. One reason for this is that there is a limit to the time and effort that respondents are prepared to devote and, if overloaded, they will start looking for short cuts to the detriment of data quality. Collecting data which are not subsequently analysed is a waste of resources and is ultimately unethical. However, surveys can also founder if some data items vital to the research aims and objectives are not collected. To ensure that adequate but not excessive quantities of data are collected, a number of techniques can be used to highlight data requirements:

- *Inventory of variables* – using the approaches described in the previous section, draw up a list of potential items for inclusion. This should include dependent and independent variables and measures of intervening, modifying and confounding factors.

- *Construction of hypothetical path diagrams* – since the relationships between independent and dependent variables are likely to be highly complex, with many possible intervening, modifying and confounding factors, path diagrams, in which the nature of these complex relationships is shown by arrows, can help to clarify what is going on. At this stage, a decision might be taken to omit some variables, perhaps because the anticipated relationship appears to be so complicated that it would be too difficult to disentangle within the design limitations of the study.

- *Tabular representation of hypotheses* – constructing path diagrams helps to specify in tabular form the hypotheses to be tested. In a tabular representation, the dependent or outcome variables are usually shown as columns and the independent variables as rows. A plus sign in the table indicates a hypothesised positive relationship between independent and dependent variables; a negative sign indicates a negative relationship; a zero indicates a hypothesis of no association; a question mark indicates that we have no prior ideas about what to expect. If we find that, for certain variables, most of the entries are zeros or question marks, we might consider dropping those variables on the grounds that they are not central to our analyses.

- *Construction of dummy tables* – a further refinement of representing hypotheses in tabular form is to draw up dummy tables just as they will appear in the survey report, but without any figures in them. This can help to ensure that data are collected on all relevant variables and in such a way as to allow the statistics of interest to be extracted or calculated (for example, if we indicate that a table of mean age is to be displayed, this will remind us to collect disaggregated data, rather than simply recording age-group).

SOURCES OF SURVEY QUESTIONS

In a later section, we discuss development and wording of questions and their associated response categories. Each survey needs to be carefully tailored to its purpose and to the type of respondent to whom it is addressed. However, many surveys on health topics will be addressing issues and concepts which have been the subject of previous research and surveys and it is important to avoid 're-inventing the wheel'. Apart from the advantages of drawing upon the expertise and experience of others, developing and refining new questions, and ensuring that they are valid and reliable, is time-consuming and expensive. In many circumstances, use can be made of existing well-validated questions or even whole questionnaires. On the other hand, the existence in the literature of a set of questions which has a relevant-sounding label does not guarantee that it is appropriate to *this* population and *this* study.

Questions on health status and quality of life
Many surveys conducted in the area of public health have the 'general health status' or 'quality of life' of respondents as the key outcome variables to be measured. As used in everyday discourse, neither of these concepts is very well defined and neither is easy to measure in ways which meet the criteria of validity, reliability, sensitivity and so on.

There is nevertheless a wealth of instruments, with established validity and reliability, for measuring health status, both in general populations and in specific disease- and age-groups. Rather than trying to develop and test a new set of questions, the researcher should first review these existing instruments and see whether any are appropriate to the aims and objectives of the planned survey. Comprehensive reviews of instruments for measuring health status and quality of life have been produced by McDowell and Newell (1987), Wilkin and colleagues (1992) and Bowling (1995, 1997b). Of course, instruments should not be chosen unthinkingly – they need to be evaluated against explicit criteria to ensure that they are appropriate to the survey's aims and objectives. It is also important to remember that validity and reliability may need to be re-established if an instrument is used in a setting other than that for which it was developed (for example, if an instrument originally intended for application in a secondary care setting is to be used in primary care). Further details of criteria by which instruments should be assessed are provided by Bentzen and colleagues (1998).

The CASS Social Survey Question Bank
The CASS Social Survey Question Bank is designed to aid questionnaire designers in search of appropriate questions for health and other surveys. It is a site on the Internet, maintained and continually developed and added to by a team at the Resource Centre supported by the Economic and Social Research Council Centre for Applied Social Surveys (CASS). The Question Bank is not a list of questions taken out of their context and listed under topic headings, but a store of questionnaires from important and established surveys, reproduced in their original format. In addition to questionnaires, it contains commentary on concepts and measurement issues, through which the wording, context, origin, purpose and performance of questions can be better understood. The site search engine enables users to scan questionnaires and to locate questions and text containing particular words or phrases. The Question Bank does not contain data sets or substantive survey reports. The surveys include successive annual versions of the Health Survey for England and the General Household Survey, and also the National Patients Survey, the Welsh Health Survey, the National Survey of Sexual Attitudes and Lifestyles and others. The address of the site is:

http://www.natcen.ac.uk/cass/

· 5 ·
SAMPLING FOR SURVEY RESEARCH

Sampling is efficient, saving time and resources that would be required for a census of all population members (for many populations a complete census would in any case be impracticable). Statistical techniques can be applied to data that have been collected using scientifically selected samples, to yield useful estimates of the prevalence and incidence of attributes, attitudes, behaviour and so on, and the distributions of scores etc in the population from which the sample is drawn. While offering these important advantages, all sampling incurs random sampling variance in the results and the extent of this needs to be taken into account both in designing samples and in interpreting results.

DEFINITION OF AN ADEQUATE SAMPLE

An adequate sample:

- is drawn using an *unbiased* method (a biased method is one which produces results which will differ from the true population values in a consistent or systematic way)

- is *representative* of the population of interest

- is *sufficiently large* to make inferences about the underlying population that have acceptable margins of random variability.

To achieve an adequate sample, the survey researcher needs to:

- state the objectives of the survey clearly and precisely

- define the population to be surveyed explicitly, in terms of inclusion and exclusion criteria

- choose a sampling frame that is appropriate to the defined study population

- specify rigorous and objective sample selection methods (preferably probability sampling methods)

- determine the required achieved sample size, taking into account the likely variation in the characteristics of interest in the population, the size of differences between sub-groups that s/he wishes to be able to detect, and the level of confidence s/he wishes to have in estimates of population values derived from the sample

- contact more than the required sample, to allow for the losses that are expected due to the occurrence of ineligibles (those who do not fit population criteria; those who have died) and to non-response (for example, non-contacts, refusals).

SOME SAMPLING TERMS

Population – the complete set of units from which a sample is selected and to which the sample-based results will apply.

Units or elements – the elements of which the population is composed, some of which are selected as the sample:

- units could be patients, or members of the public, or hospitals, but also events; such as births or attendances at a clinic

- a precise operational definition of population and units is crucial (i.e. explicit eligibility criteria)

- there could be different sampling units at different stages of selection

- the sampling unit may or may not be identical with survey respondent (for example, the sampling unit could be the seat in the waiting room, but the survey respondent would be the patient occupying that seat).

Sampling frame – a listing of all the units (elements) in the population that are eligible to be sampled:

- the sampling frame should ideally correspond exactly to target population

- in practice, the sampling frame used may itself be a sample (adequate or inadequate) of the real target population; for example, 'List of elderly people registered with this practice' as a substitute for 'List of all elderly persons residing in this Health Authority Area'

- populations and sampling frames may be implicit because no physical listing exists; for example, patients attending an STD clinic, considered as a sample from the population of all who have attended the clinic in the recent past and (barring major changes) will attend in the immediate future.

DEFINING THE TARGET POPULATION

The definition of the target population should relate explicitly to the research aims. It should specify *inclusion* criteria (for example, adult patients attending the diabetic clinic at 'X' hospital) and *exclusion* criteria (for example, those attending the clinic for a second or subsequent time during the sampling period and out-of-area cases) and usually involves a *timeframe* (for example, those attending during the months of June and July).

WHAT IS REQUIRED IN A SAMPLING FRAME

The ideal sampling frame is a listing of population units that:

- matches the target population one-to-one

- is comprehensive (has no omissions)

- has one entry only for each eligible unit

- contains no ineligible units

- contains complete, accurate and up-to-date identifying and tracing information for each unit

- contains information about each unit useful for sample stratification (for example, age, sex etc)

- is accessible and cleared for use in research

- ideally, can be manipulated by computer.

In practice, few sampling frames exactly satisfy all these criteria. Because the sampling frame is so fundamental to the enquiry and because defects can affect the validity of the sample, it is often worth spending time and effort on improving it.

AVOIDING SAMPLING BIAS

It is important to ask:

- to what population (for example, professionals, patients, institutions) do we intend our results to apply?

- does the sampling frame and selection procedure that we use to select our sample give all members of the in-scope population a known chance of selection? If not, how many and what types of population units are likely to be excluded?

- can we ensure or reasonably assume that the units to which we have access are a *random* sample of *all* in-scope population units?

If the answer to any of the preceding three questions is 'No', we have a sampling frame bias.

It is also important to ask:

- do all members of the population have a *known* probability of selection (for example, an equal chance of being chosen)?

- are some population units listed or available for selection several times? This could arise if some individuals appear more than once on the population listing or visit the surgery several times during sampling period

- if some population units are *listed* more than once, there is still bias even if they are not *selected* more than once (or at all).

It is important to remember, first, that all statistical inference to population and hypothesis testing assumes *random selection*. We need to query whether our chosen selection process is truly random. It could be non-random because of: concessions to convenience (for example, going for the 'easy-to-find' cases – in an interview survey, those people who are at home during daylight hours); a desire to include 'interesting' cases (for example, 'We must include Mrs Miggins, her symptoms are fascinating'); a desire to exclude difficult or uninteresting cases (for example, 'Let's leave out Mr Meldrew, he's so grumpy!'). It is important to recognise that human beings cannot choose a random sample by judgement – there has to be a *random selection procedure*.

Secondly, the most perfectly constructed sample can be largely invalidated, for the purposes of drawing conclusions, if there is gross and differential non-response at the data collection stage. If sample members of a particular kind are less likely than average to respond, that is equivalent to under-sampling them (and relatively over-sampling other groups) in an uncontrolled way.

SAMPLE SELECTION METHODS

Probability (random) sampling methods include:

- *simple* random sampling

- *systematic* random sampling

- *stratified* random sampling

- *multi-stage* (clustered) random sampling.

Non-probability methods include:

- *convenience* sampling

- *snowball* sampling

- *quota* sampling.

For a more detailed discussion, see Moser and Kalton, 1971.

Probability sampling: selection

For probability sampling, each unit in the target population must have a calculable, non-zero probability of being selected.

- *Simple random sampling* generally uses a paper-based random number table or a computerised random selection procedure. Each selection is made independently and each unit has *equal* probability of being selected.

- *Systematic random sampling* uses a random start in the population listing, then selects every nth unit; this has the merit of being easier to implement. It may lead to bias if the list is organised in some systematic manner. For example, in sampling ward staff from a series of wards, where each ward has around 20 staff and the staff are listed in order of seniority within ward, a low random start and a sampling interval of 10 will tend always to select one very senior staff member or one from the middle of the seniority list and to under-sample the remainder. Such risks can generally be removed through paying attention to how the list was compiled.

- *Stratified random sampling* controls the composition of the sample in relevant respect(s); it can be applied at any stage of selection (but only if information about all population units is available). Units are split into subsets (*strata*) likely to differ in terms of what the survey aims to measure (for example, defined by age and/or gender) and separate random samples are drawn within each stratum. For example, if the population contains men and women (who can be pre-identified) and if the results for men are likely to differ from the results for women, then something is gained by listing and sampling the two sexes as separate *strata*, so as to predetermine the number of men and the number of women selected. Provided the probabilities of selection are known, estimates from strata can be combined to give estimates for the total population. Stratification can significantly improve the precision of estimates, but its effect is in most applications small relative to that of *sample size*.

- *Multi-stage (clustered) random sampling* is done in stages, using different population units at each stage. For example, in a two-stage random sampling procedure the first stage units (for example, areas, hospitals) are randomly selected from an appropriate sampling frame at stage 1; and the second (final) stage units (patients) are selected at stage 2 from within selected stage 1 units. Thus the final stage units are said to be *clustered* within first stage units. Multi-stage sampling is used to reduce the amount of administrative, sample selection and data collection effort required by the survey. The results of multi-stage sampling will be unbiased, but are usually less precise (i.e. have wider confidence intervals) than those of single stage sampling.

SAMPLE SIZE

Assuming random selection, the precision of sample-based population estimates is then mainly determined by sample size. The larger the sample size, the smaller the random sampling error. With large populations (for example, 'All adult residents of a Health Authority Area'), what matters is the *absolute size* of the sample; the *proportion of the population included in the sample* is unimportant. Thus, for example, to provide results of the same level of precision for the population of

Scotland and the population of England, equal-sized samples are generally required. It is only when the number of units to be selected for the sample exceeds about 10% of the units in the population that the *finite population correction* starts to come seriously into play in calculating the precision of results.

Precision increases approximately in proportion to the *square root of sample size*. Therefore, for example, increasing sample size by a factor of ten increases precision (narrows confidence intervals) by only a factor of just over three. (For further reading on confidence intervals refer to workbook 3 in this series, *Statistical Concepts*.) The implication is that if we want to detect small differences or changes, we need very large samples! But that is usually very expensive, since sample size is also the main determinant of survey operational costs. We may therefore need to trade-off precision against cost and feasibility.

In research studies where the survey is embedded within a particular study design (for example, a randomised controlled trial), the sample size will generally be based on a calculation of the statistical power required to test specified hypotheses. If a survey is being carried out as a separate operation, sample size calculations should be based on the desired precision of the most important estimates to be made from study findings.

Table 2 shows the impact of different sample sizes on the precision of estimates of the proportion of current smokers in the population, using simple random sampling.

Table 2
Sample size and the precision of population estimates

Sample-based estimate of % of smokers in group	Sample size for group of interest	Range within which true value lies (95% confidence interval)
30%	10	1.0-59.0% (range 58)
30%	100	20.8-39.2% (range 18)
30%	1000	27.1-32.9% (range 6)
30%	10,000	29.1-30.9% (range 2)

If the aim was to estimate the proportion of smokers within sub-populations (for example, males aged 16-24) the calculation would be the same *for each sub-group*.

Estimating required sample size for major or complex studies is fundamental and requires a knowledge of sampling statistics, so consult a trained statistician if you can. However, do not expect the statistician to simply produce a number, without help from you. In particular, s/he will want to know:

- What is your null hypothesis? (for example, 'no difference in symptoms experienced between two groups')?

- How confident do you want to be in accepting or rejecting the null hypothesis (usually 95% or 99%)?

- How certain do you want to be of detecting, for example, a real (population) difference of (say) 5% in symptom prevalence (usually 80% or 90%)?

- How variable is what you are estimating (situation at a point in time, change over time) likely to be across the population? For example:

  - for a yes/no dichotomy, the proportion with that attribute (for example, proportion of the population, or change in the proportion of the population, exhibiting a particular symptom)

  - for a continuous variable, the population standard deviation of what is being measured (for example, diastolic blood pressure).

This means that in order to set a sample size, you and your adviser will have to guesstimate some of the very things you hoped to measure! Fortunately, it is usually possible to make the requisite guesses to a sufficient degree of precision, for example on the basis of published data, previous research, or pilot work. For many of the variables likely to be of interest, possible sources of information are the published results of the decennial Census of Population, or the annual reports and tables produced by the General Household Survey and the Health Surveys for England (Department of Health), Scotland (Scottish Office) and Wales (Welsh Office).

Further reading
See Article 4

EXERCISE 2

A survey is being designed to measure patient satisfaction with the inter-personal skills of the general practitioner during patient consultations. The researchers plan to use the practice's appointment book as the sampling frame for this survey. What problems might arise?

For answer, see Appendix 1.

· 6 ·

DEVISING SURVEY QUESTIONS

Surveys involve a special kind of conversation or interchange with respondents, which has the purpose of collecting information on predetermined topics. People who are naturally articulate, intuitive and interested in the lives of others may well be able to plan and manage a conversation with respondents which covers the required topics, draws out respondents and elicits relevant information in a natural and easy-going way. Those who are particularly gifted may, with further training and experience, become good *qualitative* researchers.

The designer of *quantitative* survey instruments (questionnaires) needs to have some of the same abilities. To respondents, a good set of survey questions (organised as a questionnaire) should appear as a straightforward and logical sequence of requests for information on topics, and in a form and at a level of detail that the respondent is well able to provide. Providing the information may require some mental effort, but it should always be clear exactly what information is needed.

However, the designer of quantitative instruments must also, and at the same time, pursue another, quite different scientific agenda. Questions asked on quantitative surveys should:

- provide 'meaningful numbers' for analysis (quantification)

- measure that quantity or concept that they are intended to measure and no other (validity)

- be as free as possible from systematic measurement bias (lack of bias)

- be as free as possible from random measurement variability (reliability)

- be able to detect relevant differences between respondents and groups of respondents (sensitivity)

The art and science of questionnaire design consists in reconciling these two agendas. If, on the one hand, respondents are unable to relate the questions asked to their own concepts, knowledge and experience, or if, on the other hand, the quantitative measures obtained fail seriously to meet the criteria just listed, the results of the survey will be misleading or seriously flawed.

The design of individual questions and whole questionnaires depends crucially on the particular aims of the survey (including not just the topics but the exact form and level of detail in which the data are required) and the particular characteristics (knowledge of the subject matter, language skills, literacy, age etc) of the population from which the respondents are drawn. It is therefore impossible to provide a 'questionnaire template' which will be suitable without major adaptation for all, or a wide range of applications (analogous to statistical formulae, for example). Instead, we must proceed by giving examples of widely-used information-eliciting tactics and devices that may help to satisfy the criteria mentioned above and by drawing attention to the many traps into which the unwary question and questionnaire designer can fall.

ASKING ABOUT BEHAVIOUR

The majority of health surveys ask about behaviour in some shape or form. Typical examples are questions about taking medication, about use of health services, or about health-related behaviour such as smoking, alcohol consumption, exercise or dietary behaviour.

For some types of behaviour there is a 'natural' standard unit or units to ask about. For example, for smokers 'a cigarette' or 'a pack of 10 or 20 cigarettes' fills this function and for use of health services 'a consultation' or the equivalent is also useful, though much less standardised as a quantity than a pack of 20 cigarettes. However, for other forms of behaviour defining a standard unit of behaviour is often problematic.

For example, for measuring diet the ideal, pursued by elaborate and costly dietary surveys, is to obtain weighed food intake reports classified and analysed for conversion into nutritional values. In terms of this ideal, asking respondents questions such as 'How many times in the last seven days have you eaten fried food?' is extremely crude. This is because of the vagueness and weak quantification of 'a time' as a unit of behaviour; the lack of information about the frying fat or oil used; and the difficulty of defining, in terms that respondents can recognise and understand, what is meant by 'fried' (does it include stews that are fried before further cooking?).

However, if the researcher thinks that it will still be analytically useful to have a crude measure – say, one which divides respondents into those who report never eating fried food, those who sometimes eat it and those who regularly eat it – then the data provided by the above question may serve the purpose. Lateral thinking might suggest asking about food purchases over a reference period, rather than directly about food intakes. The question might also be improved by defining more clearly what is meant by 'fried food' (for example, does it include stir-frying, pre-frying prior to using another method of cooking etc).

A second crux in producing standardised measures of behaviour is whether to pass to the respondent the task of providing frequency estimates, or to use a standard reference period. The first option typically involves asking questions containing words like 'How often...' or 'How much...' and response scales such as 'Every day'/'At least twice a week'/'Once a week' etc). The second option involves asking respondents to recall how many times they have done the behaviour, or how much of the behaviour they have done (alternative methods of quantification) over a specified 'back reference' period appropriate to the behaviour (for hospitalisation it might be 'the past 12 months', for taking strenuous exercise 'the past two weeks').

The best available tactics for obtaining information on behaviour from respondents, in terms of units and in terms of standardisation strategy, varies critically according to the level, detail and precision of the quantitative measure that is needed for analysis purposes. In slightly more generalised terms the considerations are set out in Table 3.

ASKING ABOUT ASSESSMENTS, ATTITUDES, VALUES, MOTIVES, INTENTIONS ETC

In questionnaire surveys, there is no sharp boundary between attributes that are in principle physically observable, such as behaviour, gender, age, housing and family situation etc, and attitudes and mental phenomena that are not observable, since almost everything depends to some extent on the respondent's interpretation of the question. However, questions about attitudes and values are often particularly prone to question wording effects (two wordings thought to be equivalent in meaning in fact produce different response distributions). This is a particular danger when weight is to be placed on assessments, made by members of survey samples, of their level of 'satisfaction with services received' and the like.

In order to achieve standardisation, respondents are often proffered a concept or statement and asked to respond by choosing one of a set of labelled scale points (for example, Very satisfied / Fairly satisfied / Neither satisfied nor dissatisfied / Fairly dissatisfied / Very dissatisfied). Inexperienced survey designers often focus on issues such as 'What is the correct number of scale points to offer?'. There is no standard answer to this, beyond saying that for things which are important to them and central to their day-to-day experience respondents can generally make finer meaningful distinctions than they can for issues about which they have, at best, vague and imperfectly formed views. In

Table 3
Question forms for behaviour questions

Question form	Comments
Have you ever (*done behaviour*)?	Easy to answer but uninformative for most purposes.
When did you last (*do behaviour*)?	Fairly easy to answer, but gives a biased representation of the relative positions, in terms of amount of behaviour done, of persons with regular and persons with irregular habits.
How many times per (*time period*) do you usually/ on average (*do behaviour*)?	Still relies on respondent's judgement in response to the vague word 'usually'. Subject to (often unconscious) reporting biases.
How many times have you (*done behaviour*) in the last 7 days?	This approach standardises by using a common reference period. Good for quantification if appropriate reference period is chosen. However, there may be recall problems and distortions. There may also be content effects if behaviour varies (say) with time and year, or with place
Can you now please think back over the week ending last Sunday. On Monday of that week, how many times did you (*do behaviour*)? (Or other quantification such as '*How much of (behaviour) did you do?*') *Repeat for other days.*	This approach involves more thinking back and recording by respondent. It is more burdensome and consumes more questionnaire space, but may provide a more complete and accurate record than preceding approaches.

practice, it is unusual to use more than ten points and five are commonly used. Occasionally respondents may be asked to answer in terms of a 'thermometer scale' with 100 graduations (for example, in assessing their own health) but the ground is usually prepared for this through 'priming' questions to ensure that all respondents are considering the whole domain of 'health' intended by the researchers.

Getting the form of the question and the presentation of the response categories right is generally more important than whether to use, say, five- or seven-point scales. However, the response scale must be seen as part of the question and giving the points labels at all is an issue that needs to be considered, given that respondents may be influenced by extraneous overtones of words and concepts such as (say) 'I am satisfied', rather than (say) 'The service was excellent'. Another important principle is to make it clear to respondents what are the poles of evaluation between which s/he is required to place themselves.

A device which addresses a number of these concerns is to use a format in which only the poles of the scale are labelled, as below.

Could not be better ☐☐☐☐☐ Could not be worse

Question wording effects occur particularly when respondents are asked to make judgements about matters to which they have previously devoted little systematic thought and have no pre-formed views; where the concepts embodied in the question are vague and ill-defined; or where the words used in the question have evaluative overtones. One type of effect which occurs in these circumstances is the tendency of respondents to 'play safe and avoid impoliteness' by choosing a neutral or mildly positive response from a range of labelled response categories offered (for example, 'fairly satisfied'). A related effect is the tendency to avoid endorsing statements containing drastic or extreme-sounding expressions (such as 'forbid') where a less extreme sounding, though logically equivalent, expression such as 'not allow' would have been endorsed.

In general, if evaluations are required, the more concrete and close to the respondent's experience the concept offered by the question, the more likely it is that responses will be robust to extraneous wording effects. Thus, in a survey of inpatients, responses to a question about whether meals were too cold, too hot or the right temperature when served is less prone to unwanted response effects than a more general and abstract questions about satisfaction with 'hospital catering'. This tends to create a tension with the desire of some survey sponsors and questionnaire designers to obtain 'overall' assessments. It is possible to build up to overall assessments by asking and analysing the responses to more concrete assessment questions, but a large number of such questions may be required to cover the domain.

QUESTION FORMS

A major distinction in designing survey questions is between 'open' and 'closed' questions. *Open* questions invite a verbatim response from the respondent and should be phrased in a way which does not encourage the respondent to assume that one type of answer is more acceptable than another type. *Closed* questions present the respondent with a list of possible answers, from which s/he is asked to choose either just the one that best applies, or as many as seem applicable. Quite often question designers attempt a compromise by adding at the end of the pre-specified responses: 'Other answers – please specify'. A further variant sometimes used in interview surveys is where the response is 'open' from the point of view of the respondent, but the interviewer codes the response into one or more pre-specified categories visible to them. Each type of question has its strengths and limitations. To a large extent the strengths of closed questions correspond to limitations or weaknesses of open questions and vice versa. (See Box 3).

In a survey of patient satisfaction with hospital services, an open question might read:

'In what ways do you think this hospital's services to patients need to be improved?'

followed by a space, with or without ruled lines, on which answers are to be recorded verbatim. A closed question might read:

'In which of the following ways do you think this hospital's services to patients need to be improved?'

and would be followed by a list of pre-specified response categories, which give an indication of the types of response that the researcher thinks are relevant (see below).

It is important to understand that open questions are not just non-leading versions of closed questions, but are essentially different. Repeated experiments have shown that, if the range of pre-specified responses used in a *closed* version of the question is used to code *open* responses obtained from an equivalent sample of respondents, very different distributions of coded responses can result.

In self-completion questionnaires, responses to open-ended questions are typically less full than in interview surveys. Moreover, better educated, articulate respondents tend to write more than the less educated (a subtle bias). The amount of space provided on the questionnaire for the response is taken as an indication of the level of detail required. With larger samples, the time and labour required by office coding may be an important consideration.

For these reasons, it is recommended that open questions be kept to a minimum in self-completion questionnaires addressed to the general public. Nonetheless, carefully focused open questions may have an important role, for instance in surveys of professionals who have well-developed views in their area of experience and expertise.

BOX 3

Open/closed questions

Open questions

Open questions avoid imposing the survey researcher's perspective on respondents. If the researcher does provide a list (i.e. uses a closed question), respondents will focus on the listed items and not think of other possible items or frames of reference.

Closed questions

But closed questions focus the respondent on aspects that are relevant to the research. Without prompting, respondents may find it hard to think about vague and undefined domains (for example, 'this hospital's services to patients').

Without a list of responses to choose from, different respondents may interpret the scope of the question differently. Only if the full range of responses is prompted can we be sure that all respondents have considered all the relevant response options.

Respondents will hopefully come up with open responses that reflect the issues of most importance to them.

But in practice less articulate respondents tend to give short, uninformative answers to open questions which do not necessarily do justice to more complex underlying motives etc. Many will put down the first answer that comes to mind and pass on, possibly failing to consider the full range of aspects that the researcher had in mind.

Open questions allow for unexpected responses. But it can be difficult to keep respondents focused on the issues which are most relevant to the research (for example, an open question intended to elicit suggestions for improving a hospital's services to in-patients may elicit responses about waiting times).

Closed questions with prompted response categories help to define the domain of interest to the research. But the listed answers may effectively steer the respondent towards certain types of response and away from others.

Open questions may provide vivid examples for inclusion in a report on the survey.

But this is really the province of qualitative, rather than quantitative, research.

Respondents often find answering open questions hard work and tend to feel that one answer (e.g. mention of one reason for doing something) is enough.
Coding responses to open questions is time-consuming, laborious and unreliable (different coders may assign the same response to different categories).

Closed questions make it easy for the respondent to choose several different answers if s/he so wishes. However, the choices will be limited by the options offered. This applies even if an 'Other answers – please specify' option is provided.

The following is an example of a closed question. Two alternative versions, A and B (of the prompted response categories), are shown to illustrate a point made above.

The final prompted phrase 'Other answers (please specify)' is an attempt to elicit spontaneous answers not covered by the pre-specified categories.

'In which of the following ways do you think this hospital's services to patients need to be improved?'

Version A
More nurses on the wards
More experienced doctors
Shorter treatment waiting lists

.

.

.

Other ways (please specify)

Version B
Wider choice of menus
Better quality of food
Longer visiting hours

.

.

.

Other ways (please specify)

It might be thought that respondents presented with Version A would make heavy use of the 'Other specify' option to give responses of the kind shown in Version B, and vice versa, but in practice this does not happen. The provision of a pre-specified list, even with an 'Other answers' category, tends to direct respondents' thinking towards the domain represented by the pre-specified categories (in the case of A, major changes to the resourcing of the National Health Service; in the case of B, relatively minor changes to the hospital's hotel and catering arrangements). Effectively, A and B are different questions and the response categories must be seen as part of the question. Self-confident respondents with strong and well-formed views on a topic may give those views regardless, but most respondents tend to look for clues in the question wording or format as to what kinds of answers are expected.

QUESTION WORDING

Choosing between open and closed questions is not the only decision facing the survey researcher. Other issues can be illustrated using the common case of questions intended to measure the frequency with which the respondent performs a particular type of behaviour. This may well be a 'cognitively demanding task' for the respondent – that is, it involves hard mental work by way of applying definitions, recalling and counting. In everyday conversation it is not normal to impose such tasks on the person you are talking to without warning. Instead, the parties often 'negotiate meaning', with the respondent first assuming that a quick and easy answer will suffice and the questioner 'unfolding' what s/he really wants to know through a series of 'turns'. For example:

> 'How many times have you seen a doctor over the past six months?'
> 'Oh, several times.'
> 'I meant, exactly how many times?'
> 'Well … I have seen Dr Brown my GP four times.'
> 'How about hospital doctors?...'

In designing a questionnaire, the survey researcher must somehow focus on the precise type of information required without several 'turns' of conversation. But respondents are not used to having to digest precise and elaborate definitions before attempting to answer a question. This is one of the things that makes the wording of survey questions difficult. Some common problems are the following.

- Respondents tend to revert to definitions which are familiar to them but do not necessarily correspond to the survey concept. For example, respondent and researcher definitions of 'your family' may differ – does it mean those living with you, or does it encompass the extended family?

- Lay people and health professionals may use words and concepts in quite different ways, or may not share a common vocabulary. For example, to a health professional the word 'chronic' implies a long-term, ongoing health problem, but patients may interpret 'chronic' as 'severe', or 'very painful'. In a survey on women's health, when asked 'Do you have any problems with your menstrual cycle?', one respondent replied 'I used to, but I've got a car now'!

- If forced to do mental arithmetic, many respondents will guess or make serious mistakes. For example, many adults cannot add up accurately and do not know how to define or calculate an average (arithmetic mean) or a percentage.

- The terms 'on average', 'usually', 'normally' are usually interpreted by the lay public to mean much the same thing. If behaviour is very regular, that may suffice. But if behaviour varies over the period you are interested in, 'normally' and 'on average' should imply different answers. If you require accurate numeric information, it is best to collect it by getting the respondent to enumerate instances over a reference period and doing the summarising yourself.

- There are limits on how hard respondents are prepared to work. But if they are unable or unwilling to perform the cognitive tasks imposed by a question, they seldom say so. Instead they try a 'short cut' answer that requires little thought to see if it is acceptable. Therefore, if a precise and accurate answer is needed, you need to make a special point. For example, if you are interested in the number of times on which the respondent has seen a doctor, you may need to ask:

> 'Please include all occasions on which you saw your general practitioner and all occasions when you saw a hospital doctor. Do not include occasions when you saw a nurse but not a doctor.'

- If asked (say) how many times they have suffered minor symptoms over past six months, few respondents will mentally enumerate the episodes. Instead, they may assume that 'last week' was typical to work out a 6-month estimate (often making arithmetical errors!). Such short cuts may give seriously inaccurate or biased results.

- Responses given are influenced by the choice of responses offered, especially if the concepts used in the question are vague. For example, responses to A below will produce more '2 times or less' estimates than responses to B. This is because respondents will not know what the researcher means by 'problems with neighbours' and will seek clues from the response categories offered. Asking respondents to specify a number avoids bias arising from the response categories, but 'problems with neighbours' will still be differentially interpreted and needs to be defined.

'How often have you had problems with your neighbours?'

Version A	Version B
Never	*2 times or less*
Once	*3-6 times*
Twice	*7-10 times*
More than twice	*More than 10 times*

Box 4 provides a summary of recommendations with respect to question wording, while Box 5 gives some recommendations on the presentation of response categories for closed questions. Complete Exercise 3.

Further reading
See Article 5

EXERCISE 3

A survey researcher wishes to gather data on the purchase and use of over-the-counter (OTC) drugs for self-medication. One of the questions reads as follows:

'How often in the past six months have you used OTC analgesics for the treatment of headache, backache, menorrhagia or toothache?'

Never	1
Once a week	2
Once a month	3
More frequently	4

What problems might arise with this question?

For answer, see Appendix 1.

BOX 4

Principles of question wording (after Moser and Kalton, 1971 and Oppenheim, 1992)

- Use simple language. For example, 'How often has this kind of thing happened?', rather than 'How frequently have incidents of this type occurred?'.

- Keep the question short (i.e. sentence of less than 20 words approximately) and avoid complex grammatical structures such as qualifying clauses. Two short and simple sentences are usually better than one long and complex one.

- Avoid questions which are insufficiently specific. [Often this only becomes apparent through piloting]

- Avoid ambiguity. [Often identified only through piloting]

- Avoid vague words and those with more than one meaning (for example, 'dinner'). [Often identified only through piloting] If a vague term or word (for example, 'children') is used, define it (for example, 'children under the age of 16 years').

- Avoid jargon and technical terms, including acronyms and abbreviations. [Technical terms are often identified only through piloting] Bear in mind that words commonly used and understood by health professionals (for example, 'chronic') may be misunderstood by lay people. If it is necessary to use such terms, define or paraphrase them.

- Avoid double-barrelled questions (i.e. those containing two or more different concepts or propositions to which respondents may have different reactions (for example, 'The clinic should open earlier and remain open longer' with response categories of 'Agree / Disagree').

- Avoid double negatives (for example, a negative statement followed by a 'disagree' response). These often confuse people.

- Avoid proverbs and clichés when measuring attitudes.

- Avoid leading questions (for example, 'Do you agree that the NHS is under-funded?').

- Beware of loaded words and concepts (i.e. those implying a value judgement). [Often identified only through piloting]

- Beware of presuming questions (for example, those which assume that a respondent has indulged in a specific type of behaviour).

- Be cautious in the use of hypothetical questions. People in general are poor predictors of how they would behave in novel situations.

- Do not over-tax respondents' memories (for example, by asking for detailed recall of unmemorable events or behaviour).

- Allow for 'Don't know' and 'Not applicable' responses if appropriate.

BOX 5

Recommendations for presentation of response categories (after Sudman and Bradburn, 1981)

- Use open-ended questions sparingly (because they are more resource-demanding, and are more subject to between-interviewer and between-coder variability and therefore are less reliable).

- Ensure that response categories are mutually exclusive (i.e. do not overlap) and collectively exhaustive (i.e. all possible responses are catered for).

- Present response categories in a logical order.

- If some responses are more socially desirable than others, start with the least socially desirable option.

- Limit rating scales (for example, scales to measure satisfaction or strength of attitude) to not more than five points when written descriptors are attached.

- For more than five response categories, use numeric scales.

- Consider analogues such as ladders, clocks or thermometers for numerical scales with many points.

- Ask respondents to respond to every item in a list rather than indicating only those that apply (i.e. to respond 'yes / no' or 'applies / does not apply' to each item rather than simply complying with the instruction 'circle as many as apply').

QUESTION ORDERING

A questionnaire is not just a list of topics and questions. The survey researcher also needs to pay attention to the order in which questions are presented and to logical dependencies between questions and sections of the questionnaire.

The respondent should be 'led' through the questionnaire in a logical sequence, from the general to the specific, but the sequence of topics may not be the same for all respondents. For example, there may be a section on employment for those who are economically active, which will be omitted by those who are not. Within the 'Employment' section there may be special questions for those who work in particular industries.

However, with self-completion questionnaires addressed to the general public, complicated 'skip' instructions will confuse and put off some respondents. If the respondent is required to make difficult judgements or to 'get their head around' unfamiliar concepts, lead up to these through definition and by stages.

When new topics are introduced, there should be a re-orientation statement or instruction. For example:

'*Questions 20-25 are about **the last time you visited the doctor***. *If you have **not** visited a doctor in the past six months, please go to Question 26.*'

Read Box 6, which provides a summary of recommendations on question ordering and then complete Exercise 4.

EXERCISE 4

In what order would you place the following topics in a questionnaire on health and lifestyle? Respondent's age; whether the respondent smokes; income; alcohol consumption; history of chest problems; frequency of exercise; family size and composition; dietary behaviour; beliefs about 'healthy eating'; practice of 'safe sex'; history of digestive disorders; history of headaches/migraine.

For answer, see Appendix 1.

BOX 6

Guidelines for question ordering (after Sudman and Bradburn, 1981)

- Place easy, salient and non-threatening questions first in a questionnaire.

- Place questions about personal circumstances (for example, age, financial situation, family situation) last, since they can be seen as threatening or intrusive. (Exceptions must, however, be made where they are required to determine the respondent's eligibility to complete the remainder of the questionnaire.)

- Use funnelling procedures to minimise question order effects, starting with the general and moving to the specific.

- Complete questions on one topic before embarking on a new topic.

- Use transitional phrases and instructions when switching topics.

- Order filter questions (those intended to establish who should answer what questions) in such a way as to cover all contingencies and encourage complete responses.

QUESTIONNAIRE STRUCTURE AND LAYOUT

FORMATTING QUESTIONNAIRES

No matter how good the question wording and ordering are, a poorly formatted questionnaire can contribute to poor response rates and, by misleading respondents, result in response errors.

Keep what respondents have to do as simple, natural and straightforward as possible. For example, do not start with instructions that look complicated and boring. The ideal is a well-spaced question layout, with standardised response layouts, through which the respondent works in sequence, as in the normal reading of a document.

Respondents expect to have to do one thing only to answer each question (for example, tick one box); therefore, if more than one action is needed in response to a question, make that very clear.

It should be clear where to start filling in the questionnaire. Respondents tend to go straight to Question 1 and preliminary details with no question numbers will be overlooked.

Instructions 'en route' should help respondents 'navigate' through the questionnaire (Figure 1). But complex skipping and filtering instructions in a self-completion questionnaire will confuse some respondents and make the document look more burdensome to complete than it really is. For this reason the complexity of routing must be limited.

Finally, they need to be told where to finish. For example:

'If you have not attended a hospital during the past six months, finish here. Thank you for your help.'
'If you have attended a hospital during the past six months, please answer questions 20-25.'

Spaces which are reserved for office use (for example, insertion of codes or other information in the office) should be clearly marked 'Office use only'.

The layout of questions and their associated response categories should take account of natural reading style (for readers of English, from left to right, from the top of the page to the bottom). Use a vertical response format (Figure 2) for closed questions, except for rating scales. To emphasise the underlying continuum in rating scales, a horizontal format is more appropriate (Figure 3); this format is also recommended where there is a series of questions (sometimes termed an 'item set') all involving the same response categories.

Arrangement of questions within a questionnaire needs careful attention. Avoid spreading a question, its associated response categories and instructions for answering, over two pages. A split can introduce a subtle form of bias, since respondents are more likely to endorse responses that are on the same page as the question. In questions where the list of response categories is too long to fit on a single page, continue the response categories on a facing page if possible; otherwise repeat the question on the subsequent page. Similarly, where one question is logically dependent upon another, make every effort to place both on the same page. Finally, avoid placing a short question at the foot of a page, especially if preceded by a long question with a number of sub-parts; this minimises the risk of the short question being overlooked.

Figure 1

Indicating how to move from one question to the next

Yes	1	➔	*Go to question 7*
No	2	➔	*Go to question 8*
Not sure	3	➔	*Go to question 8*

Figure 2

Example of vertical format for closed questions

1. If your doctor has advised you to take a daily dose of aspirin, how do you usually obtain them?

*(Please **circle the number** that describes you)*
Get them on prescription....................................1
Buy them over the counter..............................2
(for example, in a chemist or supermarket)
Have not been advised to take daily aspirin.......3

Figure 3

Example of horizontal format for rating scale

In the **past month**, on how many **days** have you been **short of breath during exercise** (for example going upstairs, walking up hill, gardening, taking part in sports)?

Never	On one or a few days	On several days	On most days	Every day
1	2	3	4	5

Consideration should also be given to size and font of typeface. This is very important in self-completion questionnaires, especially if it is anticipated that respondents may have problems with vision or literacy. Use a clear and distinct typeface (for example, Times Roman or Arial) and a large enough font (at least 12-point) so as not to put off those whose near sight is failing. Lower case is more readable than upper case. Avoid excessive use of italics, especially in self-completion questionnaires; however, italics and emboldening may be useful to give emphasis or to distinguish instructions and response categories from questions.

Coloured paper, especially dark or bright shades, can cause problems of legibility; white or pastel shades are to be preferred for inside pages, though brightly coloured covers can help questionnaires to stand out.

Box 7 provides a summary of recommendations on designing 'user-friendly' questionnaires.

Further reading
See Article 6

PRE-TESTING AND PILOTING QUESTIONNAIRES

Unless a questionnaire consists entirely of previously tested and validated questions which have been successfully used together before, it is advisable to go through a process of pre-testing and piloting. This process helps to ensure face and content validity, and may indicate the need for re-wording, re-formatting or other refinements to the questionnaire itself or to the proposed conduct of the survey.

The first step in pre-testing should be to show the questionnaire and any accompanying documentation to colleagues (preferably not involved in the research), family and/or friends; a fresh eye can often pick out ambiguous or confusing questions or instructions. However, colleagues and relatives may not be typical of the study population. Therefore, it is also advisable to test the questionnaire with a small sample of the target population, to ensure that it is understandable and acceptable to the target audience. The sample should ideally represent the variation in the types of respondent and respondent circumstances that will be met with on the main survey. There is no consensus as to an appropriate sample size for such pre-testing; one is

better than none, and it is unlikely that resources will allow for a pre-test sample of more than thirty.

A useful technique for pre-testing is 'cognitive interviewing', in which respondents are asked to 'think aloud' as they work their way through the questionnaire, indicating how they are interpreting the questions, what they are thinking about in giving their answers and whether they have any problems in answering the questions. Similar results can be achieved by questioning respondents retrospectively, after they have completed the questionnaire. Following this pre-testing phase, the questionnaire should be modified (if necessary) to take account of the feedback. If extensive modifications need to be made, it may be advisable to repeat the pre-test.

Once a 'final draft' questionnaire is available, it should be pilot tested, ideally with a larger sample (often 30-100, though the actual sample size will generally be dictated by resources). The sample used should again represent the variation in the types of respondent and respondent circumstances that will be met with on the main survey. In the pilot test, it is desirable to match methods of administration to 'real life' circumstances (for example, if the questionnaire is intended for self-completion in a doctor's surgery, the pilot test should be carried out under those conditions). The aims of the pilot study are to:

*   Look for 'how well questions work'. Poor questions may be indicated by:
    *   frequently omitted questions
    *   inappropriate responses
    *   inconsistent responses
    *   lack of spread of responses
    *   an apparent need for new response categories.

*   Assess likely response rates

*   Assess likely non-response bias.

Once again, the questionnaire and data collection procedures should be refined on the basis of the findings from the pilot test. As with the pre-test phase, if extensive changes are required, it may be necessary to repeat the pilot test.

Finally, when all the changes to the questionnaire have been made, it should be carefully proof-read before being printed and distributed.

BOX 7

Principles for the design of self-administered questionnaires (Jenkins and Dillman, 1997)

Principle 1: *Use the visual elements of brightness, colour, shape and location in a consistent manner to define the desired navigational path for respondents to follow when answering the questionnaire.*

Principle 2: *When established format conventions are changed in the midst of a questionnaire, use prominent visual guides to reorient respondents.*

Principle 3: *Place instruction and directions where they are to be used and where they can be seen.*

Principle 4: *Present information in a manner that does not require respondents to connect information from separate locations in order to comprehend it.*

Principle 5: *Require respondents to answer only one question at a time.*

· 8 ·

MAXIMISING RESPONSE RATES

As already noted, maximising response rates and minimising non-response bias are important in ensuring the quality of survey data. Response rates may be defined as follows:

$$\text{Overall (questionnaire) response rate} = \frac{\text{number of respondents}}{\text{number eligible to respond}}$$

$$\text{Item response rate} = \frac{\text{number of questions and parts of questions 'properly' answered}}{\text{total number of questions}}$$

Note that 'number eligible to respond' includes all those it was ideally intended to cover, including those who could not be contacted (possibly because of sampling frame defects), those who were inaccessible, unavailable or too ill to take part and those who declined to take part, as well as those who responded. Those who were contacted and found to be ineligible according to inclusion / exclusion criteria should be excluded from both numerator and denominator. It may be necessary to estimate the number of ineligibles in the denominator. Note also that 'respondents' should include only those who produced usable responses.

The principal reasons for questionnaire non-response are:

- *sample member unable to respond* (for example, too infirm, cognitively impaired, blind, illiterate, non-competent in language of survey)

- *sample member no longer at contact address*, this is also related to quality of sampling frame

- *refusals*; these may be explicit or implicit (for example, ring up and say they don't wish to participate, return questionnaire blank, simply do not return questionnaire at all)

- *away from home for duration* of survey

- *not at home when called on* (usually, this is not a major problem in postal surveys unless using recorded delivery).

In survey research (both interview surveys and self-completion questionnaires), non-respondents are likely to be significantly different from those who do respond, in respect of a range of characteristics; and the characteristics concerned are in turn likely to be associated with what the survey is trying to measure. For example, heavy drinkers are likely to be unavailable (because they are often away from home) or unwilling to respond to a survey of alcohol consumption. Since heavy drinkers are often younger men, a deficiency of younger men in the achieved sample may indicate likely bias.

Empirical evidence shows that respondents to postal surveys, particularly those returning their questionnaires early, are likely to be more interested in the survey topic, to make more favourable reports and to be more successful in their current status. But evidence of other forms of non-response bias is less clear-cut. Kanuk and Berenson (1975) concluded that the only consistent and widespread finding was that respondents to postal surveys tend to be better educated and therefore have greater facility in writing. In respect of interview surveys, Goyder (1987) demonstrated that survey response rates (given that initial contact has been made) tend to be positively correlated with socio-economic status and negatively correlated with age.

In health surveys of the general population and of specific patient groups, non-respondents to postal surveys are more likely to be in semi-skilled or unskilled manual occupations and to be from ethnic minorities, while respondents tend to be younger, have high levels of educational attainment, and have better health status. (Cartwright, 1986); this latter finding is of particular relevance when the aim is to measure health status in the underlying population, since estimates derived from survey respondents are likely to be upwardly biased.

Non-response bias also occurs in surveys of professional groups. Cartwright (1978) reported that relatively higher response rates were generally obtained in surveys of nurses; younger doctors and those with better qualifications; and consultants with university rather than NHS appointments. Single-handed general practitioners were less likely to respond and non-responding doctors were somewhat less likely to be regarded as sympathetic and helpful by their patients. However, response rates for general practitioners and consultants were broadly similar, and the gender of doctor did not generally have a significant impact on response rates. Cartwright also concluded that the number and direction of biases did not appear to be strongly related to overall response rate. But of concern was her observation that response rates among doctors appeared to be dropping in recent years, a finding echoed by McAvoy and Kaner (1996).

Reasons for item non-response (failure to answer particular questions) include:

- *accidental item non-response* (for example, poor instructions/routing; pages stuck together; respondent distracted)

- *deliberate item non-response*, including *refusal to respond* (for example, because of amount of information required or nature of information required); *inability to answer* (for example, because instructions on how to respond are unclear; the question is too complex; the respondent does not have the necessary information; the respondent's position is not catered for).

High response rates are important because:

- the higher the response rate, the less likely there is to be non-response bias

- the higher the response rate (i.e. the larger the achieved sample), the more precise are inferences drawn from the sample about the underlying population.

Table 4 provides a summary of what constitutes acceptable and unacceptable response rates in postal surveys.

However, a 100% response rate is rarely (if ever) achieved; the survey researcher therefore needs to over-

Table 4
Acceptable and unacceptable response rates
(Mangione, 1995)

Response rate	Acceptability
> 85%	Excellent
70-84%	Very good
60-69%	Acceptable
50-59%	Barely acceptable
< 50%	Unacceptable

sample to ensure that the achieved sample is big enough. It is also important to use information that may be available or inferred about the total population to compare respondents and non-respondents and thus identify potential sources of bias (for example, if respondents are older, on average, than non-respondents). If there is significant non-response bias, it may be necessary to adjust or weight responses to take account of this, but weighting generally does not remove all bias.

A number of factors influence response rates. Some are structural and beyond the control of the survey researcher, others are manipulable. Table 5 provides a summary of means of maximising response rates. Brown and colleagues (1989) drew on this to produce a 'task-analysis' model of respondent decision-making,

Table 5
Means of achieving objectives in maximising response rates (after Dillman, 1978)

Minimising cost of responding	Maximising rewards of responding	Establishing trust
Making questionnaire clear and concise • attention to issues of question wording and sequencing	*Making questionnaire interesting to respondent* • choice of topic • addition of 'interesting' questions	*Establishment of benefit of participation* • statement of how results will be used to benefit respondents / others • promise to send results of research
Making questionnaire (appear) to be simple to complete • attention to issues of questionnaire appearance	*Expression of positive regard for respondent as an individual* • stating importance of individual's contribution • individual salutation • hand-written signature • individually typed letter • stamped (not franked) mail	*Establishment of credentials of researchers* • use of headed note-paper • naming of researchers
Reduction of mental / physical effort required for completion and of feelings of anxiety / inadequacy • simple questions • clear instructions • sensitive handling of potentially embarrassing questions	*Expression of verbal appreciation* • statement of thanks in all communications • statement of thanks on questionnaire • follow up 'thank you' letter or card	*Building on other exchange relationships* • endorsement by well-regarded organisation / individual
Avoidance of subordination of respondent to researcher	*Support of respondent's values* • appeal to personal utility • appeal to altruism / social utility	
Reduction of direct monetary costs of responding • provision of pre-paid envelopes for return of postal questionnaires	*Incentives* • monetary or material incentive at time of response • provision of results of research	

summarised in Table 6, which is useful in designing and implementing questionnaire surveys.

Further reading
See Articles 7-9

Table 6

Task-analysis model of respondent decision-making (after Brown, Decker et al., 1989)

Stage 1 Interest in task	Stage 2 Evaluation of task	Stage 3 Initiation and monitoring of task	Stage 4 Completion of task

Personal contact
Personalisation of letter
Personalisation
  of envelope
Class of mail
	Time and effort required
	Length of questionnaire
	Size of pages
	Supply of addressed
	  return envelope
	Supply of stamped
	  return envelope
		Actual difficulty encountered
		Clarity of question wording
		Clarity of instructions
		Complexity of questions
			Provision of SAE

Questionnaire appearance Cover illustration Colour of cover Layout and format Quality / clarity of type	*Cursory evaluation of difficulty* Number of questions Complexity of questions	*Sensitivity of requests* Number and nature of sensitive questions	*Reminders to return*
Topic Questionnaire title Cover illustration Content of cover letter Timeliness Relevance / salience		*Actual time required*	
Source credibility / trust Image of sponsor Credentials of individual investigator Message in cover letter			
Reward for participation Tangible rewards; monetary and other incentives Intangible rewards; appeals to altruism, self-interest etc			
Persistence of source Follow-up procedures			

SURVEY MANAGEMENT

Good questionnaire and survey design is not enough – the whole survey process needs to be carefully managed. The survey researcher must estimate and procure resources, timetable the survey process and monitor progress against the defined schedule, and manage the dispatch and return of questionnaires.

Adequate time must be allowed for each stage in the survey process. The exact time required will depend on whether the questionnaire needs to be developed from scratch, the size of the sample and the number of follow-up contacts made. There are no hard and fast rules about the dispatch of reminders, but it is sensible to wait until responses to previous mailings have tailed off (generally after two to three weeks). It is also useful to specify a cut-off date after which any additional responses will be excluded from the data set. An example of a survey timetable is presented in Table 7.

It can be seen that a postal questionnaire survey, if carefully designed and prepared and conducted so as to maximise response and obtain good quality data, can easily take eight or nine months from start to finish and is therefore *not* a way of obtaining information to answer policy or administrative questions 'overnight'.

Table 7

Example of a postal survey timetable

Weeks	Activity
1-5	Design and pre-testing; preparing sample
6-9	Pilot testing
10-11	Refinement and redesign
12	Printing
13	Initial mailing
15	First reminder
17	Second reminder
21	Data set closed
21-24	Data coding, checking and cleaning
25-26	Data entry
27-28	Data validation and formatting for analysis
29-32	Analysis
33-36	Write up results
37	Finish

The need for a survey needs to be anticipated well before the information flowing from it is to be used.

COSTS AND COSTING

As well as time, the resources required to carry out a postal survey will include stationery, postage and staff time. Of these, staff time is likely to be by far the most costly item, even though with in-house surveys it may not be fully recognised in accounting terms and may make its impact as an opportunity cost of taking staff off other tasks. From this it follows that failure to estimate the staff time requirement realistically is likely to lead to difficulties and contention within the organisation and to skimping of survey tasks, particularly those related to survey quality and quality control.

It should be noted that the costing of postal surveys is not only a question of identifying operational stages and the types of resource needed at each, but also requires the making of quantitative estimates of unknown factors. For example, estimates must be made of the numbers of sample members who will respond to the initial mail-out and to successive reminders, and of the numbers of case records to be processed (particularly at the manual processing stages). To inform the planning of future surveys, it is good practice to keep careful records of these quantities.

MANAGEMENT OF MAILING OPERATIONS

Managing the dispatch of questionnaires and logging returns needs careful attention. For reasons of confidentiality, names and addresses of target respondents are not usually placed on the questionnaires themselves; rather a unique identifier (survey number) is used. Consideration needs to be given to how these numbers are added. Sophisticated printing and document reproduction systems allow for the production of 'personalised' questionnaires, using a facility akin to the mail-merge function in word-processing packages; however, this is a relatively costly option. A lower cost alternative is to use a word-processing or database package to produce individualised sticky labels which can be stuck to the questionnaires. Similarly, self-inking, automatically advancing number stamps can be used to number questionnaires sequentially. The least satisfactory alternative is to write the survey number on by hand, since this approach is error prone. Whichever method is used, care must be taken to place the correct questionnaire and any supporting documentation (for example, covering letter) in the right envelope.

Managing dispatch and return of questionnaires, and sending reminders, implies the need to know who has received a questionnaire and who has returned one. In all but the simplest surveys, the use of a computerised database facilitates survey management. Details should be regularly (preferably on a daily basis) updated. Database fields should generally include:

- personal details of sampled individuals (for example, age, date of birth) to facilitate comparisons of respondents and non-respondents

- date when initial questionnaire sent / given

- whether the individual has responded

- date when the individual responded

- whether a reminder was required (possibly distinguishing between first and second reminders, to allow comparison of early and late respondents)

- other useful details (for example, if package or letter was returned by Royal Mail as 'gone away').

Finally, when questionnaires are returned, they need to be carefully checked before data is entered on to a computer for analysis. Things to look out for include: data completeness; inconsistent or implausible answers; respondents not following instructions (for example, writing response in wrong place). Any errors should be noted and, if possible, rectified. If open questions have been used, these will need to be coded prior to analysis. Once data have been entered on to the computer, further checks will be required before these data are analysed. Things to check for include: whether skips have been followed correctly; whether the answers given are valid (for example, within a sensible range); whether responses are internally consistent (for example, that a respondent is not claiming to be male and pregnant).

Further reading
See Article 10 and complete Exercise 5

EXERCISE 5

In a survey, the initial sample size is to be 500. Two reminders are to be used: the first will be a letter; the second will include a duplicate questionnaire as well as a letter. Reply-paid envelopes will be included with the initial mailing and the second reminder. It is assumed that 40% of those contacted will respond to the initial mailing. Thirty per cent of the remaining 60% will respond to the first reminder, while 40% of the residual 42% will respond to the second reminder. Estimate the resources required to conduct this survey.

For answer, see Appendix 1.

· 10 ·
CONCLUSIONS

It is with good reason that Dillman's (1978) classic text on postal and telephone surveys is subtitled *The total design method*. The preceding sections of this workbook should have convinced the reader that the component aspects of the design and conduct of questionnaire surveys – for example, sampling or question wording – cannot and should not be considered in isolation. Excellent *execution* cannot save a survey if the design does not fit the aims; excellent *design* cannot save a survey if there are planning, resource or management deficiencies.

Dillman's *The total design method* has two components. Firstly, it is important to identify how each aspect of the survey process may affect the quantity and quality of the data collected. The survey researcher must carefully consider and manipulate each aspect to obtain the best possible responses, while operating within the constraints imposed by scarce resources of time, money, personnel and equipment. Procedures and practices should be based on sound theory and empirical evidence from previous surveys. Secondly, care must be taken that the actual conduct of the survey is in line with the design intentions.

Throughout the survey process, the survey researcher should keep the aims and objectives of the research study at the forefront of their mind. At each step, the potential for bias and error to creep in should be considered and every effort should be made to minimise these threats.

REFERENCES

Abramson JH (1990) *Survey methods in community medicine*. Edinburgh: Churchill Livingstone.

Bentzen N, Christiansen T, McColl E et al. (1990) Selection and cross-cultural adaptation of health outcome measures. *European Journal of General Practice* **4**:27-33.

Bourque LB and Fielder EP (1995). Chapter 1 – Overview of self-administered questionnaires. In Bourque LP and Fielder EP. *How to conduct self-administered and mail surveys*. Thousand Oaks: Sage Publications.

Bowling A (1995) *Measuring disease: a review of disease specific quality of life measurement scales*. Buckingham: Open University Press.

Bowling A (1997a) *Research methods in health: Investigating health and health services*. Buckingham: Open University Press.

Bowling A (1997b) *Measuring health: a review of quality of life measurement scales* (2nd edition). Milton Keynes: Open University Press.

Brown TL, Decker DJ and Connelly NA (1989) Response to mail surveys on resource-based recreation topics: A behavioral model and an empirical analysis. *Leisure Sciences* **11**;99-110.

Campbell DT and Fiske DW (1959) Convergent and discriminant validation by the multitrait-multimethod matrix. *Psychological Bulletin* **56**:81-105.

Cartwright A (1978) Professionals as responders: variations in and effects of response rates to questionnaires, 1961-77. *British Medical Journal* **2**:1419-1421.

Cartwright A (1986) Who responds to postal questionnaires? *Journal of Epidemiology and Community Health* **40**:267-273.

Crombie IK and Davies HTO (1996) *Research in health care: design, conduct and interpretation of health services research*. Chichester: John Wiley and Sons.

de Vaus DA (1991) *Surveys in social research*, 3rd edition. London: UCL Press Ltd.

Dengler R (1996) Organisation and management of postal surveys. *Survey Methods Centre Newsletter* **16(1)**: 14-16.

Dillman DA (1978) *Mail and telephone surveys: The total design method*. New York: John Wiley and Sons, Inc.

Fink A (1995) *The survey kit*. Thousand Oaks: Sage Publications.

Fishbein M (1967) A consideration of beliefs, and their role in attitude measurement. In Fishbein M (Ed). *Readings in attitude theory and measurement*. New York: John Wiley and Sons.

Fowler FJ Junior (1993) *Survey research methods* (2nd edition). Newbury Park: Sage Publications (Applied Social Research Methods Series – Volume 1).

Fowler FJ Junior (1995) *Improving survey questions – design and evaluation*. Thousand Oaks: Sage Publications (Applied Social Research Methods Series – Volume 38).

Franklin B and Osborne H (1971) *Research methods: issues and insights*. Belmont: Wadsworth Publishing Company Incorporated.

Goyder J (1987) *The silent minority: Nonrespondents on sample surveys*. Cambridge: Polity Press.

Jenkins CR (1996) Designing respondent-friendly self-completion questionnaires. *Survey Methods Centre Newsletter* **16(1)**: 9-13.

Jenkins CR and Dillman DA (1997) Towards a theory of self-administered questionnaire design. In: Lyberg L, Biemer P, Collins M et al. (eds.) *Survey Measurement and Process Quality*, pp165-196. New York: John Wiley & Sons Inc.

Kanuk L and Berenson C (1975) Mail surveys and response rates: A literature review. *Journal of Marketing Research* **12**:440-453.

Litwin MS (1995) *How to measure survey reliability and validity*. Thousand Oaks: Sage Publications.

Lynn P (1996) Quality and error in self-completion surveys. *Survey Methods Centre Newsletter* **16(1)**:4-9.

Mangione TW (1995) *Mail surveys – improving the quality*. Thousand Oaks: Sage Publications (Applied Social Research Methods Series, Volume 40).

McAvoy BR and Kaner EFS (1996) General practice postal surveys: a questionnaire too far? *British Medical Journal* **313**:732-733.

McColl E, Jacoby A, Thomas L et al. (1998) Designing and using patient and staff questionnaires. In Black N, Brazier J, Fitzpatrick R and Reeves B (eds). *Health services research methods: a guide to best practice*. London: BMJ Books.

McDowell I and Newall C (1987) *Measuring health: a guide to rating scales and questionnaires.* Oxford: Oxford University Press.

Moser CA and Kalton G (1971) *Survey methods in social investigation*. London: Gower.

Nicolaas G and Lynn P (1998) The use of respondent incentives in surveys. *Survey Methods Centre Newsletter* **18(2)**:3-8.

Oppenheim AN (1992) *Questionnaire design, interviewing and attitude measurement*, 2nd edition. London: Pinter Publishers.

Øvretveit J (1998) *Evaluating health interventions*. Buckingham: Open University Press.

Sackett DL (1979) Bias in analytic research. *Journal of Chronic Diseases* **32**:51-63.

Streiner DL and Norman GR (1989) *Health measurement scales: a practical guide to their development and use.* Oxford: Oxford University Press.

Sudman S and Bradburn NM (1981) *Asking questions – a practical guide to questionnaire design*. San Francisco: Jossey-Bass Publishers.

Tulsky DS (1990) An introduction to test theory. *Oncology* **4**:43-48.

Wilkin D, Hallam L and Doggett AM (1992) *Measures of need and outcome in primary health care*. Oxford: Oxford Medical Publications.

SUGGESTED FURTHER READING

There are a number of good texts on survey research available. They tend to cover much the same material, so choosing between them is as much a matter of availability and preferred style. The list below includes a number of the texts referenced in this workbook, including some of those from which the reprints have been taken.

Czaja R and Blair J (1996) *Designing surveys: a guide to decisions and procedures*. Thousand Oaks: Pine Forge Press. (*A reasonable introduction, though less specifically oriented to health surveys*)

de Vaus DA (1996) *Surveys in social research* (4th edition). London: UCL Press. (*A relatively recent book, regularly updated, providing a good overview of the whole survey research process*)

Dillman DA (1978) *Mail and telephone surveys: The total design method*, New York: John Wiley and Sons, Inc. (*A classic, though somewhat dogmatic and, in parts, outdated*)

Fink A (ed) (1995) *The survey kit*. Thousand Oaks: Sage Publications. (*A set of seven books, somewhat simplistic but a good introduction; volumes 1, 3 and 4 are particularly useful*)

Fowler FJ Junior (1993) *Survey research methods* (2nd edition). Newbury Park: Sage Publications (Applied Social Research Methods Series – Volume 1). (*Fairly comprehensive and up-to-date*)

Mangione TW (1995) *Mail surveys – improving the quality*. Thousand Oaks: Sage Publications (Applied Social Research Methods Series, Volume 40). (*Similar to Fowler, but focusing on postal surveys*)

Moser CA and Kalton G (1971) *Survey methods in social investigation*. London: Gower. (*A classic, though now a bit dated*)

Oppenhcim AN (1992) *Questionnaire design, interviewing and attitude measurement* (2nd edition). London: Pinter Publications. (*Another classic, but in an updated version*)

Sudman S and Bradburn NM (1981). *Asking questions – a practical guide to questionnaire design*. San Francisco: Jossey-Bass Publishers. (*A very comprehensive presentation of the wording of questions and response categories, and of questionnaire layout; little on other aspects of the survey process*)

APPENDIX 1
EXERCISE ANSWERS

EXERCISE 1

Question 1 is a behaviour question, asking for information about current behaviour in relation to consumption of aspirin. Question 2 is a knowledge question, designed to sort respondents into those who do and those who do not possess the relevant information. Question 3 is an attributes question; marital status is generally seen as an attribute rather than a behaviour (but 'Are you planning on getting married in the next 12 months?' would be an about intentions question). Question 4 is also a behaviour (or event) question, though focusing on past rather than current behaviour. Question 5 is tapping beliefs or knowledge about the efficacy of aspirin in patients who have had a heart attack. By contrast, question 6 is assessing attitudes towards the free availability of aspirin to this patient group; a respondent may know that aspirin is generally indicated in this group (i.e. have a positive belief) but may not feel that it should be available free of charge to all patients (i.e. have a negative or neutral attitude). Question 7 is once again measuring behaviour, albeit projected or planned future behaviour (note that the question does not ask whether the respondent thinks she will become pregnant – that would be a belief). Question 8 is a question about reasons; it often seems that responses to such questions will tell survey users just what they want to know, but respondents often cannot or will not fully analyse their own motives (for example, fear of needles in this case) and may offer rationalisations instead.

EXERCISE 2

The population of interest for this study is the group of patients who have experience of a patient consultation; patients who have not consulted could not be expected to offer an opinion on the interpersonal skills of the general practitioner in this context. However, it would be necessary to define how recently the consultation should have been, since recall problems may compromise the validity of responses. It would also be important to define what constitutes a 'consultation' – does it include a telephone conversation with the general practitioner? Are home visits included? The definition of what constitutes a consultation will determine how adequate the appointment book is as a sampling frame – for example, if the definition of 'consultation' includes home visits and telephone consultations, but the appointment book covers only surgery consultations, an important part of the population is not covered. Other problems could include: multiple entries for certain individuals (i.e. those attending

more than once in the period of interest), thereby increasing their chances of selection; individuals who did not attend for their appointment (and therefore could not be expected to offer an opinion on the general practitioner's interpersonal skills); multiple consultations for a single appointment ('While I'm here, could you have a look at little Johnny?'). Practical problems may also arise. If administrative data have not been registered for use for research purposes under the Data Protection Act, it will be inappropriate to use them in this way. The appointment book may not be computerised, thereby hampering sampling and contacting research subjects.

EXERCISE 3

A lay respondent might not understand the abbreviation OTC or the words 'analgesics' or 'menorrhagia'. The question is double-barrelled (indeed, multiple barrelled!) in asking about use of medication for a range of conditions. It is not clear whether the question refers solely to treatment of self, or whether administration of analgesics to other family members should be included. Occasional use (i.e. less than once a month) or usage more frequently than once a month but less frequently than once a week are not catered for. The order of the response categories is illogical and as a result, the interpretation of 'more frequently' is clouded.

EXERCISE 4

There is no single right answer here! But questions on related topics should be grouped together – for example, those on health-related behaviour (smoking, alcohol consumption, exercise, dietary behaviour, practice of safe sex) should be in the same section, while those on health problems (chest problems, digestive disorders, headache) should also be grouped. Within each section, it would be appropriate to put the more 'contentious' or potentially sensitive questions (for example, practice of safe sex) towards the end of the section. Consideration should also be given to the relative placement of sections. For example, asking about actual dietary behaviour after a series of questions on beliefs about healthy eating might lead to biased responses in which respondents report healthier eating behaviour than is actually the case. Since income and age are sensitive issues for many respondents, these questions should be placed towards the end of the questionnaire. Although family size and composition may be less sensitive, it would be logical to include this question with the other 'personal details' of income and age.

EXERCISE 5

Mailing	No. sent	% returned	No. returned
1	500	40%	200
2 (first reminder)	300	30%	90
3 (second reminder)	210	40%	84
Total	1010		374

Overall response rate = 374 / 500 = 75%

Materials needed:
- questionnaires = 500 + 210 (initial mailing + 2nd reminder)
- letterhead = 500 + 300 + 210 (all mailings)
- large envelopes
    → for posting out = 500 + 210 (initial mailing + 2nd reminder)
    → for return post = 500 + 210 (to be enclosed with initial mailing + 2nd reminder)
    → small envelopes 300 (1st reminder)

Costs:
- printing of questionnaires (unit cost x [500 + 210])
- stationery (envelopes, letterhead – quantities as above)
- postage
    → outgoing = (500 + 210) x cost of package of questionnaire, letter + envelope + 300 x cost of letter
    → return = (200 + 90 + 84) x cost of package

APPENDIX 2
SAMPLE QUESTIONNAIRE

An example questionnaire on cigarette smoking by children aged 11-15

In order to illustrate some of the points raised throughout the workbook, a sample questionnaire, in three parts, has been provided. This is reproduced by kind permission of the Social Surveys Division of the Office of National Statistics.

OPCS Survey of Smoking among Secondary School Children 1984. Office for National Statistics.
© Crown copyright.

QUESTIONNAIRE 1

Office of Population Censuses and Surveys   1215/02

Survey of Smoking

Most of the questions can be answered by putting a tick in the box next to the answer which applies to you – like this

Yes ☐ 1

No ☐ 2

1. (a) In which month is your birthday?

TICK ONE BOX

January	1
February	2
March	3
April	4
May	5
June	6
July	7
August	8
September	9
October	10
November	11
December	12

15-16

1. (b) On what date in that month is your birthday?

WRITE THE DATE IN THE BOX

17-18

2

2. How old are you?

TICK ONE BOX

10 years old	1	
11 years old	2	
12 years old	3	
13 years old	4	19
14 years old	5	
15 years old	6	
16 years old	7	
17 years old	8	

TICK ONE BOX

3. Are you? . . . . a boy?

a boy?	1	20
or a girl?	2	

4. Which year are you in at school?

TICK ONE BOX

1st year	1	
2nd year	2	
3rd year	3	21
4th year	4	
5th year	5	

5. Now read all the following statements carefully and tick the box next to the one which best describes you.

TICK ONE BOX

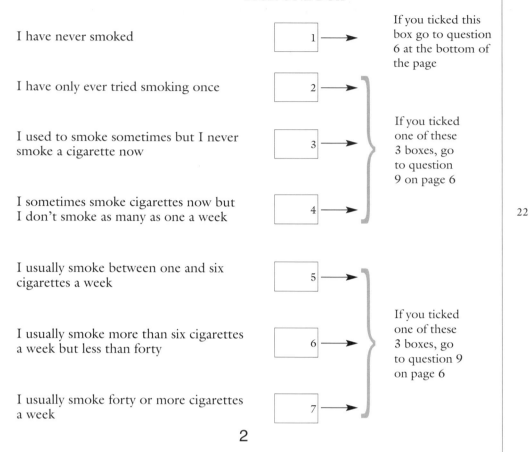

I have never smoked — 1 → If you ticked this box go to question 6 at the bottom of the page

I have only ever tried smoking once — 2 →

I used to smoke sometimes but I never smoke a cigarette now — 3 →

I sometimes smoke cigarettes now but I don't smoke as many as one a week — 4 →

If you ticked one of these 3 boxes, go to question 9 on page 6

I usually smoke between one and six cigarettes a week — 5 →

I usually smoke more than six cigarettes a week but less than forty — 6 →

I usually smoke forty or more cigarettes a week — 7 →

If you ticked one of these 3 boxes, go to question 9 on page 6

22

2

6. Just to check, read the statements below carefully and tick the box next to the one which best describes you.

TICK ONE BOX

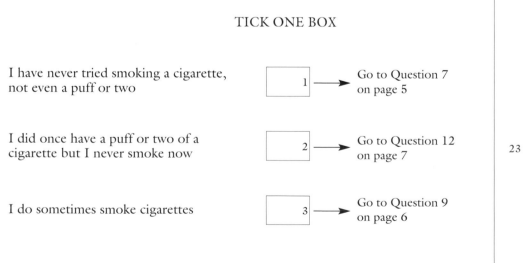

I have never tried smoking a cigarette, not even a puff or two — 1 → Go to Question 7 on page 5

I did once have a puff or two of a cigarette but I never smoke now — 2 → Go to Question 12 on page 7

I do sometimes smoke cigarettes — 3 → Go to Question 9 on page 6

23

And now a couple of questions about whether you are going
to smoke in the future.

7. Do you think you will try smoking a cigarette before you leave school?

TICK ONE BOX

Yes, I think I will ☐ 1   Go to question 8

No, I don't think I will ☐ 2   Go to question 8

24

8. A REGULAR SMOKER is someone who smokes every day.
   After you leave school, do you think you will be a regular smoker?

TICK ONE BOX

Yes, I think I will ☐ 1

No, I don't think I will ☐ 2

25

THANK YOU

YOU SHOULD STOP HERE – DON'T ANSWER ANY MORE
OF THE QUESTIONS AS THE REST OF THEM ARE FOR
PEOPLE WHO HAVE TRIED SMOKING.

WERE THERE ANY QUESTIONS THAT YOU MEANT TO
GO BACK AND COMPLETE?

PLEASE CHECK

9. When you smoke a cigarette, do you usually take the smoke down into your lungs?

TICK ONE BOX

Yes, I do [1]

No, I don't [2]

26

---

10. Where do you usually get your cigarettes from?

TICK ONE OR MORE BOXES

I buy them from a shop [1]

I buy them from a machine [2]

I buy them from other people [3]

Friends give them to me [4]

My brother or sister gives them to me [5]

My mother or father gives them to me [6]

I take them [7]

I get them in some other way [8]

27-30

---

11. When you smoke, who are you usually with?

TICK ONE OR MORE BOXES

With my friend or friends [1]

With my brother [2]

With my sister [3]

With my mother [4]

With my father [5]

With some other person [6]

On my own [7]

31-34

6

Now some questions about the first time you tried smoking a cigarette

12. How old were you the first time you tried smoking a cigarette, even if it was only a puff or two?

WRITE IN THE BOX YOUR AGE WHEN YOU
FIRST TRIED SMOKING (numbers not words)

I was [   ] years old   35-36

13. Who were you with the first time you tried smoking?

TICK ONE OR MORE BOXES

With my friend or friends	1
With my brother	2
With my sister	3
With my mother	4
With my father	5
With some other person	6
On my own	7
Can't remember	8

37-40

14. And where were you the first time you tried smoking a cigarette?

TICK ONE BOX

At home	1	
At a friend's house	2	
On the way to or from school	3	
At school	4	41
At a youth club, disco or other social event	5	
Somewhere else	6	
Can't remember	7	

15. Still thinking about the first time you tried smoking a cigarette, where did you get the cigarette?

TICK ONE BOX

A friend gave it to me	1	
My brother or sister gave it to me	2	
My mother or father gave it to me	3	
Some other person gave it to me	4	42
I bought it	5	
I found it	6	
I just took it	7	
I got it some other way	8	

8

16. And how did you feel the first time you tried smoking a cigarette?

TICK ONE OR MORE BOXES

I enjoyed it	1
I felt grown up	2
I felt nothing	3
I was disappointed	4
I felt sick/ill	5
I felt sorry	6
I can't remember	7

43-46

Finally a couple of questions about whether you are going to smoke in the future

17. Do you think you will smoke a cigarette again before you leave school?

TICK ONE BOX

Yes, I think I will	1
No, I don't think I will	2

47

18. A REGULAR SMOKER is someone who smokes everyday.
   After you leave school, do you think you will be a regular smoker?

TICK ONE BOX

Yes, I think I will	1
No, I don't think I will	2

48

THANK YOU
WERE THERE ANY QUESTIONS THAT YOU MEANT
TO GO BACK AND COMPLETE? PLEASE CHECK

QUESTIONNAIRE 2

For each part of the day: 1) answer the question about what you did by ticking yes or no

		YES	NO
EARLY MORNING	Did you get up and go to school?	1	2
MORNING	Were you at school all morning?	1	2
DINNER TIME	Did you stay on the school premises all dinnertime?	1	2
AFTERNOON	Were you at school all afternoon?	1	2
TEA TIME	Did you have your tea at home?	1	2
EVENING	Did you stay at home all evening?	1	2

and 2) IF YOU DID NOT SMOKE during that part of the day leave the box blank

IF YOU SMOKED during that part of the day write in the box the number of cigarettes you smoked yourself

NUMBER OF CIGARETTES SMOKED

$\longrightarrow$ I smoked [   ] cigarettes

$\longrightarrow$ I smoked [   ] cigarettes

$\longrightarrow$ I smoked [   ] cigarettes

$\longrightarrow$ I smoked [   ] cigarettes

$\longrightarrow$ I smoked [   ] cigarettes

$\longrightarrow$ I smoked [   ] cigarettes

QUESTIONNAIRE 3

81215/02

SERIAL NUMBER

☐ ☐ ☐ ☐   ☐ ☐

SCHOOL NO.   PUPIL NO.

On this page are a few things people say about smoking.
Some people think they are true and some people think they are not true.
What do you think?

AGAINST EACH SENTENCE TICK ONE BOX TO
SHOW IF YOU THINK IT IS TRUE OR NOT TRUE

TICK ONE BOX

	TRUE	NOT TRUE	
1. Smoking gives people confidence	☐ 1	☐ 2	49
2. Smoking makes people worse at sport	☐ 1	☐ 2	50
3. Smokers stay slimmer than non-smokers	☐ 1	☐ 2	50
4. If a woman smokes when she is pregnant, it can harm her unborn baby	☐ 1	☐ 2	52
5. Smoking helps people relax if they are nervous	☐ 1	☐ 2	53
6. Smoking can cause heart disease	☐ 1	☐ 2	54
7. Smoking is not really dangerous. It only harms people who smoke a lot	☐ 1	☐ 2	55
8. Smokers get more coughs and colds than non-smokers	☐ 1	☐ 2	56
9. Other people's smoking can harm the health of non-smokers	☐ 1	☐ 2	57
10. Smoking helps people cope better with life	☐ 1	☐ 2	58
11. Smokers are more fun than non-smokers	☐ 1	☐ 2	59
12. Smoking can cause lung cancer	☐ 1	☐ 2	60

1

13. Who in your family at home smokes?

TICK A BOX AGAINST EACH ONE WHO SMOKES.
LEAVE IT BLANK IF THEY DON'T SMOKE OR IF
THEY DON'T LIVE AT HOME WITH YOU.
IF NO ONE AT HOME SMOKES JUST TICK BOX 6

Mother	1
Father	2
Sister (s)	3
Brother (s)	4
Anyone else who lives at home with you	5
No one at home smokes	6

61-65

14. How do you think your family feel or would feel about you smoking

TICK ONE BOX

They (would) stop me	1
They (would) try to persuade me not to smoke	2
They (would) do nothing	3
They (would) encourage me to smoke	4
I don't know	5

66

15. Are you allowed to smoke at home if you want to?

TICK ONE BOX

Yes	1
No	2
I don't know	3

67

2

16.　A regular smoker is someone who smokes cigarettes every day

Do you think that adults who are regular smokers become less healthy because of their smoking than adults who never smoke?

TICK ONE BOX

Yes　　　　　　　　　　　☐ 1

No　　　　　　　　　　　☐ 2　　　　68

I don't know　　　　　　　☐ 3

17.　What about when <u>you</u> become an adult?

If you become a regular smoker, do you think your smoking will make <u>you</u> less healthy than you would be if you didn't smoke at all?

TICK ONE BOX

Yes　　　　　　　　　　　☐ 1

No　　　　　　　　　　　☐ 2　　　　69

I don't know　　　　　　　☐ 3

18.　During the last 12 months, have you had any lessons, films or discussions in class about smoking?

TICK ONE BOX

Yes　　　　　　　　　　　☐ 1

No　　　　　　　　　　　☐ 2　　　　70

I don't know　　　　　　　☐ 3

3

19. Each week, how much money do you have of your own to spend as you like?

TICK ONE BOX

Nothing	1
Less than £1 a week	2
£1 or more but less than £5	3
£5 or more but less than £10	4
£10 or more but less than £20	5
£20 or more	6

71

20. If you spend any of this money on cigarettes, how do you usually buy them?

TICK ONE BOX

Never buy cigarettes	1
Buy them one at a time	2
Buy them in packets of 10	3
Buy them in packets of 20	4
Buy them in larger packs	5

72

WERE THERE ANY QUESTIONS THAT YOU
MEANT TO GO BACK AND COMPLETE?
PLEASE CHECK
OTHERWISE, THIS IS THE END

THANK YOU VERY MUCH FOR YOUR HELP

4

QUESTIONNAIRES

Each questionnaire needs to be designed for its specific purpose, with many factors in mind. Some of the more important factors relevant to questionnaire design are:

A. the aims of the enquiry, including the specific information needs of a sponsor;

B. any specific hypotheses that it is intended to test;

C. the population from which the survey sample is drawn and the likely distribution of respondent characteristics (age, motivation, literacy and comprehension levels etc);

D. the style of research and data collection (flexible qualitative, standardised quantitative etc);

E. the chosen mode of data collection (personal interview, self-completion questionnaire etc);

F. the conditions under which data are to be collected (in school, in the home, with or without precautions to ensure privacy etc);

G. the ethical basis on which the research is conducted, for example with respect to confidentiality;

H. the method of sample selection;

I. the time available for data collection from each research subject;

J. any related research literature and direct survey precedents;

K. the survey timetable;

L. the survey budget.

GENERAL DESIGN OF THE SMOKING AMONG SCHOOLCHILDREN SURVEY

The above survey was carried out by the Social Survey Division of the (then) Office of Population Censuses and Surveys on behalf of the Department of Health. The primary aim (A) was to obtain estimates of the prevalence and incidence of cigarette smoking amongst children in the first five years of secondary education (C), corresponding approximately to the age range 11-15 years. Secondary aims (A) were to measure the children's attitudes and expectations with respect to smoking, to learn about the social environment in which smoking behaviour begins and the habit is established and to find out how children of different ages obtained cigarettes. There were no formal hypotheses (B), but there were some informal hypotheses about the causes of smoking behaviour implicit in the choice of questions on attitudes and beliefs about smoking and on social environment. The research took the form of a standardised, quantitative survey of a sample drawn from the population of school children (D).

The survey followed on earlier ones in a series and the methodology used was constrained by the need for comparability (J). The mode of data collection was self completion questionnaires administered in a supervised classroom situation (E). The advantages of this were economy (many respondents dealt with simultaneously in one location) (L), control over sampling from school registers (H), control over data collection giving high response and limitation was the level of literacy and form-filling speed and stamina that could be expected of younger pupils in particular (C), given that data collection had to be contained with a school period (I) in order to minimise inconvenience and disruption to the schools.

The co-operation of school management had to be obtained and their ethical requirements (e.g. asking parental permission for child to take part) had to be sought (G), adding to the required timetable (K). The time of year at which data collection was to be carried out was also constrained, since smoking behaviour was known to change rapidly with age and a later survey would produce higher prevalence estimates (K). From a quality control viewpoint it was a great advantage that the methodology had already been tested in a strictly similar research context and, in particular, that the wording of questions had been piloted (J).

QUESTIONNAIRE DESIGN

The following questionnaire design points should be noted

FIRST QUESTIONNAIRE (MARKED QUESTIONNAIRE 1)

Page 1. Note the example to children on how to complete questions. No question texts are given in the example, so there is no suggestion that particular questions 'ought to' be answered by copying the example.

Note the keying design (assigning items of information to card columns on right).

Note the carefully designed sampling unit (school, pupil) date and document identification numbers. These carry information and are essential for survey administration and survey analysis purposes. They were inserted by the supervisor, using pupil numbers assigned at the sampling stage (see Interviewer Classroom Instructions).

Page 2. Q1 It is necessary to obtain and record birthday, from which calendar age can be inferred when school year is known (see Q4). Exact age is an important analysis variable.

Young children do not necessarily know and follow the standard 'DD/MM/YY' way of recording dates, so it is best to rely on ticking boxes.

Page 4. Q5 is a filter question, always a point of potential confusion. The wording and layout shown may or may not be the optimum compromise between explicitness of instruction and too many words to read.

The smoking behaviour categories have been carefully devised to match the spasmodic pattern of smoking known to be typical of younger smokers. Q6 is designed to identify conflicted individuals who have tried smoking but do not like to identify themselves as 'smokers'.

Page 5. At Q8 genuine 'Never tried smoking' cases are filtered out. Note the use of arrows.

Never-smokers (as well as smokers) still need to go to both the smoking diary (labelled Questionnaire 2) and the second questionnaire (labelled Questionnaire 3). This enables the home background and attitudes of non-smokers as well as smokers to be captured for comparison.

Two separate questionnaire documents are used to help those supervising the self-completion to monitor the children's progress and ensure that all complete the questionnaires. The different questionnaires would have been printed on different coloured paper.

Page 6. At Q9 use of technical word 'inhale' is avoided.

At Q10 code 7 the more emotive word 'steal' is avoided, but perhaps with some loss of clarity. At Questionnaire 1 Q15 the wording used is 'I just took it'.

At Q10 and Q11 the instruction is 'TICK ONE OR MORE BOXES'. This could easily be missed since up to now only one tick per question has been required. The habit of not noticing such instructions could affect completion of other questions.

Page 7. At Q12 note the explicitness of instructions on how to answer.

Page 8. At Q14 code 5 'social event' would probably not have been understood by some children.

Page 9. At Q16 code 6 'sorry' is probably better wording than 'guilty'.

Note the reminder to ensure that all questions are answered.

SMOKING DIARY (MARKED QUESTIONNAIRE 2)

This instrument was intended as a means of checking the validity of responses to Q5-6 in the first questionnaire. Since only one week's smoking behaviour was recorded, the diary measure (even assuming it was completed honestly and accurately) is unreliable as an indicator of the smoking behaviour of individuals. However overall statistical estimates of smoking behaviour resulting from questions and the diary can be compared.

For administration of the diary see Interviewer Classroom Instructions at the end of this section. [In point (v) the words 'smoked/drank' were mistakenly carried over from another survey and should have read just 'smoked'.]

Note that the diary contained seven pages labelled with days of the week. The diary was handed to pupils ready-open at yesterday; they began recording yesterday's smoking behaviour and then worked through the seven days of the diary, finishing with the day a week ago (which would be the same day as the one on which they were completing the diary).

THIRD QUESTIONNAIRE (MARKED QUESTIONNAIRE 3)

Page 1. Note the school and pupil identification numbers inserted by the supervisor.

Note that pupils only have to tick either 'True' or 'Not true'. Finer discrimination of the individual's attitudinal position on a particular item (e.g. 'Strongly agree', 'Agree on the whole' etc) is sacrificed to simplicity.

The items have been designed to get at several dimensions of belief and attitude about smoking which were suggested by earlier research as being important in turning children off or on to smoking. However, this is a non-experimental study and therefore it is very hard to determine whether belief 'causes' smoking or smoking 'causes' belief (or both or neither).

Page 2. At Q13 completion instruction is rather complicated. Intention was to identify possible smoking role models actually living in a child's household. This is emphasised by use of 'at home' in question text.

At Q14 wording 'feel or would feel' and use of brackets may have confused some children. Such problems are likely to arise where the same questions are intended to be answered by individuals in different circumstances, so that for some the question is factual, but for others hypothetical. The alternative is to have separate question sequences tailored to smokers and non-smokers, but that would require filtering and lengthen the questionnaire.

Page 3. At Q16-17 note how question wording avoids complicated concepts such as probability.

Page 4. At Q19 note careful definition, rather than vague term such as 'pocket money'.

Remember amounts relate to 1984 prices.

INTERVIEWER CLASSROOM INSTRUCTIONS*

Interviewers' instructions on procedure for administering the survey documents in the classroom

At most schools you will have selected a sample of approximately 39 pupils for the smoking survey and you should divide the sample into two groups and administer the questionnaire to first one group and then the other. Generally you should take the younger pupils, the 1st and 2nd years (approximately 16 pupils) as the first group and the 3rd, 4th and 5th years (approximately 24 pupils) as the second group. You may, if necessary, divide the pupils in a different way – if the school is on two sites, for instance, there may be a more appropriate way to divide the pupils according to which site they are on.

At middle schools you will have selected a sample of approximately 13 pupils for the smoking survey so these can all be dealt with in one group.

The school will provide a room, probably a classroom, for the completion of the questionnaire and you will have given them lists of the selected pupils in each group at the end of your sampling visit. Arrive at the classroom early, before the first group of pupils. This gives you and your helper time to get organised and rearrange or separate the desks if necessary. (It is also helpful to have discussed the procedure for the main visit with your helper to decide who will do what).

The school should also have arranged for the groups of selected pupils to come to the classroom at the agreed times, but if necessary the helper could assist in doing this. Remember to check with your contact what the pupils should do or where they should go when they have completed the documents. Some contacts may be willing to check the registers on the day of your main visit and inform you whether any of the sampled pupils are absent. This is useful so suggest it if you feel you can.

REMEMBER TO HAVE THE DIARIES OPEN AT THE CORRECT DAY – YESTERDAY

The procedure for each group of selected pupils should then be:

(i) As the pupils come into the classroom, ask for their names and tick them off on your sampling sheet. Note how many there are.

(ii) *Introductions*
When all the pupils who are in school that day are settled in their seats you should introduce yourself and your helper. The introduction should include a short description of Social Survey Division, a statement about confidentiality (particularly in relation to the school and the teachers) and a brief explanation of the survey and what they will have to do. Explain a little about the background and purpose. It may be worth explaining how the sample was selected so that they do not feel unfairly singled out, and that it is important for us to have both smoker/drinkers and non-smokers/non-drinkers in the sample. If the school took part in the 1982 survey it will be particularly relevant to mention that this is a repeat. Pupils seem to find it reassuring to realise that you only serial number the questionnaires after they have been completed so that even *you* cannot tell which questionnaire a particular pupil completed. It may therefore be worth explaining that this is what you will do.

(iii) Tell the pupils to put their hand up whenever they have a query or problem so that one of you can provide assistance.

(iv) Give a copy of the first questionnaire and a pen to each pupil and briefly explain the method of completion – reiterating what is written on the front of the questionnaire and explaining the signposting. Then ask them to complete the questionnaire.

(v) When they have all finished, give out a diary to each pupil, *ready opened at the correct page i.e. yesterday.* Explain the diary briefly, using one or two examples, and including both the possibility that pupils smoked/drank during a particular part of the day and the possibility that they did not. Then ask them to complete the diaries.

(vi) (Smoking groups only) When they have all finished, give out the second questionnaire, containing the 'new' questions. Another brief explanation may be useful, particularly in relation to the statements on the front page.

(vii) When they have all finished, ask them to tag the documents together (you should give out the tags at some time during the self-completion session). Then allow them to return to their classes or whatever you agreed with the school.

(viii) Complete the response summary on the school sheet. Repeat this procedure for each group. Before you leave, remember to thank your contact and/or whoever helped with the organisation. Discuss arrangements for a follow-up visit if necessary.

* The text above is taken directly from the Interviewer Classroom Instructions provided to interviewers on the smoking survey. This is reproduced by kind permission of the Social Surveys Division of the Office for National Statistics.

Reading Material

1. Bourque LB and Fielder EP (1995) Overview of self-administered questionnaires. In: *How to conduct self-administered and mail surveys*. CA, Sage.

2. McColl E, Jacoby A, Thomas L et al (1998) Designing and using patient and staff questionnaires. In: Black N, Fitzpatrick R and Reeves B (eds) *Health Services Research Methods – Mail Surveys – a guide to best practice*, London, BMJ Books.

3. Lynn P (1996) Quality and error in self-completion surveys. *Survey Methods Centre Newsletter* **16** (1).

4. Fowler FJ Junior (1993) Sampling. In: *Survey Research Methods* (2nd edn), CA, Sage.

5. Fowler FJ Junior (1995) Some general rules for designing good survey instruments. In: *Improving Survey Questions – Design and Evaluation*, CA, Sage.

6. Jenkins CR (1996) Designing respondent-friendly self-completion questionnaires. In: *Survey Methods Centre Newsletter* **16** (1).

7. Mangione TW (1995) The basics of avoiding non-response errors. In: *Mail Surveys – improving the quality*, CA, Sage.

8. Mangione TW (1995) Additional ways to reduce non-response errors. In: *Mail Surveys – improving the quality*, CA, Sage.

9. Nicolaas G and Lynn P (1998) The use of respondent incentives in surveys. In: *Survey Methods Centre Newsletter* **18** (2).

10. Dengler R (1998) Organisation and management of postal surveys. In: *Survey Methods Centre Newsletter* **19** (1).

This chapter was first published by Sage Publications and is reproduced by permission of Sage Publications
How to Conduct Self-Administered and Mail Surveys, CA: Sage (1995)
Linda B Bourque and Eve P Fielder

Chapter 1
Overview of Self-Administered Questionnaires

Self-administered questionnaires are one of the most frequently used methods for collecting data in research studies. Furthermore, self-administered questionnaires appear in many areas of our lives. Think, for example, of the testing strategies used in most classrooms from kindergarten through graduate school. Classroom tests are a type of self-administered questionnaire. Similarly, we fill out forms or "questionnaires" to obtain everything from a driver's license to a death certificate.

Unfortunately, this very proliferation and familiarity of self-administered "questionnaires" in a wide variety of daily life settings results in neophyte surveyors often assuming that they can develop a self-administered questionnaire literally overnight and use it to collect data that will be available immediately. Like any research endeavor and the use of any procedure for collecting data, the development and administration of self-administered questionnaires takes time and thought. This book outlines the circumstances under which self-administered questionnaires provide a good or at least an adequate method for collecting information, what must be considered in designing such questionnaires, and the methods used in administering them while maximizing the collection of complete, reliable, and valid data.

Types of Self-Administered Questionnaires

A self-administered questionnaire is an instrument used to collect information from people who complete the instrument themselves. The stimulus is exclusively visual. As we noted at the outset, such instruments are not used exclusively for research purposes but can be used to collect information for a wide variety of purposes and in a wide variety of settings. To date 'self-administered questionnaires have almost always been administered using paper-and-pencil techniques, but with the rapid proliferation of computers and the information superhighway it is likely that such procedures will increasingly be adapted to electronic mediums. To the extent that such developments occur, it is entirely possible that auditory stimuli could be added to the visual in soliciting information through such means in much the same way that sophisticated voicemail systems now route telephone requests for information, service, or appointments. For the purposes of this book, however,

we will stick with the traditional method by which such questionnaires have been historically administered—namely, each respondent receives a printed questionnaire, which is filled out using a pen or pencil.

There are two types of self-administered questionnaires, best described as the ends of a unidimensional continuum. At one end are questionnaires that people answer in the presence of the surveyor or other supervising personnel. At the opposite end of the continuum are questionnaires completed by the respondent outside the presence of the surveyor or other monitoring personnel.

Questionnaires sent through the mail provide the most common example of unsupervised administration. Such questionnaires—frequently called "mail questionnaires"—are the major focus of this book both because of their frequent use and because almost everything that applies to a mail questionnaire has equal applicability to self-administered questionnaires distributed through other means and administered in other environments. Before turning our attention to mail questionnaires, we briefly describe some of the different kinds of supervised or partially supervised environments in which self-administered questionnaires are distributed.

Supervised Administration
One-to-One Supervision
In the most extreme form of group administration, the respondent is in a one-to-one situation with the surveyor and the surveyor is available to answer any questions that the respondent has about the questionnaire. This type of administration is rarely used because, as we discuss later, a major reason for using self-administered questionnaires is to reduce costs. The costs associated with one-to-one administration would more closely resemble those of telephone or personal interviewing than those of self-administration.

Nonetheless, one-to-one supervision is, on occasion, used—often within the context of a study where face-to-face interviewing provides the major method of data collection. For example, under the auspices of the National Institute for Drug Abuse (NIDA) self-administered questionnaires were developed for use in ascertaining respondents' current and historical use of drugs. The questionnaires were given to respondents as part of a face-to-face interview. Their format was such that the time taken to complete the questionnaire did not differ with current or past drug history. In other words, persons who had never used drugs took just as long to complete the questionnaire as did those who had used many drugs. Within the context of the face-to-face interview, elaborate procedures were developed to ensure that the interviewer did not see the questionnaire either while it was being completed or once it was completed. The purpose here was to maximize confidentiality, the assumption being that people generally underreport the use of drugs. At the same time, the interviewer was available to answer questions or to clarify concepts should it be necessary.

Group Administration

Far more common is the situation where questionnaires are passed out in a classroom, workplace, or other group setting. Each person is expected to complete the questionnaire without consulting other persons in the group, but the surveyor or other supervisory person is available to provide introductory instructions, answer questions, and monitor the extent to which questionnaires are completed and individual respondents communicate with each other during the period of administration. Depending on the purpose of the study, the administrator may be instructed to answer and clarify any and all questions that come up or may be instructed to defer or deflect all or most questions.

For example, when group self-administration is being used to develop a questionnaire, the surveyor will probably want to learn as much as possible about how the questionnaire "works," whether respondents understand the questions asked, whether the information requested is accessible to respondents, and whether the response categories provided are exhaustive, mutually exclusive, and readily understood. In such instances, the surveyor may invite respondents to raise questions as they move through the questionnaire, or, alternatively, the surveyor may ask the respondents to first complete the questionnaire and then solicit questions, comments, and problems as part of a general discussion following the administration of the questionnaire. In either case, the person supervising the group administration must keep careful notes of the issues raised by respondents because many of the questions and comments may necessitate changes in the questionnaire.

When, in contrast, a finalized questionnaire is being administered in a group setting, supervisory personnel often are instructed to deflect any questions or comments raised by respondents. Many of the instruments used to measure attitudes, opinions, physical health status, psychological distress, and a number of other things were developed to be administered as paper-and-pencil tests in either individual or group settings. Generally, these instruments have been developed over time and with substantial attention to establishing the validity and reliability of the measure. They also were developed to assess how a particular individual respondent compares with other groups of respondents.

When such instruments are administered, the surveyor wants to do everything possible to ensure that each respondent gets an identical stimulus and that the information obtained represents that individual's feelings, attitudes, or health status. In such cases, the administrator in a group setting will generally have a scripted set of instructions used to introduce the questionnaire. These instructions may or may not be repeated on the questionnaire itself. Included in the instructions will be a statement to the effect that there are no right or wrong answers to the questions being asked, that the purpose is to find out how this particular person feels about or experiences the topic under investigation, and, when pertinent, instructions are given on how to complete the questionnaire.

Semisupervised Administration

In group administrations, as described above, it is assumed for our purposes that everyone is in the same place—usually a room—for the duration of the administration period or at least for the beginning part of it. Everyone hears the same set of verbal instructions, and everyone's questions or comments are handled in a similar way. Self-administered questionnaires are also distributed in an almost infinite variety of semisupervised administrations. For example, questionnaires might be distributed in the waiting room of a well-baby clinic by a receptionist. In such a situation, no formal presentation of verbal instructions will be given to the potential group of respondents as a whole. Rather, the receptionist will give each respondent pertinent instructions when the questionnaire is passed out. Because personnel may change during the week and the activity level in the clinic will vary the content and extent of instructions that a given respondent receives is also likely to vary. Respondents who arrive when the clinic is quiet may receive detailed instructions, whereas those who arrive when the patient load is heavy may receive no instructions. Clearly, the constancy of the stimulus provided in such situations, at least as indicated in instructions, has the potential to influence the validity and reliability of the data obtained. Nonetheless, someone—namely, the receptionist—is, at least titularly, available to answer questions about the questionnaire and monitor the data collection effort at some minimal level.

Questionnaires are also passed out in environments such as registration lines, auditoriums, amusement centers, and airplanes and as persons are entering or exiting a store or other site. Such questionnaires can also be considered "semisupervised" to the extent that the person who distributes and collects the questionnaires is available to answer questions or provide instructions. The amount of control the surveyor exerts in such an environment is, however, limited to the selection of who will receive a questionnaire, the ability to ensure that distributed questionnaires are completed and returned, and the consistency with which any verbal instructions beyond those printed on the hard copy of the questionnaire are, in fact, solicited by or available to respondents.

Unsupervised Administration

To our knowledge, no statistics exist regarding the number of self-administered questionnaires that are used in research projects or how they distribute between supervised and unsupervised administration, but when people think of self-administered questionnaires within a research context, in all probability they are referring to questionnaires sent through the mail, which is the primary method by which unsupervised questionnaires are administered.

When a questionnaire is administered in a completely unsupervised administration, it is imperative that the questionnaire be completely self-sufficient, or able to "stand alone." When questionnaires are sent through the mail, no member of the research staff is available to answer questions or ensure that the correct person completes the questionnaire or, indeed, that anyone completes it. Even though the questionnaire's cover sheet can include a contact name and phone number for the potential respondent's use if clarification or information is needed, the respondent must initiate such contacts. Hence, the motivation to seek information must be high.

The remainder of this book focuses on the design of mail questionnaires because the requirement that they be able to stand alone places greater restrictions on what can be included in them and requires the surveyor to pay careful attention to how clearly the questionnaire is written and presented so as to maximize the response rate.

A summary of the advantages and disadvantages of using the aforementioned ways of administering questionnaires is provided in Example 1.1.

Example 1.1
Four Ways of Administering
Respondent-Completed Questionnaires

Type of Administration	Advantages	Disadvantages
One-to-one	Interviewer available to answer questions	Expensive
	Maximizes confidentiality in face-to-face interviews	
	Provides in-depth data on the answerability of questions	
Group	Consistent instructions	Not usable with general populations
	Simultaneous administration to all respondents.	
	Administrator can answer questions	
	Provides some information on the answerability of questions	
	Monitor communication between respondents	
	Monitor completion by respondents	
	Useful in pretesting	
Semisupervised	Administrator can answer questions	Samples are frequently unrepresentative
	Efficient	
	Some ability to monitor communication, between respondent and others	Inconsistent instructions
	Some ability to monitor completion	
	Useful in pretesting	
	Inexpensive	
Unsupervised	Consistent stimulus to all respondents	No control over who responds
	Possibility of more representative samples	No direct information on answerability of questions
		Questionnaire must stand alone

ADVANTAGES OF SELF-ADMINISTERED QUESTIONNAIRES

Cost

The single greatest advantage of self-administered questionnaires is their lower cost compared to other methods (e.g., in-person and telephone interviews). Given the same-length questionnaire and same objective, a completed questionnaire administered by mail costs approximately 50% less than one administered by telephone and 75% less than one administered by personal interview.

Sample Related

Mail questionnaires have three sample-related advantages: geographic coverage, larger samples, and wider coverage within a sample population. Although the three are interrelated, both with each other and with issues of cost, each advantage is briefly recognized.

Geographic Coverage

Mail questionnaires allow for wider geographic coverage. This is particularly true when mail questionnaires are compared to personal or face-to-face interviewing. A questionnaire can be mailed anywhere in the world, whereas face-to-face interviews tend to be restricted to a defined geographic area or areas where trained interviewers are available, can be monitored, and are able to physically contact intended respondents. Telephone interviewing also allows for a wider geographic coverage and, for all practical intents and purposes, can be conducted anywhere within the United States from a single site, assuming that funds are available for covering long-distance charges and the population under study has access to telephones. Telephone interviewing becomes problematic, however, if a substantial number of the designated respondents reside outside the United States.

For example, we used mail questionnaires to contact both undergraduate and graduate alumni of UCLA. Although most potential respondents lived in the United States (many of them in Southern California), a certain proportion of both groups resided in other countries. Because little money was available for either study, data collection using either telephone or face-to-face interviewing techniques would have prevented any attempt to obtain information from non-U.S. residents. In contrast, sending questionnaires through the mail allowed a substantial proportion of such respondents to be contacted and yielded response rates comparable to those of the sample as a whole.

Larger Samples

The lower unit cost of a mail questionnaire combined with its ability to cover a wider geographic area with little additional cost for respondents at a distance allows surveyors to study a larger sample of persons or groups. Thus, where available funds might allow for only 100 persons within a limited geographic area to be interviewed, they may allow for questionnaires to be mailed to 400-500 persons over a much larger geographic area.

Wider Coverage Within a Sample Population

Some people are reluctant to talk with people either in person or on the phone. This reluctance to talk with strangers has increased particularly in large urban areas. For example, it may be difficult or impossible to get residents of high-security buildings to agree to be interviewed—particularly if the interview is to be conducted in the home. These same persons may, however, be willing to respond to a mail questionnaire. Similarly, some persons do not have access to telephones or are reluctant to be interviewed by telephone. Again, some percentage of these persons may be willing and able to respond to a self-administered questionnaire.

In some cases, respondents are much more willing to complete a self-administered questionnaire when it can be done at their convenience rather than having to make a commitment to an interviewer to be available at an appointed time for a specific length of time to do an interview.

Implementation

Mail and other self-administered questionnaires are much easier to implement than other kinds of questionnaires. First, the number of personnel needed is substantially less because interviewers and those who hire, train, and supervise them are not needed. As is discussed in Chapter 2, self-administered questionnaires are shorter and simpler in structure, so fewer personnel and less complicated procedures are required for processing data once obtained. In contrast to telephone interviewing and particularly computer-assisted telephone interviewing (CATI), minimal equipment is needed to conduct a study by mail. In the simplest case, a single person can conduct an entire mail survey from start to finish.

Timing

Unlike almost all other methods of data collection, it can be assumed that when a questionnaire is sent through the mail all members of the sample receive it simultaneously. Thus, the potential influence of events outside or unrelated to the study that might influence a potential respondent's experiences, opinions, or attitudes are reduced and can be assumed to be equal for all recipients of the questionnaire. For example, in our study of assault in the workplace, all questionnaires were mailed on the same day and were received by all respondents within the same 2- or 3-day period. Imagine telephone interviews being conducted with the same group of respondents. It is generally not possible to conduct 1,000 telephone interviews within a 2- or 3-day period—more likely, it would take weeks or even months.

Suppose that during that period of time an employee of the Los Angeles County Health Department is assaulted on the job and this assault is prominently featured in the *Los Angeles Times*. Clearly, persons interviewed *after* the assault are likely to have different attitudes and opinions about assault in the workplace than those interviewed *before* the assault. The questionnaire that the two groups of respondents received cannot be assumed to have had an identical impact on their responses. In contrast, had the questionnaires been mailed on the same day, they can be assumed to have created a similar stimulus for all potential respondents. That is not to say that an event cannot occur at some point during the conduct of a mailed survey; however, the "window of opportunity" is greatly lessened.

Sensitive Topics

Earlier, we discussed the use of self-administered questionnaires to collect information about drug use within the context of an interview. Many surveyors believe that people are more likely to give complete and truthful information on sensitive topics if a self-administered questionnaire rather than an interview is used. Early methodological studies tended to support this perception on the part of surveyors, but more recent studies suggest that sensitive information may be collected as effectively or with even greater accuracy through telephone and face-to-face interviews.

The reason for the variation in findings across time and studies probably relates to the overall objectives of studies, the environments in which they are conducted, the ability of interviewers to establish rapport, the extent to which respondents believe that the data provided is both anonymous and confidential, and the ways in which both the overall questionnaire and individual questions are structured. We are of the opinion that sensitive topics can be effectively studied using all kinds of questionnaires.

DISADVANTAGES OF SELF-ADMINISTERED QUESTIONNAIRES

Mail and self-administered questionnaires have a number of disadvantages that limit or prohibit their use in many research projects. These disadvantages can be grouped under three general headings: sample related, questionnaire construction, and administration.

Sample Related

Availability of Lists

Although self-administered questionnaires are administered to admittedly nonrepresentative convenience samples, many surveyors want to use self-administered questionnaires and particularly mail questionnaires to collect data from samples that can be considered representative of the population from which they were drawn. The ability to do this—particularly when questionnaires are sent through the mail—is dependent on having a complete and accurate list of the population. To the extent that lists are unavailable, incomplete, or inaccurate, the data obtained cannot be assumed to represent the population to which the surveyor wishes to generalize.

In the worst-case scenario, the surveyor must either resort to other methods of sample generation and data collection (e.g., random digit dialing and telephone interviewing), conduct a census to establish the population from which the sample is to be drawn, or resort to convenience sampling techniques.

Response Rates

One of the greatest and most studied disadvantages to mail questionnaires is their low response rate. When a single mailing that incorporates no incentives is made to a sample of the general community, the surveyor can probably expect no better than a 20% response rate. The use of premailings, follow-up contacts, incentives, targeted populations, and a variety of other procedures combine to increase response rates, but even in the best case, response rates for mail questionnaires will be lower than those for telephone and face-to-face interviews.

Literacy and Language

One of the reasons why response rates are poor—particularly in studies targeted at general community samples—is because persons who are illiterate or who have difficulty reading simply are unable to respond even if they want to. The rate of adult illiteracy in the United States is estimated to be 20%. Obviously, persons who are functionally illiterate will be unable to complete a self-administered questionnaire and will be missed in *any* study in which they are part of the target population.

Visual acuity of the respondent can have an effect on response. Individuals who have problems with reading, such as the elderly, the visually impaired, or the dyslexic, may find the effort required to read the questionnaire too great and may not complete and return it to the surveyor. Obviously, if the target population tends to overrepresent any of these groups, it may be wise to consider an alternative method for collecting the data.

An additional problem—particularly in large urban areas on the East and West Coast—is the wide range of languages spoken in the home. For example, in Los Angeles County, 13% of the population is linguistically isolated—meaning that they speak no English—and an additional 28% report that a language other than English is the primary or only language spoken in the home. Obviously, when target populations include substantial proportions of respondents who are non-English speakers, self-administered questionnaires must be translated and some mechanism devised for ensuring that each respondent receives a questionnaire in the correct language. As a result, data from multiple-language populations generally cannot be adequately or accurately collected using self-administered questionnaires.

Questionnaire Construction

Objective

Self-administered questionnaires can be used only when the objective of the study is clear and not complex. For example, you would not want to use a mail questionnaire if you needed to collect an entire occupational history on respondents and wanted to investigate their satisfaction with their current worksite, job, employment benefits, and co-workers, and how these factors correlated with or interacted with lifestyle.

Obviously, surveyors hope to have motivated subjects in any research study, but motivation is particularly important when self-administered questionnaires are used for data collection. In the case of the workplace assault study, we decided that mail questionnaires could be used because union representatives informed us that many of their members had expressed concern about the physical safety of the environments where they worked. Thus, we believed that the topic under study would be considered important by potential respondents and that this heightened salience of the topic would increase respondents' motivation to participate in the study and hence increase our response rate.

Format

The need for a clear and noncomplex data-collection objective has ramifications for how the questionnaire is constructed and precludes the use of many strategies typically used in designing questionnaires. Chapters 2 through 4 discuss this issue in detail, so only some of these limitations are briefly noted here.

First, self-administered questionnaires must be shorter than questionnaires administered in other ways. If the questionnaire must be shorter, then obviously the number of questions asked and topics covered is reduced.

Second, the questions on self-administered questionnaires must be closed-ended ones. Although highly motivated respondents may be willing to answer a few open-ended questions, the surveyor who writes a self-administered questionnaire dominated by open-ended questions will find that few questionnaires will be returned and that those that are returned will frequently have substantial amounts of missing or irrelevant data.

Third, the questionnaire must "stand alone." In other words, all the information that the potential respondent needs to answer the questions must be provided on the questionnaire itself, as there is no interviewer available to clarify instructions or provide additional information to eliminate confusion. The objective is to make the questionnaire as easy as possible for the respondent to complete without assistance from others. This restriction means that cue cards or other visual aids cannot be used with self-administered questionnaires. It also means that the number of possible responses to a question must be limited to a number that can be readily assimilated by respondents and from which they can reasonably select those that apply to them. Thus, the need to create exhaustive lists of mutually exclusive responses may be impossible if the list becomes excessively long. Nor is it reasonable to expect respondents to rank order large numbers of alternatives. Not only are such lists burdensome for respondents to read, assimilate, and select from, but the issue of *primacy effect* becomes relevant. By primacy effect we mean respondents' tendency to select the *first* response they come to that reflects how they feel or behave even if it is not the best or most representative response available. Once a response is selected, the respondent ignores the rest of the list and goes to the next question. The necessity that the questionnaire be totally self-explanatory is probably one of the most difficult objectives to achieve in designing self-administered questionnaires.

Fourth, as part of the objective of simplifying the task for respondents, the surveyor needs to create a questionnaire without branches or skips. In other words, every question asked in the questionnaire should contain a response category that each respondent can comfortably use to describe his or her attitudes, behavior, knowledge, or characteristics. In some instances, this means that a "not applicable" alternative must be included among the responses provided for a question or series of questions.

Order Effects

When questionnaires are administered by telephone or face-to-face interviewer, the interviewer controls the order in which the questions are asked and controls whether or not the answer alternatives are made available to respondents—either by reading aloud the alternatives or by presenting them in written form on a cue card. In a self-administered questionnaire, everything is simultaneously available to the respondent. As a result, respondents can complete sections of the questionnaire in any order they choose, can refer to other sections in providing answers, and can complete the questionnaire over a series of days or even weeks. Thus, the surveyor cannot use self-administered questionnaires when one set of questions is likely to "contaminate," "bias," or "influence" answers to another section of the questionnaire.

For example, political scientists and politicians often are interested in knowing what the members of a community perceive to be the greatest problems facing their community today. What is typically asked next in the interview is a series of questions to ascertain respondents' concern over specific problems the surveyor assumes face that community. When respondents have the ability to look ahead in an interview and see the topics the surveyor selects as problems for their community, they are more likely to respond by selecting the topics that are specifically selected out later in the interview.

Similarly, it is not possible to build validity checks into a self-administered questionnaire. If, for example, the surveyor is suspicious that respondents are more likely to underreport their age when asked "How old were you on your last birthday?" than when they are asked "When were you born?", a self-administered questionnaire would not be a good way to check the "match" between the answers given to the two questions because respondents can compare their answers and change them to be consistent, if necessary. Opportunities to change answers are significantly reduced or even eliminated when interviewers control the order in which questions are asked and have been given instructions regarding the legitimacy of letting a respondent "change" an answer to a question.

Administration

No Control Over Who Responds

The single biggest administrative disadvantage to mail questionnaires is the fact that once the questionnaire leaves the surveyor's office, he or she has no control over who, in fact, fills it out and whether that person "consults" with others when completing it. Thus, in the Workplace Assault Study, we had a list of persons and addresses that was provided by the union. We addressed our cover letter and envelope to one union person. Once we sent the questionnaires out, however, we had no way to be sure that the designated respondent, who was a member of the union, completed the questionnaire and, furthermore, completed it without talking about it with other members of his or her household, workplace, or social group.

We know of one study conducted many years ago where questionnaires were passed out by a receptionist in a clinic waiting room. One day, the surveyor happened to walk through the waiting room just as one waiting patient was reading the questions to the rest of the waiting patients, who were then essentially "voting" on what answer should be selected. The resultant answers essentially represented a consensus of those available in the waiting room at that time rather than the opinions or behaviors of the person completing the questionnaire. Needless to say, the surveyor quickly changed his mode of administering questionnaires to a system that allowed for greater control over the number and identity of the persons completing the questionnaire. Unfortunately, when questionnaires are mailed, the surveyor has no way of checking up on these issues and must accept completed questionnaires "on faith."

Quick Turnaround

Earlier, we said that one of the advantages of mail questionnaires is that it can be assumed that all of them were administered on the same date and that all respondents received the questionnaire on the same date. In general, this means that data collected by mail will be more quickly completed than data collected by telephone or in face-to-face interviews.

There are exceptions to this. Generally, it takes a minimum of 2 weeks after each mailing for completed questionnaires to be returned to the surveyor. To the extent that the surveyor tries to maximize a good response rate by using follow-up mailings and telephone calls, the data collection period may extend to 2 or 3 months. In contrast, it is possible to conduct a telephone survey literally "overnight" if the surveyor has the resources necessary to hire a large number of interviewers and the necessary number of telephones *and if* the surveyor is willing to sacrifice a certain representativeness of the sample obtained. If, for example, all data are collected in one night from a sample of 500 persons, it clearly means that persons not

at home that night have no chance of being in the sample. Also, persons whose lines were busy at the time of the attempted call will likely not be in the sample because, unlike regular telephone surveys, little or no redialing is done.

However, for interviews about fast-breaking events such as the Oklahoma City bombing on April 19, 1995, a quick telephone survey is the only way to measure rapidly changing opinions.

SELF-ADMINISTERED QUESTIONNAIRES BY EXAMPLE: ASSAULT AND VISION STUDIES

The remainder of this book explains and describes how self-administered questionnaires are developed and administered. Two ongoing studies are used as examples.

The questionnaire used in the first study examined the extent to which members of two locals of the Service Employees International Union (SEIU) perceived their workplace sites as safe, the incidence of physical assaults experienced while at work during the preceding year, and the incidence of threats of assault within the past month. Questionnaires were sent by mail to the homes of a stratified random sample of 1,744 potential respondents on January 17, 1995 (for more information on stratified random sampling, see **How to Design Surveys** and **How to Sample in Surveys**, Vols. 5 and 6, respectively, in this series).

The questionnaire used in the second study examined the visual functioning, satisfaction, and experiences with side effects following radial keratotomy. Radial keratotomy is a surgical procedure that reduces myopia, or nearsightedness, by making slices in the patient's cornea. The questionnaire used here was administered as part of the 10-year follow-up examination in the Prospective Evaluation of Radial Keratotomy (PERK) Study, a multisite clinical trial of the 435 respondents who entered the study. In this study, questionnaires were administered at one of the nine clinical sites by clinic coordinators (for more information on clinical trials and other survey designs, see **How to Design Surveys** and **How to Sample in Surveys**, Vols. 5 and 6, respectively, in this series).

To reflect the normal progress and problems often associated with the design of data collection instruments, we discuss what worked, what did not work, and what could have been improved in our two questionnaires. Although most of our examples are drawn from these two studies, examples are also drawn from other studies where appropriate.

This chapter was first published by BMJ Books and is reproduced with permission of BMJ Books

Health Services Research Methods – A guide to best practice. London: BMJ Books, 1998
Edited by Nick Black, John Brazier, Ray Fitzpatrick and Barnaby Reeves

CHAPTER 5

DESIGNING AND USING PATIENT AND STAFF QUESTIONNAIRES

Elaine McColl, Ann Jacoby, Lois Thomas, Jennifer Soutter, Claire Bamford,
Andrew Garratt, Emma Harvey, Roger Thomas and John Bond

In health services research, questionnaires are frequently the method of choice for gathering primary quantitative data from patients and health care professionals. The aim is to gather valid and reliable data from a representative sample of respondents. However, in common with other approaches to data collection, the information yielded by questionnaires is subject to error and bias from a range of sources. Close attention to issues of questionnaire design and survey administration can reduce these errors. However, many of the classic texts on questionnaire development, on which many researchers and health surveyors rely, are now quite dated [1,2] and most lack a scientific base, drawing instead on the accumulated experience and views of the authors.

Our aims in this chapter are to address this evidence gap by identifying established and innovative approaches to questionnaire design and administration, particularly those supported by evidence from experimental studies, and thereby to identify current best practice with respect to the design and conduct of surveys. The principal foci were:

- modes of questionnaire administration (face-to-face and telephone interviews; mailed and "captive audience" self-completion questionnaires; computer-assisted techniques);
- issues of question wording, choice of response formats, and question sequencing;
- issues of questionnaire formatting and other aspects of presentation; and
- techniques for enhancing response rates, with particular emphasis on mailed surveys.

We defined "questionnaire" to mean "structured schedules used to elicit predominantly quantitative information, by means of direct questions, from informants, either by self-completion or via interview".

NATURE OF THE EVIDENCE
We were interested both in high grade evidence from comparative studies, and in lower grade evidence from descriptive studies and previous reviews, especially where higher grade evidence was lacking; we also sought information on the theoretical underpinnings of survey response. We used the PsychLIT and MEDLINE databases as much of the innovative work on survey methods has been carried out in social and market research, rather than in the health sector; we searched for papers published between 1975 and 1996. Secondary references, cited in identified papers, were also obtained.

In synthesising our findings, we first reviewed "expert opinion" as expressed in the classic texts [1-3] and in papers on the theory of survey response, and then examined the identified evidence to see whether findings supported or refuted this conventional wisdom. With respect to many aspects of questionnaire design and administration, we found that evidence for the relative effectiveness of different approaches was scant. Moreover, we identified a number of limitations to the interpretation and applicability of the evidence. In particular, many comparative studies involved the manipulation of only one factor; yet as Dillman recognises, "the decision to respond (to a survey) is based on an overall, subjective evaluation of all the study elements visible to the prospective respondent".[2] We also recognised the existence of practical and ethical constraints in implementing some of the recommendations in a health setting.

FINDINGS
Mode of administration
The two principal modes of questionnaire administration are self-completion by the respondent (traditionally this has been a pencil-and-paper exercise, but more recently computer presentation has been tried) or via an interviewer (either face-to-face or over the telephone; computers may be used for data capture). Expert opinion suggests that each mode has its advantages and disadvantages, as summarised in Table 5.1.

We identified six studies comparing face-to-face interviews with self-completion questionnaires. The two studies[4,5] which measured response rates reported significantly higher rates for interviews, while Cartwright also found that Asian women were under-represented in respondents to the mailed approach.[5] Five of the six studies[5-9] examined responses to sensitive questions; it is often asserted that the greater anonymity afforded by a self-completion questionnaire leads to greater honesty and that this approach is therefore more appropriate for surveys on sensitive or embarrassing topics. However, there was no clear evidence from these five studies that mailed survey subjects do respond more truthfully to questions on sensitive issues or make more critical or less socially acceptable answers than in an interview.

We also identified four studies in which telephone interviews were compared with mailed questionnaires; all were on health-related topics. Two of the studies found significantly higher response rates for the telephone approach,[4,10] and two found this approach cheaper.[4,11] One study reported a significantly higher response rate from the mailed questionnaire and a higher cost for the telephone survey; however, the rate of missing responses to individual questions was significantly higher in the mailed survey.[12]

In summary, evidence from the identified studies did not provide a consistent picture of the superiority of any one mode of questionnaire administration. In choosing a method, the researcher needs to consider trade-offs, for example between response rate and cost.

Question wording and sequencing

Most experts agree on general principles of question wording, as summarised in Box 5.1. We identified 11 studies on this issue, though only two were on health-related topics. Evidence from these supported the notion that question wording and framing can have an important impact on the responses given. For example, Larsen *et al.* conducted two experiments on the use of quantifiers – verbal descriptors such as "often", "regularly", "sometimes"

– in assessing symptom frequency; these words may be seen to be vague and different respondents may interpret them in different ways.[13] Findings showed that, while there were no statistically significant differences in the mean number of headaches reported, the quantifier "frequently" appeared to lead to under-reporting of this symptom.

Findings on whether a "don't know" category should be included were equivocal. Poe *et al.*, in a postal questionnaire containing only factual questions and sent to close relatives of recently deceased persons, found that the inclusion of a "don't know" option had no effect on overall response rates or item response rates, but that, for a quarter of the items in the questionnaire, the percentage of substantive replies (that is, endorsing one of the specific response categories) was significantly higher in the version without this option.[14] By contrast, Hawkins and Coney[15] and Bishop *et al.*[16] found that including a "don't know" option reduced the rate of uninformed response (that is, expressing a definite opinion on a fictitious matter) and concluded that offering such an option might reduce bias arising from a desire to appear knowledgeable or to hold a definite opinion.

Question ordering has received rather more attention. The conventional wisdom is that general questions should precede specific questions. Evidence from a number of studies supported this assertion. For example, Schuman *et al.*[17] found that general attitudinal questions (for example with respect to abortion) received significantly more positive endorsement when posed before a specific question on the same topic. Colasanto *et al.*,[18] in a study of HIV infection, looked at the effect of placing a question about whether HIV could be transmitted by donating blood before or after a question on transmission via blood transfusion. When the donation question was posed first, a significantly higher proportion thought it was possible to contract the disease through donating blood. It appeared that the question on blood transfusion, when it appeared first, helped to clarify the meaning of a potentially ambiguous question by means of a "contrast" effect and so reduced the number of erroneous responses.[19]

In summary, evidence from the identified studies generally supported the conventional wisdom on issues of question wording (though comparative studies were few), definition of response categories, and question sequencing.

Questionnaire appearance

Attention to the appearance of a questionnaire, including its length and layout, is important. As Sudman and Bradburn noted, in interview surveys, a well-designed questionnaire can simplify the tasks of both interviewers and data processors.[20] Through good design, the risk of errors in posing questions and coding responses can be reduced and potential variability between interviewers or coders can be minimised, thus reducing bias.

Evidence from comparative studies on aspects of questionnaire appearance was scant. However, we identified a number of papers outlining a theoretical basis to issues of design. Brown *et al.*[21] proposed a "task analysis" model of questionnaire response, based on social

---

Box 5.1
Principles of question wording [1,31]

- Use simple language; avoid acronyms, abbreviations, jargon and technical terms

- Keep the question short (i.e. sentence of less than 20 words approximately)

- Avoid questions which are insufficiently specific

- Avoid ambiguity

- Avoid vague words and those with more than one meaning (e.g. "dinner")

- Avoid double-barrelled questions (those with an "and" or an "or" in the wording)

- Avoid double negatives (e.g. a negative statement followed by a "disagree" response)

- Avoid proverbs and clichés when measuring attitudes

- Avoid leading questions (e.g. "Do you agree that the health service is underfunded?")

- Beware loaded words and concepts

- Beware of presuming questions

- Be cautious in use of hypothetical questions

- Do not overtax respondents' memories (e.g. by asking for detailed recall of trivial issues)

- Allow for "don't know" and "not applicable" responses if appropriate

Table 5.1

Advantages and disadvantages of different modes of questionnaire administration

Mode of administration	Advantages	Disadvantages
Mailed self-completion	Cheaper than interviews No interviewer effects Greater anonymity for respondent Good for named individual and special population samples	Lower response rates than interviews – no-one to motivate respondent No control over response process (e.g. order in which questions are answered) Cannot ensure target recipient fills it in No opportunity to prompt or probe More errors in data Delay in getting back questionnaires through mail Not suitable for respondents with literacy problems
Supervised self-completion	Similar to mailed self-completion but interviewer/researcher available to help and explain Can be used for groups More timely return of questionnaires vis à vis postal self-completion	Generally as for mailed self-completion and only suitable if target group of respondents comes together naturally
Face-to-face interviewing	Better for open ended questions Flexible – interviewer can explain, probe and check Can have complex instructions and definitions High response rates – interviewer can motivate respondent Can use visual aids Can validate responses by observation	Interviewer may influence answers Inter-interviewer differences are a source of bias Other people may be present High cost
Telephone interviewing	Similar to face-to-face interviews Quicker than face-to-face interviews Cheaper than face-to-face interviews Greater anonymity for respondent Easier supervision and monitoring of interviewers	Coverage problems (those with no phone or ex-directory) Generally lower response rates than face-to-face interviews Less flexible than face-to-face interviews Cannot use visual aids Long interviews impractical Less intimate/poorer rapport Complex open-ended questions more difficult
Computer-assisted methods (questions presented on screen and answers entered directly into computer by interviewer or respondent)	Allows "tailoring" of questionnaire to individual respondent Extra step of data entry eliminated, thereby reducing costs Faster than traditional pencil-and-paper methods Improved data quality, since on-line data validation and editing possible Better control of fieldwork	High set-up costs Writing and testing questionnaire presentation/data capture program time consuming and error prone

2

exchange theory,[22] which suggested that issues of questionnaire appearance can influence respondents' decisions at several stages. The first stage is arousal of interest in the task of questionnaire completion. The second stage is evaluation of the task, involving perceptions of the time and effort required to complete the questionnaire. The third stage is initiation and monitoring of the task of completion; here the actual burden of response becomes apparent. Appropriate design, in particular a layout that is clear, consistent, and uncluttered, can reduce the perceived and actual burden of response.

Jenkins and Dillman sought to develop a theory of self-administered questionnaire design, with particular emphasis on issues of format.[23] They emphasised the need for an understanding of "graphic non-verbal language", in other words the spatial arrangement of information and other visual phenomena such as colour and brightness. Drawing on theories of cognition, perception, and pattern recognition/processing, they argued for the need for consistency in the presentation of visual information, and derived five principles of design for self-administered questionnaires (Box 5.2).

Enhancing response rates

In any survey a high response rate is desirable, since it increases the precision with which underlying population values can be estimated from sample results. In addition, a high response rate reduces the risk of bias; respondents are typically different from non-respondents in many respects – they are generally better motivated and more interested in the topic, are usually better educated, and the age and ethnic mix is often different (the very elderly and people from minority ethnic groups tend to be underrepresented).[5,25,26]

The theory of social exchange postulates that the actions of individuals are influenced by the rewards they expect to get from completing these actions and the costs of doing so.[22] This suggests that many factors combine to influence the decision of a recipient of a questionnaire to respond. Potential respondents must have both the means to complete the questionnaire and the will to do so; the perceived costs of responding must not exceed the benefits of doing so. Many primary studies and reviews have addressed factors influencing the decision and ability to respond; most have focused on overall response rates, but the time to respond, response bias, and cost of the survey have also been considered by some authors.

In their review, Heberlein and Baumgartner showed that "saliency" – the apparent relevance, importance, and interest of the survey to the respondent – was the single most important factor affecting response rates.[24] Perhaps surprisingly, length of questionnaire appears to be less important; they found no significant first order correlations between length and response, although on controlling for saliency, longer questionnaires had poorer response rates. Health-related surveys, however, are likely to be seen as salient by the respondents, an assertion borne out by the findings of Cartwright[25] and Jacoby[26] who found no significant effect of length of questionnaire on response rates.

The number of contacts made with sampled individuals is another powerful factor in influencing response rates. Some researchers advocate prenotification, so that the recipients are primed for the arrival of the questionnaire. Linsky reported that prenotification significantly increased response rates.[27] However, Heberlein and Baumgartner demonstrated no advantage of advance contacts after controlling for total number of contacts, including reminders.[24] Almost all experts in survey design recommend the use of reminders. For example, Linsky showed that follow-up almost invariably increased response rate and that postcard reminders were as effective as letters.[27] Heberlein and Baumgartner showed that the first follow-up netted an additional return of 20% of the initial sample, while second and third follow-ups brought in an extra 12% and 10% respectively.[24]

Other factors which have been shown to influence response rates include making a self-interest/utility appeal to the respondent, the use of incentives, and the type and rate of postage used (for example, higher response rates are generally demonstrated for stamped mail by comparison with franked or reply-paid envelopes). Perhaps surprisingly, anonymity (exclusion of any identifier, even a survey number) was shown to have no effect on initial response rates; or on item omission or completeness of response.[28,29] However, the use of numbered questionnaires (providing confidentiality rather than anonymity) was shown to boost overall response rates significantly, since targeted reminders could be used.

As already mentioned, a weakness of many of the studies we identified was that they sought to manipulate only one or two factors potentially influencing response rates; it is therefore difficult to interpret and generalise findings. In practice, the aim should be "to identify each aspect of the survey process that may influence either the quality or quantity of response and to shape each one of them in such a way that the best possible responses are obtained".[2] Moreover, few of the identified studies included an economic evaluation – for example, studies of

---

Box 5.2
Principles of questionnaire design [23]

1. Use the visual elements of brightness, colour, shape and location in a consistent manner to define the desired navigational path for respondents to follow when answering the questionnaire.

2. When established format conventions are changed in the midst of a questionnaire, prominent visual guides should be used to redirect respondents.

3. Place directions where they are to be used and where they can be seen.

4. Present information in a manner that does not require respondents to connect information from separate locations in order to comprehend it.

5. Ask people to answer only one question at a time.

the impact of reminders did not generally indicate whether the marginal benefit of the additional responses outweighed the marginal cost. Similarly, ethical considerations might preclude the application of some of the recommendations from social or market research in the health sector – for instance, postcard reminders might violate principles of confidentiality.

RECOMMENDATIONS

There can be no universal recommendations with respect to best practice in respect of questionnaire design and survey conduct. Rather, the researcher needs to take into account the aims of the study, the general study design, the population under investigation and the resources available. In a given study, trade-offs between the ideal and the possible are likely to be needed. However, some general principles can be stated.

• The principal objective should always be to collect reliable and valid data, in a timely manner, and within given cost and resource constraints, recognising that there may need to be a trade-off.
• In choosing a mode of questionnaire administration, consideration needs to be given to:

- availability of an appropriate sampling frame
- anticipated response rates
- the potential for bias from sources other than non-response
- the acceptability of candidate methods to respondents
- the time available for data collection
- the financial budget and
- availability of other resources (such as skills and equipment).

While it may not be possible to quantify these parameters, some attempt should be made to estimate their relative magnitude for competing modes.
• In formulating questions and response categories, and in determining question order, researchers should bear in mind that survey respondents employ a wide range of cognitive processes in formulating their responses. To minimise bias and to reduce spurious inter-respondent variation, careful attention must be given to these issues. The established principles (Box 5. 1) laid down in the traditional texts still hold good today.
• The task analysis model of Brown and colleagues [21] and the theory of social exchange [22] should underpin decisions regarding the physical design of questionnaires, as well as strategies for delivering and returning them. The aim should be to enhance the perceived and actual benefits of responding and to minimise the perceived and real costs.
• The saliency of the survey to respondents is a key factor in effecting high response rates; fortunately, surveys on health-related topics are likely to be viewed as relevant, important, and interesting. The perceived benefits of responding can also be enhanced by emphasising the self-interest/utility (rather than the altruistic) aspects of participating in the survey.
• The perceived and actual burden of responding can be reduced through appropriate question wording and an attractive questionnaire design and layout, drawing on the principles presented in Box 5.2. The aim should be to make the task of interpreting the questions and providing responses as easy as possible.
• Strategies for reducing the monetary cost to respondents include the use of prepaid and addressed envelopes for returning completed questionnaires (a must in mailed surveys). Financial incentives are often offered in social and market research as token compensation for the time required to complete a questionnaire; however, such incentives are generally regarded as unethical in health research, and grant-awarding bodies tend to disapprove of the practice.[30]
• Above all, careful piloting and testing of draft versions of any questionnaire with the appropriate population is a vital step in questionnaire development. Questioning of respondents can indicate problems of comprehension. Analysis of responses can show whether all reasonable and relevant alternatives are included in response categories for closed questions. Data from the pilot study can also indicate the likely rate of response and inform sample size calculations for the main survey.

References

1 Moser CA, Kalton G. *Survey methods in social investigation.* London: Gower, 1971.
2 Dillman DA. *Mail and telephone surveys – the total design method.* New York: John Wiley & Sons Inc., 1978.
3 Fink A. (ed.) *The survey kit.* Thousand Oaks: Sage, 1995.
4 Hinkle AL, King GD. A comparison of three survey methods to obtain data for community mental health program planning. *Am J Community Psychol* 1978;**6**:389-97.
5 Cartwright A. Interviews or postal questionnaires? Comparisons of data about women's experiences with maternity services. *Milbank Quart* 1988;**66**:172-89.
6 Newton RR, Prensky D, Schuessler K. Form effect in the measurement of feeling states. *Social Sci Res* 1982;**11**:301-17.
7 Nederhof AJ. Visibility of response as a mediating factor in equity research. *J Social Psychol* 1984;**122**:211-15.
8 Oei TI, Zwart FM. The assessment of life events: self-administered questionnaire versus interview. *J Affective Disorders* 1986;**10**:185-90.
9 Boekeloo BO, Schiavo L, Rabin DL, Conlon RT, Jordan CS, Mundt DJ. Self-reports of HIV risk factors by patients at a sexually transmitted disease clinic: audio vs written questionnaires. *Am J Public Health* 1994;**84**:754-60.
10 Talley JE, Barrow JC, Fulkerson KF, Moore CA. Conducting a needs assessment of university psychological services: a campaign of telephone and mail strategies. *J Am Coll Health* 1983;**32**:101-3.
11 Pederson LL, Baskerville JC, Ashley MJ, Lefcoe NM. Comparison of mail questionnaire and telephone interview as data gathering strategies in a survey of attitudes toward restrictions on cigarette smoking. *Can J Public Health* 1994; **3**:179-82.

12 McHorney CA, Kosinski M, Ware Jr JE. Comparisons of the costs and quality of norms for the SF-36 health survey collected by mail versus telephone interview: results from a national survey. *Med Care* 1994;**32**:551-67.

13 Larsen JD, Mascharka C, Toronski C. Does the wording of the question change the number of headaches people report on a health questionnaire? *Psycholog Record* 1987;**3**:423-7.

14 Poe GS, Seeman I, McLaughlin J, Mehl E. "Don't know" boxes in factual questions in a mail questionnaire: effects on level and quality of response. *Public Opinion Quart* 1988;**52**:212-22.

15 Hawkins DI, Coney KA. Uninformed response error in survey research. *J Marketing Res* 1981;**18**:370-4.

16 Bishop GF, Tuchfarber AJ, Oldendick RW. Opinions on fictitious issues: the pressure to answer survey questions. *Public Opinion Quart* 1986;**50**:240-50.

17 Schuman H, Presser S, Ludwig J. Context effects on survey responses to questions about abortion. *Public Opinion Quart* 1981;**45**:216-23.

18 Colasanto D, Singer E, Rogers TF. Context effects on responses to questions about AIDS. *Public Opinion Quart* 1992;**56**:515-18.

19 Schuman H, Presser S. *Questions and answers in attitude surveys: experiments on question form, wording and context.* New York: Academic Press, 1981.

20 Sudman S, Bradburn NM. *Asking questions.* San Francisco: Jossey-Bass Publishers, 1981.

21 Brown TL, Decker DJ, Connelly NA. Response to mail surveys on resource-based recreation topics: a behavioral model and an empirical analysis. *Leisure Sciences* 1989;**11**:99-110.

22 Thibaut JW, Kelley HH. *The social psychology of groups.* New York: Wiley, 1959.

23 Jenkins CR, Dillman DA. Towards a theory of self-administered questionnaire design. In: Lyberg L, Biemer P, Collins M *et al.* (eds) *Survey measurement and process quality.* New York: John Wiley & Sons Inc., 1997.

24 Heberlein TA, Baumgartner R. Factors affecting response rates to mailed questionnaires: a quantitative analysis of the published literature. *Am Sociolog Rev* 1978;**43**:447-62.

25 Cartwright A. Some experiments with factors that might affect the response of mothers to a postal questionnaire. *Statist Med* 1986;**5**:607-17.

26 Jacoby A. Possible factors affecting response to postal questionnaires: findings from a study of general practitioner services. *J Public Health Med* 1990;**12**: 131-5.

27 Linsky AS. Stimulating responses to mailed questionnaires: a review. *Public Opinion Quart* 1975;**39**: 82-101.

28 Campbell MJ, Waters WE. Does anonymity increase response rate in postal questionnaire surveys about sensitive subjects? A randomised trial. *J Epidemiol Community Health* 1990;**4**:75-6.

29 McDaniel SW, Rao CP. An investigation of respondent anonymity's effect on mailed questionnaire response rate and quality. *J Market Res Soc* 1981;**23**: 150-60.

30 Bowling A. *Research methods in health – investigating health and health services.* Buckingham: Open University Press, 1997.

31 Oppenheim AN. *Questionnaire design, interviewing and attitude measurement.* London: Pinter Publishers, 1992.

2

This article was first published in the Survey Methods Centre Newsletter and is reproduced by permission of the Survey Methods Centre

Survey Methods Centre Newsletter Volume 16 No. 1

QUALITY AND ERROR IN SELF-COMPLETION SURVEYS

Peter Lynn

Peter Lynn's presentation consisted of an overview of precision and other quality issues in self-completion surveys, and a review of what is known about factors that affect precision and quality, and what can be done by the survey designer to maximise quality and minimise error. The aims of the paper were to identify relevant quality measures for self-completion surveys, to discuss how aspects of quality can be assessed, to review work which has attempted to make assessments of this sort, and to draw some conclusions about the relative importance of different aspects of the design and execution of self-completion surveys.

Peter Lynn suggested that the most important quality measure for a survey may be the standard definition of statistical error – the difference between a survey estimate of a quantity and the true population value. There are of course many aspects of survey design and execution that contribute to the overall error, and some of these are <u>random</u> errors (e.g. sampling variation). It would therefore be misleading to use <u>realised</u> error to measure the quality of execution of a survey. One should instead think in terms of <u>expected</u> error. Many components of survey design influence expected error, and it may be necessary to attempt to quantify a number of these before it is possible to get an idea of the overall quality of a survey.

However, there are important aspects of a survey that cannot be incorporated in a measure of error. Survey cost is one. Surveys should be value for money, in the sense that the value of the information provided by a survey should exceed the cost of obtaining it. One way of considering error and cost simultaneously is to think in terms of precision per unit cost, rather than just precision regardless of cost.

Timeliness is also relevant. Precise, and cheap, estimates, may be of little value if they are not available until the deadline for influencing some important process has passed. Peter Lynn suggested that timeliness can be thought of as one aspect of value – timely results are more valuable than untimely ones.

The burden caused by a survey is also important. Data collection can be a burden on sample members, on "gatekeeper" organisations involved in the survey process, and others. Other things being equal, a survey which avoids being disruptive and imposing a burden is better than one which imposes a greater burden. Burden can be thought of as part of the cost of a survey, albeit a non-monetary cost.

Another important concept is validity. Is the survey measuring the thing that it is supposed to be measuring, or the most appropriate thing for its purpose? Peter Lynn argued that validity too is an aspect of value – invalid information is less valuable than valid information.

Figure 1 summarises Peter Lynn's conceptual model of survey quality. It is a simple model, consisting only of two quantities which must be weighed up against one another – value, and cost. The aim is to maximise the ratio of value to cost. Value has a number of components – notably precision or error, but also the utility and validity of the survey measures, and timeliness. And cost incorporates not only monetary payments, but also some rather difficult to measure costs.

SOURCES OF ERROR

Peter Lynn then concentrated on survey error. He attempted to identify the likely main sources of error in self-completion surveys by starting with the classification of error sources presented by Bob Groves[1], and proposing that certain sources of error were of little or no importance in the context of self-completion. He concluded that the three most important sources of error were likely to be sampling variance, non-response bias, and response errors.

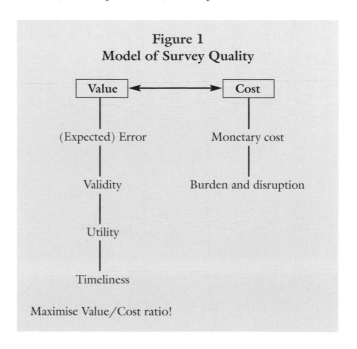

Figure 1
Model of Survey Quality

SAMPLING VARIANCE

The nature and treatment of sampling variance is not specific to self-completion surveys. Consequently, Peter Lynn did not discuss it further except to emphasise that it is an important element of survey error, and therefore should be considered in parallel with other sources of error.

NON-RESPONSE BIAS

Non-response bias in self-completion surveys is a highly researched area. However, much of the literature does not directly address bias, but merely addresses response rates. The literature is dominated by studies based on postal surveys. Response rate is indicative of the scope for non-response bias, but does not directly tell us anything about the nature of bias. However, studies where something has been known about the nature of non-response bias tend to show that response rate often is related to bias, so Peter Lynn reviewed some of the factors affecting response rates. The methodological work carried out in this area is useful as, in the absence of other information about non-respondents (e.g. information from the sampling frame), response rate is often the only available indicator of non-response bias.

FACTORS AFFECTING RESPONSE RATE

Many factors affect the response rate achieved by postal surveys, but they can be thought of as falling into two categories. Following Don Dillman[2], Peter Lynn referred to these as structural factors, and manipulable factors. Structural factors are an inherent characteristic of a particular survey, but can vary between surveys. They include the subject of the survey, the nature of the population to be sampled, and the nature of the sponsoring organisation. Manipulable factors are those which the survey research team can influence at the design stage, such as questionnaire length, class of postage, and number of mailings.

Two quantitative analyses of previous research, each carried out about fifteen years ago[3,4], found that just two factors accounted for over half of the variance in response rates to postal surveys. These were the number of contacts, and the salience of the topic. Salience is largely a structural factor, though it is possible to increase the perceived salience of a survey through appropriate wording of covering letters, and careful questionnaire design. Number of contacts is obviously manipulable, and the conclusion is clear – more contacts means better response. There are diminishing returns to extra contacts, but Peter Lynn thought it would be rare for it not to be effective to have at least three contacts altogether. Some postal surveys have as many as six.

Figure 2 is a typical graph of speed of response to a postal survey. It plots the cumulative number of respondents over time. The survey upon which it is based had three reminders at intervals of about two weeks. A rapid response immediately after the initial mailing can be seen. This then begins to tail off, but picks up again just after the first reminder, and then tails of again until the second reminder, and so on. One could extrapolate and predict that the final response rate would have been lower had any one of the reminder stages been omitted.

However, it is not only the number of reminders that is important, but also their nature. Reminder mailings which include another copy of the questionnaire tend to elicit more response than a postcard, for example. But they are also more expensive. A common strategy is to use a postcard as the first reminder, then re-administrations of the questionnaire as the second and third reminders.

Other factors found by the earlier studies to be important are summarised in table 1.

These findings are all broad generalisations of average effects, and one can look more closely at any one aspect. For example, there are suggestions in the literature that sponsorship may be more important for low salience topics than for high salience topics; that an enclosed incentive might work better than a promise to

Figure 2: Speed of Response to a postal survey

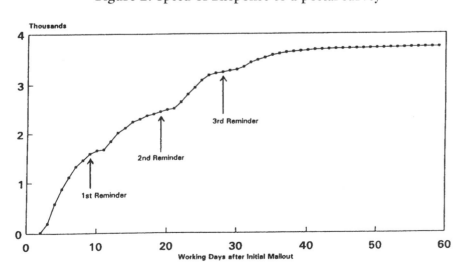

Table 1:
Important Influences on Response Rate

Structural Factors		Manipulable Factors	
Salience	(salient ↑↑)	No. of contacts (more↑↑)	
Sponsor	(government ↑)	Length	(longer ↓)
	(market research ↓)		
Population	(employees, school ↑)		
	(general ↓)	Incentive on first contact (↑)	

send one later; that a small amount of money might work better than a lottery chance to win a large amount; and of course the most promising form of incentive, and its effect, is likely to depend on the nature of the population being sampled, and the nature of the survey. In general, manipulable factors are more likely to have an effect the lower the response rate.

Dillman talks about a "theoretical maximum response asymptote", which one cannot hope to exceed, except perhaps by the use of culturally unacceptable inducements. For some populations, that asymptote may be close to 100%, but for others it might only be around 75-80%. So, a survey which already has a 70% response rate might be hard pushed to find design improvements which bring a 5% improvement in response, whereas a survey with 50% response may find it much easier to identify ways of gaining an extra 5%, or even 10%.

All the manipulable factors could potentially interact with one another, and many do. They probably also interact with structural factors. This makes it hard to make generalisations about main effects. The effect on response of increasing a questionnaire from 8 pages to 12 pages, for example, will depend on other characteristics of the survey. So, for any particular survey there is probably no direct experimental evidence which can be used to anticipate the effect of questionnaire length, say, on response rate.

Two alternative conclusions could be drawn. One is that the only way of assessing the effect of a manipulable factor on a particular survey is to manipulate it experimentally on that survey. But that ignores the considerable existing experience in these matters. Also, that conclusion is of no help to someone who is only doing a survey once, and has no feasibility study on which to carry out tests. The alternative conclusion is that we need to understand more about the process underlying the effects on response. Knowledge of the process can then be applied to new situations.

For example, when someone receives a questionnaire through the post, there may be a process of recognition – they look at the mailing to ascertain what it is – a process of assimilation – they read through some or all of the mailing in an attempt to understand what they are being asked to do – a process of evaluation – evaluating

the costs and benefits of co-operation – and so on. It may be via these processes that the researched factors, have their effect. For example, the design of the questionnaire cover might influence the process of recognition, whereas the wording of the covering letter might influence assimilation.

With some feeling for what the important processes are, and how factors are likely to affect those processes, along with a large body of empirical evidence of the effects that manifest themselves, and some common sense, survey researchers will be in a strong position to extrapolate to the likely effects of some manipulation on a survey upon which that particular factor has not been manipulated experimentally.

As an example of what he meant, Peter Lynn discussed questionnaire length. He suggested that it is fairly meaningless to talk about questionnaire length, as measured by number of pages, as it is entirely defined by the combination of two relevant manipulable factors, questionnaire content (what questions are asked), and questionnaire layout (how the questions appear on the page). He suspected that it is the confounding of these two issues that has led to conflicting findings on the effect of questionnaire length on response.

The volume of questionnaire content may be related to a number of relevant factors. First, if the questionnaire is too short, it may be perceived that the survey cannot be of much use. Or the recipient may think that the researcher has not gone to much effort, so why should they? On the other hand, volume of content is related to the burden to the respondent of co-operating, in terms of time and effort. So by thinking about the process underlying the relationship between volume of content and response rate, we may hypothesise a U-shaped relationship, with there perhaps existing an optimum volume for a given population.

The layout of the questions might also affect response. For example, the same questions spread out over more pages with clearer signs and instructions might elicit a greater propensity to respond, because the task of completing the questionnaire may be easier (even though the questionnaire is now "longer").

Many of the factors discussed above in relation to postal surveys will also be important determinants of response to other forms of self-completion survey. For example, in the case of a self-completion adjunct to a face-to-face survey, salience, sponsorship, the nature of the survey population, and the content and layout of the questionnaire will all be important. But some issues will be slightly different. For example, a questionnaire left behind with respondents after an interview may get a higher response rate if collected later in person rather than being returned by post (though costs should also be taken into account). Response to a questionnaire administered during a face-to-face interview may depend on the stage of the interview at which the questionnaire is introduced. Unfortunately, there is little published work on response rates to self-completion surveys other than postal surveys.

Nature of Non-Response Bias

Peter Lynn then considered the nature of the bias introduced to self-completion surveys by non-response. What evidence there is suggests some fairly consistent patterns. The less educated, less well qualified, lower social classes, those in manual jobs, and men, seem to be less likely than others to complete self-completion questionnaires. Peter Lynn showed some examples of evidence of bias of this sort – table 2 shows a big difference in response rate for people with different levels of educational qualifications.

Peter Lynn suggested that the sorts of people who are more likely to respond to a self-completion questionnaire may not be the same groups who are more likely to respond to a request for an interview. For example, availability and time pressure constraints may be more important for personal interviewing, while literacy skills and ability to cope with form-filling may be more important for self-completion surveys. If so, this would suggest that the most effective mode of data collection might be different for different populations, or different subgroups. This is why dual-mode or multi-mode designs are sometimes used. Nevertheless, little is known about non-response bias for the same population under different data collection modes.

But even if a survey is well designed to minimise non-response bias, some will remain. However, the impact of this bias on survey error can often be reduced by some appropriate statistical adjustment typically weighting. So, when considering overall survey error, weighting for non-response should be taken into account too. What is important is not just how successful a survey is at avoiding non-response bias at the data collection stage, but rather the <u>combination</u> of this <u>and</u> the effectiveness of subsequent weighting to reduce residual bias.

Table 2:
Differential Response by Qualification Levels

Example 1: England and Wales Youth Cohort Study (c5s2)

Qualifications	Response Rate
5+ GCSEs, 5+ ABC	86%
5+ GCSEs, 1-4 ABC	73%
5+ GCSEs, no ABC	67%
1-4 grades	58%
No grades	51%

Example 2: Scottish School Leavers Survey (1994)

Qualifications	Response Rate
5+ Highers	91%
3-4 Highers	85%
1-2 Highers	82%
5+ Standard 1-3	76%
3-4 Standard 1-3	74%
1-2 Standard 1-3	69%
Standard 4-7 only	63%
No grades	60%

Response Errors

The third main source of error in self-completion surveys is response errors. These can be sub-divided into two main classes. Respondents may omit to answer one or more questions (item non-response) or they might answer incorrectly. Those two classes of error are considered in turn.

Item Non-Response

Item non-response might occur for a number of reasons (table 3). The cause might be poor questionnaire design. For example, unclear instructions or a confusing layout may cause a respondent to fail to read a question which they should have answered. Alternatively, a burdensome questionnaire might cause respondents consciously to omit to answer certain questions, because complete response would require more effort than they are prepared to put in. Some item non-response may be related to the substance of the question – a respondent may not want to answer a question about a particular issue, no matter how well the question is designed. Income may be an example of this. And some item non-response may be purely accidental.

Table 3
Reasons for Item Non-Response

Accidental	• Poor instructions/routeing
	• Pages stuck together
	• Other (distracted, etc.)
Deliberate	• Refusal because of amount of effort required
	• Refusal because of nature of information
	• Inability to answer

Peter Lynn then showed an example of the effect of poor questionnaire design on item non-response rates. A question asked respondents their current activity status, and their status six months ago. Six alternative answer categories were provided, listed one below the other, with two parallel columns of tick boxes alongside, one for each of the two time points. The instruction asked respondents to tick one box in each column. The survey found that 0.8% of respondents omitted to answer the first part of the question, and 1.8% omitted the second part. The survey was repeated the following year and the layout of the question improved – it appeared as two separate questions, one below the other. The item non-response rates then dropped to 0.4% and 0.3% respectively. The relationship between questionnaire design and potential error is obvious.

As with unit non-response, item non-response <u>rate</u> provides only an <u>indication</u> of the scope for bias. If failure to answer the question was a purely random event, no bias would result. But, as with unit non-response, there is evidence to suggest that item non-response is not a random event – particular subgroups are more prone to it than others. Peter Lynn showed examples where item non-response rates were higher for the less well-qualified and the lower social classes.

INCORRECT RESPONSES

The discussion of incorrect responses was based on the assumption that there was such a thing as the "correct" response, or the response that the questionnaire designer intended the respondent to give. This may not apply to all types of questions. For example, there is discussion in the literature of the nature of response effects on attitudinal or opinion questions.

In general, there are a number of reasons why a respondent may give an incorrect response.

• They may <u>misunderstand</u> the question, so they answer a question to the best of their ability, but it's not the question that the researcher intended.

• The respondent may understand the question but be <u>unable</u> to provide an accurate response. In some cases the respondent might not know the answer at all – for example, if asked for details of parents' employment. In other cases they may be able to provide only an estimate – this is common with numerical data such as expenditure, income, and distances travelled.

• The respondent may be unwilling to answer the question honestly, but rather than leave it unanswered gives a false answer. This is probably uncommon, but undoubtedly happens.

Again, the effect of these phenomena on the error of survey estimates will depend on the extent to which the response errors are themselves random, or systematic. For some numeric data, where respondents tend to give rounded answers, it may be the case that the rounding errors are fairly random, and therefore the effect on estimates of means, for example, may be random. But in general, there is usually likely to be something systematic underlying response errors, so researchers should be concerned.

CONCLUSION

Classical survey error is the main component of survey quality. Other components are validity, utility, timeliness and cost. The three main sources of survey error in the context of self-completion are sampling error, non-response bias and response error. Clearly, researchers can influence all of these elements of survey quality. The quality of the researchers and the work they do is therefore important. Management, clients and/or funding bodies can also influence research in ways pertinent to quality, and their input should not be underestimated. Finally, it must be recognised that some components of survey error can not be completely controlled by the researchers. Ultimately, it is the actions of sample members that introduce (some) non-response bias and (some) response errors.

References

[1] Groves, R. (1989), *Survey Errors and Survey Costs*. New York: Wiley.

[2] Dillman, D (1991), The Design and Administration of Mail Surveys, *American Review of Sociology* vol. 17: 225-249.

[3] Heberlein and Baumgartner (1978), Factors affecting response rates to mailed questionnaires: A quantitative analysis of the published literature, *American Sociological Review*, vol. 43: 447-462.

[4] Goyder (1982), further evidence on factors affecting response rates to mailed questionnaires, *American Sociological Review*, vol.47: 550-553.

3

This chapter was first published by Sage Publications and is reproduced with permission of Sage Publications
Survey Research Methods, 2edn. CA: Sage Publications.

CHAPTER 2

SAMPLING

Floyd J Fowler, Jr

How well a sample represents a population depends on the sample frame, the sample size, and the specific design of selection procedures. If probability sampling procedures are used, the precision of sample estimates can be calculated. This chapter describes various sampling procedures and their effects on the representativeness and precision of sample estimates. Two of the most common ways of sampling populations, area probability and random-digit dialing samples, are described in some detail.

There are occasions when the goal of information gathering is not to generate statistics about a population. Journalists, people developing products, political leaders, and others sometimes just want a general sense of people's feelings without great concern about numerical precision. Researchers do pilot studies to measure the range of ideas or opinions that people have or the way that variables seem to hang together. For these purposes, people who are readily available (friends, coworkers) or people who volunteer (magazine survey respondents, people who call talk shows) may be useful. Not every effort to gather information requires a strict probability sample survey. For the majority of occasions when surveys are undertaken, however, the goal is to develop statistics about a population. This chapter is about sampling when the goal is to produce numbers that can be subjected appropriately to the variety of statistical techniques available to social scientists. Although many of the same general principles apply to any sampling problem, the chapter focuses on sampling people.

The way to evaluate a sample is not by the results—the characteristics of the sample—but by examining the process by which it was selected. There are three key aspects of sample selection:

1. The sample frame is the set of people that has a chance to be selected, given the sampling approach that is chosen. Statistically speaking, a sample only can be representative of the population included in the sample frame. One design issue is how well the sample frame corresponds to the population a researcher wants to describe.

2. Probability sampling procedures must be used to designate individual units for inclusion in a sample. Each person should have a known chance of selection set by the sampling procedure. If researcher discretion or respondent characteristics such as respondent availability or initiative affect the chances of selection, there is no statistical basis for evaluating how well or how poorly the sample represents the population; commonly used approaches to calculating confidence intervals around sample estimates are not applicable.

3. The details of the sample design—its size and the specific procedures used for selecting units—will influence directly the precision of sample estimates, that is, how closely a sample is likely to approximate the characteristics of the whole population.

These details of the sampling process, along with the rate at which information actually is obtained from those selected, constitute the facts needed to evaluate a survey sample.

Response rates are discussed in Chapter 3, which also includes a brief discussion of quota sampling, a common modification of probability sampling. In this chapter, sampling frames and probability sampling procedures are discussed. Several of the most common practical strategies for sampling people are described. Interested readers will find much more information on sampling in Kish (1965), Sudman (1976), Kalton (1983), Groves (1989), and Henry (1990). Researchers planning to carry out a survey almost always would be well advised to obtain the help of a sampling statistician. This chapter, however, is intended to familiarize readers with the issues to which they should attend, and that they will likely encounter, when evaluating the sampling done for a survey.

THE SAMPLE FRAME

Any sample selection procedure will give some individuals a chance to be included in the sample while excluding others. The first step in evaluating the quality of a sample is to define the sample frame. Most sampling schemes fall into three general classes:

1. Sampling is done from a more or less complete list of individuals in the population to be studied.

2. Sampling is done from a set of people who go somewhere or do something that enables them to be sampled (e.g., patients who received medical care from a physician, or people who attended a meeting). In these

cases, there is not an advance list from which sampling occurs; the creation of the list and the process of sampling occur simultaneously.

3. Sampling is done in two or more stages, with the first stage involving sampling something other than the individuals finally to be selected. In one or more steps, these primary units are sampled, and eventually a list of individuals (or other sampling units) is created, from which a final sample selection is made. One of the most common such sampling schemes is to select housing units, with no prior information about who lives there, as a first stage of selecting a sample of people living in those housing units. These multistage procedures will be described in more detail later in this chapter.

There are three characteristics of a sample frame that a researcher should evaluate:

1. *Comprehensiveness.* A sample can only be representative of the sample frame—that is, the population that actually had a chance to be selected. Most sampling approaches leave out at least a few people from the population the researcher wants to study. For example, household-based samples exclude people who live in group quarters such as dormitories, prisons, and nursing homes, as well as those who are homeless. Available general lists, such as those of people with driver's licenses, registered voters, and homeowners, are even more exclusive. Although they cover large segments of some populations, they also omit major segments with distinctive characteristics. As a specific example, published telephone directories omit those without telephones, those who have requested that their numbers not be published, and those who have been assigned a telephone number since the most recent directory was published. In some central cities, such exclusions amount to almost 50 percent of all households. In such cities, a sample drawn from a telephone directory would be representative of only about half the population.

A key part of evaluating any sampling scheme is determining the percentage of the study population that has a chance of being selected and the extent to which those excluded are distinctive. Very often a researcher may make a choice between an easier or less expensive way of sampling a population that leaves out some people and a more expensive strategy that is also more comprehensive. If a researcher is considering sampling from a list, it is particularly important to evaluate the list to find out in detail how it was compiled, how and when additions and deletions are made, and the number and characteristics of people likely to be left off the list.

2. *Probability of selection.* Is it possible to calculate the probability of selection of each person sampled? A procedure that samples records of visits to a doctor over a year will give individuals who visit the doctor numerous times a higher chance of selection than those who see the doctor only once. It is not necessary that a sampling scheme give every member of the sampling frame the same chance of selection, as would be the case if each individual appeared once and only once on a list. It is essential, however, that the researcher be able to find out the probability of selection for each individual selected. This may be done at the time of sample selection by examination of the list. It also may be possible to find out the probability of selection at the time of data collection.

In the above example of sampling patients by sampling doctor visits, if the researcher asks selected patients the number of visits to the physician they had in a year, it would be possible to adjust the data at the time of analysis to take into account the different chances of selection. If it is not possible to know the probability of selection of each selected individual, however, it is not possible to estimate accurately the relationship between the sample statistics and the population from which it was drawn.

3. *Efficiency.* In some cases, sampling frames include units that are not among those that the researcher wants to sample. Assuming that eligible persons can be identified at the point of data collection, being too comprehensive is not a problem. Hence a perfectly appropriate way to sample elderly people living in households is to draw a sample of all households, find out if there are elderly persons living in selected households, then exclude those households with no elderly residents. Random-digit dialing samples telephone numbers (many of which are not in use) as a way of sampling housing units with telephones. The only question about such designs is whether or not they are cost-effective.

Because the ability to generalize from a sample is limited by the sample frame, when reporting results the researcher must tell readers who was or was not given a chance to be selected and how those omitted were distinctive.

SELECTING A ONE-STAGE SAMPLE

Once a researcher has made a decision about a sample frame or approach to getting a sample, the next question is specifically how to select the individual units to be included. In the next few sections the various ways that samplers typically draw samples are discussed.

Simple Random Sampling

Simple random sampling is, in a sense, the prototype of population sampling. The most basic ways of calculating statistics about samples assume that a simple random sample was drawn. Simple random sampling approximates drawing a sample out of a hat: Members of a population are selected one at a time, independent of one another and without replacement; once a unit is selected, it has no further chance to be selected.

Operationally, drawing a simple random sample requires a numbered list of the population. For simplicity, assume that each person in the population appears once and only once. If there were 8,500 people on a list, and the goal was to select a simple random sample of 100, the procedure would be straightforward. People on the list would be numbered from 1 to 8,500. Then a computer, a table of random numbers, or some other generator of random numbers would be used to produce 100 different numbers in the same range. The individuals corresponding to the 100 numbers chosen would constitute a simple random sample of that population of 8,500.

Systematic Samples

Although simple random samples are easy to understand, in practice they are relatively rare. Unless a list is short, has all units prenumbered, or is computerized so that it can be numbered easily, drawing a simple random sample as described above can be laborious. With most lists, there is a way to use a variation called systematic sampling that will have precision equivalent to a simple random sample and will be mechanically easier to create. Moreover, the benefits of stratification (discussed in the next section) can be accomplished more easily through systematic sampling.

When drawing a systematic sample from a list, the researcher first determines the number of entries on the list and the number of elements from the list that are to be selected. Dividing the latter by the former will produce a fraction. Thus, if there are 8,500 people on a list and a sample of 100 is required, 1/85 of the list (i.e., 1 out of every 85 persons) is to be included in the sample. In order to select a systematic sample, a start point is designated by choosing a random number from 1 to 85. The randomized start ensures that it is a chance selection process. Given that start, the researcher proceeds to take every 85th person on the list.

Most statistics books warn against systematic samples if a list is ordered by some characteristic, or has a recurring pattern, that will differentially affect the sample, depending on the random start. As an extreme example, if members of a couples club were listed with the male partner always listed first, a systematic sample could be drawn that consisted of only one gender. It definitely is important to examine a potential sample frame from the perspective of whether or not there is any reason to think that the sample resulting from one random start will be systematically different from those resulting from other starts in ways that will affect the survey results. In practice, most lists or sample frames do not pose any problems for systematic sampling. When they do, by either reordering the lists or adjusting the selection intervals, it almost always is possible to design a systematic sampling strategy that is at least equivalent to a simple random sample.

Stratified Samples

When a simple random sample is drawn, each new selection is independent, unaffected by any selections that came before. As a result of this process, any of the characteristics of the sample may, by chance, differ somewhat from the population from which it is drawn. Generally, little is known about the characteristics of individual population members before data collection. It is not uncommon, however, for at least a few characteristics of a population to be identifiable at the time of sampling. When that is the case, there is the possibility of structuring the sampling process to reduce the normal sampling variation, thereby producing a sample that is more likely to reflect the total population than a simple random sample. The process by which this is done is called stratification.

For example, suppose one had a list of college students. The list is arranged alphabetically. Members of different classes are mixed throughout the list. If the list identifies the particular class to which a student belongs, it would be possible to rearrange the list to put freshmen first, then sophomores, then juniors, and finally seniors, with all classes grouped together. If the sampling design calls for selecting a sample of 1 in 10 of the members on the list, the rearrangement would ensure that exactly 1/10 of the freshmen were selected, 1/10 of the sophomores, and so forth. On the other hand, if a simple random sample were selected from the list, or a systematic sample from the alphabetical list, the proportion of the sample in the freshman year would be subject to normal sampling variability and could be slightly higher or lower than was the case for the population. Stratifying in advance ensures that the sample will have exactly the same proportions in each class as the whole population.

Consider the task of estimating the average age of the student body. The class in which a student is a member almost certainly is correlated with age. Although there still will be some variability—in sample estimates because of the sampling procedure, structuring the representation of classes in the sample also will constrain the extent to which the age of the sample will differ by chance from the population as a whole.

Almost all samples of populations of geographic areas are stratified by some regional variable so that they will be distributed in the same way as the population as a whole. National samples typically are stratified by region of the country and also by urban, suburban, and rural locations. Stratification only increases the precision of estimates of variables that are related to the stratification variables. Because some degree of stratification is relatively simple to accomplish, however, and because it never hurts the precision of sample estimates (as long as the probability of selection is the same across all strata), it usually is a desirable feature of a sample design.

Differential Probabilities of Selection

Sometimes stratification is used as a first step to vary the rates of selection of various population subgroups. When probabilities of selection are constant across strata, a group that constitutes 10% of a population will compose about 10% of a selected sample. With such a sample design, if a researcher wanted a sample of at least 100 of a population subgroup that constituted 10% of the population, a simple random sampling approach would require an overall sample of 1,000. Moreover, if the researcher decided to increase the sample size of that subgroup to 150, this would entail taking an additional 500 interviews into the sample, bringing the total to 1,500.

Obviously, there are occasions when increasing a sample in this way is not very cost-effective. In the latter example, if the researcher is satisfied with the size of the samples of other groups, the design adds 450 unwanted interviews in order to add 50 interviews that are wanted. In some cases, therefore, an appropriate design is to select some subgroup at a higher rate than the rest of the population.

As an example, suppose that a researcher wished to compare black and white students, with a minimum of 100 black respondents, at a particular college where only 10% of the students are black. Thus a sample of 500 students would include 50 black students. If black students could be identified in advance, however, one could select black students at twice the rate at which other students were selected. In this way, rather than adding 500 interviews to increase the sample by 50 blacks, an additional 50 interviews over the basic sample of 500 would produce a total of about 100 interviews with blacks. Thus, when making black-white comparisons, one would have the precision provided by samples of 100 black respondents and 450 white respondents. To combine these samples, the researcher would have to give black respondents a weight of half that given to others to compensate for the fact that they were sampled at twice the rate of the rest of the population.

In the table below, it can be seen that 18.2% of those interviewed are black (100 out of 550). When the weight is applied, though, blacks constitute 10% of the weighted total, which corresponds to their percentage in the population as a whole.

Even if individual members of a subgroup of interest cannot be identified with certainty in advance of sampling, sometimes the basic approach outlined above can be applied. For instance, it is most unusual to have a list of housing units that identifies the race of occupants in advance of contact. It is not uncommon, however, for

black families to be more concentrated in some neighborhood areas than others. In that instance, a researcher may be able to sample households in areas that are predominantly black at a higher than average rate to increase the number of black respondents. Again, when any group is given a chance of selection different from other members of the population, appropriate compensatory weighting is required in order to generate accurate population statistics for the combined or total sample.

A third approach is to adjust the chance of selection based on information gathered after making contact with potential respondents. Going back to the college student survey, if student race could not be ascertained in advance, the researchers could select an initial sample of 1,000 students, have interviewers ascertain the race of each student, then have them conduct a complete interview with all black students (100) but only half of the white students they identified (450). The result would be exactly the same as in the table above.

Finally, one other technical reason for using different probabilities of selection by stratum should be mentioned. If what is being measured is much more variable in one group than in another, it may help the precision of the resulting overall estimate to oversample the group with the high level of variability. Groves (1989) provides a good description of the rationale and how to assess the efficiency of such designs.

MULTISTAGE SAMPLING
Overview

When there is no adequate list of the individuals in a population and no way to get at the population directly, multistage sampling provides a useful approach.

In the absence of a direct sampling source, a strategy is needed for linking population members to some kind of grouping that can be sampled. These groupings can be sampled as a first stage. Lists then are made of individual members of selected groups, with possibly a further selection from the created list at the second (or later) stage of sampling. The following section illustrates the general strategy for multistage sampling by describing its use in three of the most common types of situations in which a list is not available.

	Whites	*Blacks*
Number in population	4,500	500
Percentage of population	90	10
Sampling fraction	$^1/_{10}$	$^1/_5$
Number selected in sample	450	100
Unweighted percentage of sample	81.8	18.2
Weight (to adjust for probability of selection)	1	1/2
Weighted number in sample	450	50
Weighted percentage of sample	90	10

Three Common Applications

Sampling Students From Schools

If one wanted to draw a sample of all students enrolled in the public schools of a particular city, it would not be surprising to find that there was not a complete list of such individuals. There is, however, a sample frame that enables one to "get at" and include all the students in the desired population—namely, the list of all the public schools in that city. Because every individual in the study population can be attached to one and only one of those units, a perfectly acceptable sample of students can be selected using a two-stage strategy: first selecting schools, and then selecting students from within those schools.

Assume the following data:

20,000 students

40 schools

Desired sample = 2,000 = $^1/_{10}$ of students

Four different designs or approaches to sampling are presented below. Each would yield a probability sample of 2,000 students.

The four approaches listed all yield samples of 2,000; all give each student in the city an equal (1 in 10) chance of selection. The difference is that from top to bottom, the designs are increasingly less expensive—with each approach, lists have to be collected from fewer schools and fewer schools need to be visited. At the same time, the precision of each sample is likely to decline as fewer schools are sampled and more students are sampled per school. The effect of this and other multistage designs on the precision of sample estimates is discussed in more detail in a later section of this chapter.

Area Probability Sampling

Area probability sampling is one of the most generally useful multistage strategies because of its wide applicability. It can be used to sample any population that can be defined geographically—for example, the people living in a neighborhood, a city, or a country. The basic approach is to divide the total target land area into exhaustive, mutually exclusive subareas with identifiable boundaries. A sample of subareas is drawn. A list then is made of housing units in selected subareas, and a sample of listed units is drawn. As a final stage, all people in selected housing units may be included in the sample, or they may be listed and sampled as well.

This approach will work for jungles, deserts, sparsely populated rural areas, or downtown areas in central cities. The specific steps to drawing such a sample can be very complicated. The basic principles, however, can be illustrated by describing how one could sample the population of a city using city blocks as the primary subarea units to be selected at the first stage of sampling. Assume the following data:

A city consists of 400 blocks

20,000 housing units are located on these blocks

Desired sample = 2,000 housing units = 1/10 of all housing units

Given this information, a sample of households could be selected using a strategy parallel to the above selection of students. In the first stage of sampling, blocks are selected. Second, housing units on selected blocks are listed and selected from the lists. Two approaches to selecting housing units are as follows:

	Probability of Selection at Stage 1	x	Probability of Selection at Stage 2	=	Overall Probability of Selection
(a) Select all schools, list all students, and select $^1/_{10}$ students in each school	$^1/_1$	x	$^1/_{10}$	=	$^1/_{10}$
(b) Select $^1/_2$ the schools, then select $^1/_5$ of all students in them	$^1/_2$	x	$^1/_5$	=	$^1/_{10}$
(c) Select $^1/_5$ schools, then select $^1/_2$ of all students in them	$^1/_5$	x	$^1/_2$	=	$^1/_{10}$
(d) Select $^1/_{10}$ schools, then collect information about all students in them	$^1/_{10}$	x	$^1/_1$	=	$^1/_{10}$

	Probability of Selection at Stage 1 (blocks)	x	Probability of Selection at Stage 2 (housing units)	=	Overall Probability of Selection
(a) Select 80 blocks ($^1/_5$), then take $^1/_2$ of units on those blocks	$^1/_5$	x	$^1/_2$	=	$^1/_{10}$
(b) Select 40 blocks ($^1/_{10}$), then take all units on those blocks	$^1/_{10}$	x	$^1/_1$	=	$^1/_{10}$

Parallel to the school example, the first approach, involving more blocks, is more expensive than the second; it also is likely to produce more precise sample estimates for a sample of a given size.

None of the above sample schemes takes into account the size of the stage 1 unit or groupings (i.e., the size of the blocks or schools). Big schools and big blocks are selected at the same rate as small ones. If a fixed fraction of each selected group is to be taken at the last stage, there will be more interviews taken from selected big schools or big blocks than from small ones; the size of the samples taken at the last stages (cluster sizes) will be very divergent.

If there is information available about the size of the stage 1 units, it is usually good to use it. Sample designs of a given size often provide the most precise estimates if the number of units taken in all clusters at the last stage of selection is approximately equal. Other advantages of such designs are that sampling errors are easier to calculate and the total size of the sample is more predictable. To produce equal-sized clusters, stage 1 units should be sampled proportionate to their size.

The following example shows how blocks could be sampled proportionate to size as the first stage of an area probability approach to sampling housing units. The same approach could be applied to the school example above, treating schools in a way analogous to blocks in the following process.

1. Decide how many units are to be selected at the last stage of sampling—the average cluster size. Let us choose 10, for example.
2. Make an estimate of the number of housing units in each stage 1 unit (block).
3. Order the blocks so that geographically adjacent or otherwise similar blocks are contiguous. This effectively stratifies the sampling to improve the samples, as discussed above.
4. Create a cumulative count across all blocks of estimated housing units. A table like the one below will result.
5. Determine the interval between clusters. If we want to select 1 in 10 housing units and a cluster of about 10 on each selected block, we need an interval of 100 housing units between clusters. Put another way, instead of taking 1 unit at an interval of every 10 houses, we take 10 units at an interval of every 100 houses; the rate is the same, but the pattern is "clustered."
6. After first choosing a random number from 1 to 100 (the interval) as a starting point, proceed systematically through the cumulative count, designating the primary units (or blocks) "hit" in this first stage of selection. In the example, the random start chosen (70) missed block 1 (though 43 times in 100 it would have been "hit"); the 70th housing unit was in block 2; the 170th housing unit was in block 3; and the 270th housing unit was located in block 5.

Block Number	Estimated Housing Units	Cumulative Housing Units	"Hits" (Random Start = 70; Interval = 100 HUs)
1	43	43	—
2	87	130	70
3	99	229	170
4	27	256	—
5	15	271	270

A list then is made of the housing units on the selected blocks (2, 3, and 5), usually by sending a person to visit the blocks. The next step is to select housing units from those lists. If we were sure the estimates of the sizes of blocks were accurate, we simply could select 10 units off each selected block, using either simple random or systematic sampling; a systematic sample would usually be best because it would distribute the chosen units around the block.

It is common for estimates of the size of stage 1 units such as blocks to be somewhat in error. We can correct for such errors by calculating the rate at which houses are to be selected from blocks as:

$$\frac{\text{rate of HU}}{\text{selection on block}} = \frac{\text{ave. cluster size}}{\text{Estimated HUs on block}} \overset{\text{(on Block 2)}}{=} \frac{10}{87} = \frac{1}{8.7}$$

In our example, we would take 1 per 8.7 houses on block 2, 1 per 9.9 houses on block 3, and 1 per 1.5 houses on block 5. If a block is bigger than expected (e.g., because of new construction), more than 10 houses will be drawn; if it is smaller than expected (e.g., because of demolition), fewer than 10 units will be drawn. If it is exactly what we expected (e.g., 87 units on block 2), we take 10 homes ($87 \div 8.7 = 10$). In this way, the procedure is self-correcting for errors in initial estimates of block size, while maintaining the same chance of selection for units on all blocks. No matter the estimated or actual size of the block, the chance of any housing unit being selected is 1 in 10.

The area probability sample approach can be used to sample any geographically defined population. Although the steps are more complicated as the area gets bigger, the approach is the same. The key steps to remember are the following:

- All areas must be given some chance of selection. Combine areas where no units are expected with adjacent areas to ensure a chance of selection; new construction may have occurred or estimates may be wrong.
- The probability of selecting a block (or other land area) times the probability of selecting a housing unit from a selected block should be constant across all blocks.

Finally, even careful field listers will miss some housing units. Therefore, it is good practice to include checks for missed units at the time of data collection.

Random-Digit Dialing
Random-digit dialing provides an alternative way to draw a sample of housing units in order to sample the people in those households. Suppose the 20,000 housing units in the above example are covered by six telephone exchanges. One could draw a probability sample of 10% of the housing units that have a telephone as follows:

1. There is a total of 60,000 possible telephone numbers in those 6 exchanges (10,000 per exchange). Select 6,000 of those numbers (i.e., 10%), drawing 1,000 randomly generated, four-digit numbers per exchange.

2. Dial all 6,000 numbers. Not all the numbers will be household numbers; in fact, many of the numbers will not be working, will be disconnected or temporarily not in service, or will be businesses. Because 10% of all possible telephone numbers that could serve the area have been called, about 10% of all the households with telephones in that area will be reached by calling the sample of numbers.

This is the basic random-digit dialing approach to sampling. The obvious disadvantage of this approach is the large number of unfruitful calls. Nationally, fewer than 25% of possible numbers are associated with residential housing units; the rate is about 30% in urban areas and about 10% in rural areas. Waksberg (1978) has developed a method of taking advantage of the fact that telephone numbers are assigned in groups. Each group is defined by a three-digit area code, a three-digit exchange, and two additional numbers. By carrying out an initial screening of numbers, then calling additional random numbers only within the groups of 100 numbers (area code-555-12—) where a residential number was found, the rate of hitting housing units can be raised to more than 60%.

Listings in a telephone directory also may be used as a surrogate for the initial screening. Use of a directory, however, is subject to the assumption that listed numbers are distributed in the same way as all currently working residential numbers. Newly developed areas may be assigned new groups of numbers that may be underrepresented among listed numbers. There are also ways of combining lists and random-digit dialing techniques to improve the efficiency of these designs. Lepkowski (1988) provides a good, comprehensive summary of the various strategies for sampling telephone numbers as a way of sampling households.

There are two problems to note about the random-digit dialing approach to sampling. First, it omits those who live in housing units without telephones. Nationally, this is about 5% of the households; in some areas, particularly central cities or rural areas, the rate of omission may be greater than that. Thornberry and Massey (1988) provide an extensive analysis of the differences between those who do and those who do not have telephones. Second, it is a problematic way to sample people within small areas where telephone exchanges do not correspond to area boundaries. Unless the telephone exchanges exactly correspond to the study area, interviewers will need to have respondents tell them whether or not they live in the study area. Respondents who live in small, poorly defined areas—such as neighborhoods—may perform that task unreliably.

Like any particular sampling approach, random-digit dialing is not the best design for all surveys. The pros and cons will be discussed in detail in Chapter 4. The introduction of random-digit dialing as one tool in the survey researcher's arsenal, however, has made a major contribution to expanding survey research capabilities in the last 20 years.

Respondent Selection

Both area probability samples and random-digit dialing designate a sample of housing units. There is then the further question of who in the household should be interviewed.

The best decision depends on what kind of information is being gathered. In some studies, the information is being gathered about the household and about all the people in the household. If the information is easy to report, perhaps any adult who is home can answer the questions. If the information is more specialized, the researcher may want to interview the household member who is most knowledgeable. For example, in the National Health Interview Survey, the "person who knows the most about the health of the family" is to be the respondent.

There are, however, many things that an individual can report only for himself or herself. Researchers almost universally feel that no individual can report feelings, opinions, or knowledge for some other person. There are also many behaviors or experiences (e.g., what people eat or drink, what they have bought, what they have seen, or what they have been told) that usually can only be reported accurately by self-reporters.

When a study includes variables for which only self-reporting is appropriate, the sampling process must go beyond selecting households to sampling specific individuals within those households. One approach is to interview every eligible person in a household. Because of homogeneity within households, however, as well as concerns about one respondent influencing a later respondent's answers, it is more common to designate a single respondent per household. Obviously, taking the person who happens to answer the phone or the door would be a nonprobabilistic and probably biased way of selecting individuals; interviewer discretion, respondent discretion, and availability (which is related to working status, life-style, and age) would all affect who turned out to be the respondent. The key principle of probability sampling is that selection is carried out through some chance or random procedure that designates specific people. The procedure for generating a probabilistic selection of respondents within households involves three steps:

1. Ascertain how many people living in a household are eligible to be respondents (e.g., how many are 18 or older).
2. Number these in a consistent way in all households (e.g., order by increasing age).
3. Have a procedure that objectively designates one person to be the respondent.

Kish (1949) created a detailed procedure for designating respondents using a set of randomized tables that still is used widely today. The critical features of such a system are that no discretion be involved and that all eligible people in selected households have a known (and nonzero) probability of selection. Groves and Lyberg (1988) review several strategies for simplifying respondent selection procedures.

When only one person is interviewed in a household, a differential rate of selection is introduced. If an adult lives in a one-adult household, he or she will be the respondent with certainty if the household is selected. In contrast, an adult living in a three-adult household only will be the respondent one third of the time. Whenever an identifiable group is selected at a different rate from others, weights are needed so that oversampled people are not overrepresented in the sample statistics. In the example earlier in this chapter, when black students were selected at twice the rate of white students, their responses were weighted at one half so that their weighted proportion of the sample would be the same as in the population. The same general approach applies when one respondent is chosen from households with varying numbers of eligible people.

The simplest way to adjust for the effect of selecting one respondent per household is to weight each response by the number of eligible people in that household. Hence, if there are three adults, the weight is three; if there are two eligible adults, the weight is two; and if there is only one eligible adult, the weight is one. If a weighting scheme is correct, the probability of selection times the weight is the same for all units.

There are some variables that are associated strongly with the number of adults in the household. For example, married people are much more likely than unmarried people to live in households with at least two adults, and married people are different from singles in numerous ways. Any estimate of something related to marital status will be distorted if the data are not weighted.

It also is true that some variables are unrelated to the number of adults in a household, in which case weighting will not affect descriptive results. When descriptive statistics (e.g., means or distributions) are desired, it always is appropriate to adjust for differential rates of selection of households and/or individuals through weighting. Moreover, weighting for descriptive purposes is easy with most standard analysis packages. There are, however, some complexities in using statistical tests based on weighted data. Estimates used in statistical tests are related to the number of actual interviews, as well as other sample design features, and using weights can distort the calculations if a program assumes there are more or fewer observations than there actually were. Sometimes it is not easy to do statistical tests properly when the design of a survey is complex. Moreover, for some correlational analyses, weighting may be unnecessary (Groves, 1989). This is one more example of why the involvement of a sampling statistician is important to appropriate design and analysis of survey data.

MAKING ESTIMATES FROM SAMPLES AND SAMPLING ERRORS

The sampling strategies presented above were chosen because they are among the most commonly used and they illustrate the major sampling design options. A probability sampling scheme eventually will designate a specific set of households or individuals without researcher or respondent discretion. The basic tools available to the researcher are simple random and systematic sampling, which are modified by stratification, unequal rates of selection, and clustering. The choice of a sampling strategy rests in part on feasibility and costs; it also involves the precision of sample estimates. A major reason for using probability sampling methods is to permit use of a variety of statistical tools to estimate the precision of sample estimates. In this section, the calculation of such estimates and how they are affected by features of the sample design are discussed.

Researchers usually have no interest in the characteristics of a sample per se. The reason for collecting data about a sample is to reach conclusions about an entire population. The statistical and design issues in this chapter are considered in the context of how much confidence one can have that the characteristics of a sample accurately describe the population as a whole.

Many common images have been used to explain probability theory. Perhaps the easiest one to understand is flipping a coin. If a perfectly fair coin is flipped 10 times, on any given set of 10 flips it may not come out exactly 5 heads and 5 tails. Sometimes there will be 6 heads, occasionally 7 heads, and once in a very great while one even might get 10 heads. In essence, one could think of any 10 flips as one of many possible samples. If one executed a series of 10 flips, flipping the coin 10 times and calculating the number of heads, flipping it another 10 times and keeping track of the number of heads again, and so forth, a distribution would result. If it was a fair coin, there would be more samples of 10 flips that produced 5 heads than any other number. There also would be a distribution around 5 heads with the extremes, 10 heads and no heads, occurring at the lowest frequency.

Although some sources of error in surveys are biasing and produce systematically distorted figures, sampling error is a random (and hence not a systematically biasing) result of sampling. When probability procedures are used to select a sample, it is possible to calculate how much sample estimates will vary by chance because of sampling.

If an infinite number of samples are drawn, the sample estimates of descriptive statistics (e.g., means) will form a normal distribution around the true population value. The larger the size of the sample and the less the variance of what is being measured, the more tightly the sample estimates will bunch around the true population value, and the more accurate a sample-based estimate will be. This variation around the true value, stemming from the fact that by chance samples may differ from the population as a whole, is called *sampling error*. Estimating the limits of the confidence one can have in a sample estimate, given normal chance sampling variability, is one important part of evaluating figures derived from surveys.

The design of sample selection (specifically, whether it involves stratification, clustering, or unequal probabilities of selection) affects the estimates of sampling error for a sample of a given size. The usual approach to describing sampling errors, however, is to calculate what they would be for a simple random sample, and then to calculate the effects of deviations from a simple random sampling design. Hence, the calculation of sampling errors for simple random samples is described first.

CALCULATING SAMPLING ERRORS FOR SIMPLE RANDOM SAMPLES

This is not a textbook on sampling statistics. Estimating the amount of error one can expect from a particular sample design, however, is a basic part of the survey design process. Moreover, researchers routinely provide readers with guidelines regarding error attributable to sampling, guidelines that both the knowledgeable reader and the user of survey research data should know and understand. To this end, a sense of how sampling error is calculated is a necessary part of understanding the total survey process.

Although the same logic applies to all statistics calculated from a sample, the most common sample survey estimates are means or averages. The statistic most often used to describe sampling error is called the standard error (of a mean). It is the standard deviation of the distribution of sample estimates of means that would be formed if an infinite number of samples of a given size were drawn. When the value of a standard error has been estimated, one can say that 67% of the means of samples of a given size and design will fall within the range of ±1 standard error of the true population mean; 95% of such samples will fall within the range of ±2 standard errors. The latter figure (±2 standard errors) often is reported as the *confidence interval* around a sample estimate.

The estimation of the standard error of a mean is calculated from the variance and the size of the sample from which it was estimated:

$$SE = \sqrt{\frac{Var}{n}}$$

SE = standard error of a mean
Var = the variance (the sum of the squared deviations from the sample mean over n)
n = size of the sample

The most common kind of mean calculated from a sample survey is probably a proportion, that is, the percentage of a sample that has a certain characteristic or gives a certain response. It may be useful to show how a proportion is the mean of a two-value distribution.

A mean is an average. It is calculated as the sum of the values divided by the number of cases: $\Sigma\, X/n$. Now suppose there are only two values, 0 (no) and 1 (yes). There are 50 cases in a sample; 20 say "yes" when asked if they are married, and the rest say "no." If there are 20 "yes" and 30 "no" responses, calculate the mean as

$$\Sigma X = 20 \times 1 + 30 \times 0 = 20; \qquad \frac{\Sigma X}{n} = \frac{20}{50} = .40$$

A proportion statement, such as that 40% of respondents are married, is just a statement about the mean of a 1/0 distribution; the mean is .40. The calculation of standard errors of proportions is facilitated by the fact that the variance of a proportion can be calculated readily as $p \times (1 - p)$, where p = proportion having a characteristic (e.g., the 40% married in the above example) and $(1 - p)$ is the proportion who lack the characteristic (e.g., the 60% not married).

We have already seen that the standard error of a mean is as follows:

$$\sqrt{\frac{Var}{n}}$$

Because $p(1 - p)$ is the variance of a proportion,

$$\sqrt{\frac{p(1 - p)}{n}}$$

is the standard error of a proportion. In the previous example, with 40% of a sample of 50 persons being married, the standard error of that estimate would be as follows:

$$\sqrt{\frac{p(1 - p)}{n}} = \sqrt{\frac{.40 \times .60}{50}} = \sqrt{\frac{.24}{50}} = .07$$

Thus we would estimate that the probability is .67 (i.e., $\pm$ 1 standard error from the sample mean) that the true population figure (the proportion of the whole population that is married) is between .33 and .47 (.40 $\pm$ .07). We are 95% confident that the true population figure lies within two standard errors of our sample mean, that is, between .26 and .54 (.40 $\pm$ .14).

Table 2.1 is a generalized table of sampling errors for samples of various sizes and for various proportions, provided that samples were selected as simple random samples. Each number in the table represents two standard errors of a proportion. Given knowledge (or an estimate) of the proportion of a sample that gives a particular answer, the table gives 95% confidence intervals for various sample sizes. In the example above, with 50 cases yielding a sample estimate of 40% married, the table reports a confidence interval near .14, as we calculated. If a sample of about 100 cases produced an estimate that 20% were married, the table says we can be 95% sure that the true figure is 20% $\pm$ 8 percentage points (i.e., 12% to 28%).

Several points about the table are worth noting. First, it can be seen that increasingly large samples always reduce sampling errors. Second, it also can be seen that adding a given number of cases to a sample reduces sampling error a great deal more when the sample is small than when it is comparatively large. For example, adding 50 cases to a sample of 50 produces a quite noticeable reduction in sampling error. Adding 50 cases to a sample of 500, however, produces a virtually unnoticeable improvement in the overall precision of sample estimates.

Third, it can be seen that the absolute size of the sampling error is greatest around proportions of .5 and decreases when the proportion of a sample having a characteristic approaches either zero or 100%. We have seen that standard errors are related directly to variances. The variance— $p \times (1 - p)$—is smaller as the proportions get further from .5.

Fourth, Table 2.1 and the equations on which it is based apply to samples drawn with simple random

Table 2.1
Confidence Ranges for Variability Attributable to Sampling*

Percentage of Sample With Characteristic

Sample Size	5/95	10/90	20/80	30/70	50/50
35	7	10	14	15	17
50	6	8	11	13	14
75	5	7	9	11	12
100	4	6	8	9	10
200	3	4	6	6	7
300	3	3	5	5	6
500	2	3	4	4	4
1,000	1	2	3	3	3
1,500	1	2	2	2	2

NOTE: Chances are 95 in 100 that the real population figure lies in the range defined by $\pm$ number indicated in table, given the percentage of sample reporting the characteristic and the number of sample cases on which the percentage is based.
*This table describes variability attributable to sampling. Errors resulting from nonresponse or reporting errors are not reflected in this table. In addition, this table assumes a simple random sample. Estimates may be subject to more variability than this table indicates because of the sample design or the influence of interviewers on the answers they obtained; stratification might reduce the sampling errors below those indicated here.

sampling procedures. Most samples of general populations are not simple random samples. The extent to which the particular sample design will affect calculations of sampling error varies from design to design and for different variables in the same survey. More often than not, Table 2.1 will constitute an underestimate of the sampling error for a general population sample.

Finally, it should be emphasized that the variability reflected in Table 2.1 describes potential for error that comes from the fact of sampling rather than collecting information about every individual in a population. The calculations do not include estimates of error from any other aspects of the survey process.

EFFECTS OF OTHER SAMPLE DESIGN FEATURES ON SAMPLING ERRORS

The preceding discussion describes the calculation of sampling errors for simple random samples. Estimates of sampling errors will be affected by different sampling procedures. Systematic sampling should produce sampling errors equivalent to simple random samples if there is no stratification. Stratified samples will produce sampling errors that are lower than those associated with simple random samples of the same size for variables that differ (on average) by stratum, if rates of selection are constant across strata.

Unequal rates of selection (selecting subgroups in the population at different rates) are designed to increase the precision of estimates for oversampled subgroups. They generally will produce sampling errors for the whole sample that are higher than those associated with simple random samples of the same size for variables that differ by stratum, except when oversampling occurs in strata that have higher than average variances. In the latter case, overall sampling errors will be lower than for a sample of the same size with equal probabilities of selection.

Clustering will produce sampling errors that are higher than those associated with simple random samples of the same size for variables that are more homogeneous within clusters than in the population as a whole. Also, the larger the size of the cluster at the last stage, the larger the impact on sampling errors will be.

One clear complexity of sampling is anticipating the effects of design features on the precision of estimates. They differ from study to study and for different variables in the same survey. To illustrate, suppose every house on various selected blocks was the same with respect to type of construction and whether or not it was occupied by the owner. Once an interview at the first selected housing unit on a block determined that it was a single-family house and was owner occupied, the additional interviews on that block would yield absolutely no new information about the rate of home ownership or the rate of single-family houses in the population as a whole. For that reason, whether the researcher took 1 interview per block or 20 interviews per block, the reliability of estimates of those variables would be exactly the same, basically proportionate to the number of blocks from which any interviews at all were taken. At the other extreme, the height of adults is likely to be unrelated to what block a person lives on. If clusters of interviews on a block are as heterogeneous as the population as a whole, clustering would not decrease the precision of estimates of height from a sample of a given size. One has to look at the nature of the clusters or strata and what estimates are to be made in order to evaluate the likely effect of clustering on sampling errors.

The effects of the sample design on sampling errors often are unappreciated. It is not uncommon to see reports of confidence intervals that assume simple random sampling when the design was clustered. It also is not a simple matter to anticipate design effects beforehand or to calculate them after a study is complete. As noted, the effects of the sample design on sampling errors are different for every variable; their calculation is particularly complicated when a sample design has several deviations from simple random sampling, such as clustering and stratification. Because the ability to calculate sampling errors is one of the principal strengths of the survey method, it is important that a statistician be involved in a survey with a complex sample design to ensure that sampling errors are calculated and reported appropriately.

Finally, the appropriateness of any sample design feature can be evaluated only in the context of the overall survey objectives. Clustered designs are likely to save money both in sampling (listing) and in data collection. Moreover, it is common to find many variables for which clustering does not inflate the sampling errors much. Oversampling one or more groups often is a cost-effective design. As with most issues discussed in this book, the important point is for a researcher to be aware of the potential costs and benefits of the options and to weigh them in the context of all the design options and the main purposes of the survey.

HOW BIG SHOULD A SAMPLE BE

Of the many issues involved in sample design, one of the most common questions posed to a survey methodologist is how big a survey sample should be. Before providing an approach to answering this question, perhaps it is appropriate to discuss three common but inappropriate ways of answering it.

One common misconception is that the adequacy of a sample depends heavily on the fraction of the population included in that sample—that somehow 1%, or 5%, or some other percentage of a population will make a sample credible. The estimates of sampling errors discussed above do not take into account the fraction of a population included in a sample. The sampling error estimates from the preceding equations and from Table 2.1 can be reduced by multiplying them by the value $(1-f)$, where f = the fraction of the population included in a sample.

When one is sampling 10% or more of a population, this adjustment can have a discernible effect on sampling error estimates. The vast majority of survey samples, however, involve very small fractions of populations. In such instances, small increments in the fraction of the population included in a sample will have no effect on the ability of a researcher to generalize from a sample to a population.

The converse of this principle also should be noted. The size of the population from which a sample of a particular size is drawn has virtually no impact on how well that sample is likely to describe the population. A sample of 150 people will describe a population of 15,000 or 15 million with virtually the same degree of accuracy, assuming that all other aspects of the sample design and sampling procedures were the same. Compared to the total sample size and other design features such as clustering, the impact of the fraction of a population sampled on sampling errors is typically trivial. It is most unusual for it to be an important consideration when deciding on a sample size.

A second approach to deciding on sample size is somewhat easier to understand. Some people have been exposed to so-called standard survey studies, and from these they have derived a "typical" or "appropriate" sample size. Thus some people will say that good national survey samples generally are 1,500, or that good community samples are 500. Of course, it is not foolish to look at what other competent researchers have considered to be adequate sample sizes of a particular population. The sample size decision, however, like most other design decisions, must be made on a case-by-case basis, with the researchers considering the variety of goals to be achieved by a particular study and taking into account numerous other aspects of the research design.

A third wrong approach to deciding on sample size is the most important one to address, for it can be found in many statistical textbooks. The approach goes like this: A researcher should decide how much margin of error he or she can tolerate or how much precision is required of estimates. Once one knows the need for precision, one simply uses a table such as Table 2.1, or appropriate variations thereon, to calculate the sample size needed to achieve the desired level of precision.

In some theoretical sense, there is nothing wrong with this approach. In practice, however, it provides little help to most researchers trying to design real studies. First, it is unusual to base a sample size decision on the need for precision of a single estimate. Most survey studies are designed to make numerous estimates, and the needed precision for these estimates is likely to vary.

In addition, it is unusual for a researcher to be able to specify a desired level of precision in more than the most general way. It is only the exception, rather than the common situation, when a specific acceptable margin for error can be specified in advance. Even in the latter case, the above approach implies that sampling error is the only or main source of error in a survey estimate. When a required level of precision from a sample survey is specified, it generally ignores the fact that there will be error from sources other than sampling. In such cases, the calculation of precision

based on sampling error alone is an unrealistic oversimplification. Moreover, given fixed resources, increasing the sample size even may decrease precision by reducing resources devoted to response rates, questionnaire design, or the quality of data collection.

Estimates of sampling error, which are related to sample size, do play a role in analyses of how big a sample should be. This role, however, is complicated.

The first prerequisite for determining a sample size is an analysis plan. The key component of that analysis plan usually is not an estimate of confidence intervals for the overall sample but rather an outline of the subgroups within the total population for which separate estimates are required, together with some estimates of the fraction of the population that will fall into those subgroups. Typically, the design process moves quickly to identifying the smaller groups within the population for which figures are needed. The researcher then estimates how large a sample will be required in order to provide a minimally adequate sample of these small subgroups. Most sample size decisions do not focus on estimates for the total population; rather, they are concentrated on the minimum sample sizes that can be tolerated for the smallest subgroups of importance.

The process then turns to Table 2.1, not at the high end but at the low end of the sample size continuum. Are 50 observations adequate? If one studies Table 2.1, it can be seen that precision increases rather steadily up to sample sizes of 150 to 200. After that point, there is a much more modest gain to increasing sample size.

Like most decisions relating to research design, there is seldom a definitive answer about how large a sample should be for any given study. There are many ways to increase the reliability of survey estimates. Increasing sample size is one of them. Even if one cannot say that there is a single right answer, however, it can be said that there are three approaches to deciding on sample size that are inadequate. Specifying a fraction of the population to be included in the sample is never the right way to decide on a sample size. Saying that a particular sample size is the usual or typical approach to studying a population also is virtually always the wrong answer. Finally, it is very rare that calculating a desired confidence interval for one variable for an entire population is the best way to decide how big a sample should be.

SAMPLING ERROR AS A COMPONENT OF TOTAL SURVEY ERROR

The sampling process can affect the quality of survey estimates in three different ways:

• If the sample frame excludes some people whom we want to describe, sample estimates will be biased to the extent that those omitted differ from those included.
• If the sampling process is not probabilistic, the relationship between the sample and those sampled is problematic. One can argue for the credibility of a sample on grounds other than the sampling process;

however, there is no statistical basis for saying a sample is representative of the sampled population unless the sampling process gives each person selected a known probability of selection.

• The size and design of a probability sample, together with the distribution of what is being estimated, determine the sampling errors—that is, the chance variations that occur because of collecting data about only a sample of a population.

Often sampling errors are presented in ways that imply they are the only source of unreliability in survey estimates. In fact with large samples, other sources of error are likely to be more important. A main theme of this book is that nonsampling errors warrant as much attention as sampling errors. Also, it is not uncommon to see sampling errors reported that assume simple random sampling procedures when the sample design involved clusters, or even when it was not a probability sample at all. In these ways, ironically, estimates of sampling errors can mislead readers about the precision or accuracy of sample estimates.

Sampling and analyzing data from a sample can be fairly straightforward if a good list is used as a sampling frame, if a simple random or systematic sampling scheme is used, and if all respondents are selected at the same rate. With such a design, Table 2.1 and the equations on which it is based will provide good estimates of sampling errors. Even with such straightforward designs, however, researchers need to consider all sources of error—including the sample frame, nonresponse, and response errors (all discussed in subsequent chapters)—when evaluating the precision of survey estimates. Moreover, when there are doubts about the best way to sample, or when there are deviations from simple random sampling, it is virtually essential to involve a sampling specialist both to design an appropriate sampling plan and to analyze results properly from a complex sample design.

EXERCISE

In order to grasp the meaning of sampling error, repeated systematic samples of the same size (with different random starts) can be drawn from the same list (e.g., a telephone directory). The proportions of those samples having some characteristic (e.g., a business listing) taken together will form a distribution. That distribution will have a standard deviation that is about one half the entry in Table 2.1 for samples of the sizes drawn. It is also valuable to calculate several of the entries in Table 2.1 (i.e., for various sample sizes and proportions) to help understand how the numbers were derived.

4

This chapter was first published by Sage Publications and is reproduced by permission of Sage Publications

Improving Survey Questions – Design and Evaluation. CA: Sage Publications, 1995

Floyd J Fowler, JR

CHAPTER 4
SOME GENERAL RULES FOR DESIGNING GOOD SURVEY INSTRUMENTS

In the preceding two chapters, we have discussed in some detail the problems associated with writing good survey questions and some general approaches to solving common problems. In this chapter, we attempt to lay out some general principles for how to write and design good survey instruments.

A good survey instrument must be custom made to address a specific set of research goals. It literally is impossible to identify the best question for a particular purpose out of context. Nonetheless, there are some general principles that affect the quality of measurement that emerges from survey questions.

WHAT TO ASK ABOUT

Principle 1: *The strength of survey research is asking people about their firsthand experiences: what they have done, their current situations, their feelings and perceptions.*

Yet, surprisingly, a good bit of survey research is devoted to asking people questions to which most people do not have informed answers.

Principle 1a: *Beware of asking about information that is acquired only secondhand.*

For research regarding crime, people can report when and how they were victimized, when they feel safe and when they feel fearful, and what steps they have taken to reduce their fears or their risk of being victims. People can describe their experiences with calling the police, the response of the police to their calls, and the quality of their interactions with police officials. In contrast, most people cannot report accurately about the real rates of crimes in their neighborhoods or in their communities. They may have opinions about how well the police do their jobs, but, except for their own experiences, they are unlikely to have much specific information about police performance.

People are likely to have informed opinions about the schools that their own children attend. They are unlikely to have informed opinions about what goes on in other schools, in schools throughout their communities, or in schools throughout the nation.

Regarding their health, people can reliably report how they feel, what they can do, and how they see themselves to be affected by their physical condition. They may or may not be able to reliably report what

their physicians named their health conditions or what procedures or diagnostic tests their physicians performed. People almost certainly are not the best sources of information about the medical name for their health conditions or how much money was spent to provide them with medical care.

To study the effect of race or ethnicity on employment opportunities, one can obtain descriptions of the jobs people have, their perceptions of the appropriateness of their pay or responsibilities, and whether or not they believe they have been treated unfairly or inappropriately by employers. Comparing the answers of people of different ethnic groups may be important to identifying the relationship between ethnicity and quality of employment. However, asking people for their opinions or perceptions of how fairly different groups are treated in employment situations is asking them questions about which most people are uninformed.

There may be occasions when it is important and valuable to measure peoples' relatively uninformed opinions. Such opinions and perceptions constitute a reality of sorts. If people think that crime is rising and the police are doing a poor job, those perceptions may be important in and of themselves, even if they are inaccurate by objective standards. However, researchers should not confuse opinions with objective results.

There are numerous examples of major differences between generalizations derived from people's secondhand perceptions and the results of their direct reports. Although the general perception in the United States is that the quality of schools has been deteriorating for years, most people report positive experiences with their own schools. Although in the early 1990s perceptions of ever-increasing rates of crime and drug use are common, in fact objective measures of rates of crime and drug use have been gradually and steadily declining over the past two decades. Although physicians report a perception of declining quality of life for people practicing medicine, the average ratings by physicians of their own quality of life are extraordinarily high. When studying a general problem, it often is tempting to ask respondents for their perceptions of the problems and possible solutions. Although the answers to such questions may be informative, in particular when they identify misperceptions or distortions, researchers should not forget the main strength of the survey research method. To repeat, the strength of surveys is to collect information about the firsthand knowledge and experiences of a probability sample of some population.

Principle 1b: *Beware of hypothetical questions.*

People are not good at predicting what they will do, or how they will feel, in a circumstance they have not yet encountered. Often researchers want to predict the future or estimate how people will respond to something new: a new television program, a new light bulb, or a new health care proposal. There are some reasons why this is very hard to do. First, behavior is largely determined by situations. Whether or not a person will give money to a specific charity depends more on how and by whom the request is presented than the particular cause. Questions about future behavior cannot reproduce the behaviorally relevant issues very well. Second, new programs or products consist of many components that are hard to describe fully in an interview. The researchers will pick out key features for a description, but it is hard to be sure the features that matter most to each respondent are included.

To the extent that questions about the future can build on relevant past experiences and direct knowledge, the answers will be more accurate. Women who have previously delivered babies do a better job of predicting their likely use of anaesthesia in a future delivery than women who have not had a baby. People can predict their buying intentions regarding products with which they are familiar better than if the product is merely described in a question; giving a respondent a chance to "try" the product improves the correspondence between reported intentions to buy and behavior. Nonetheless, in general, asking people to predict their response to a future or hypothetical situation should be done with considerable caution – particularly when respondents are likely to have limited direct experience on which to base their answers.

Principle 1c: *Beware of asking about causality.*

It is hard for social scientists to establish causal patterns. Many events have multiple origins. Few of us are able to report validly on the reasons we do what we do. Survey researchers often wish to identify the reasons for things, but asking the respondents to provide those reasons is unlikely to produce credible or useful data.

Example 4.1: Were you limited in your everyday activities because of your back problem?

Example 4.2: What is the main reason you did not vote?

Example 4.3: Were you homeless because of the high cost of housing?

Some people, whose only physical problem is lower back pain, may be able to answer Question 4.1, but people with various health problems will have difficulty sorting out the effects of back pain from those of their other problems to answer 4.1. Example 4.2 highlights the complexity of motivation and causality. Respondents can report barriers (trouble getting off work) or motivational issues (did not like either candidate). Yet, there will be people in exactly the same situations who voted anyway. Did we really learn anything interesting by asking people for the way they perceive causality—especially for not doing something? It is hard to make the case that we do.

Finally, Example 4.3 is the epitome of a question that will not produce useful information. Perhaps there are some people who would be homeless even if nice homes were free. For anyone who is interested in a home, however, their resources, their priorities, their standards for housing, and the cost of various housing features will interact in some complex way to determine if they do or do not choose to devote some of their resources to acquiring housing. This is known in advance, and it is hard to think what the respondents' analysis of these issues will add.

In general, surveys should address the things respondents can reliably report: what resources did they have, what were minimum housing requirements, and, perhaps, what is the perception of the cost of minimally adequate housing? The researcher can then describe the situation and identify conclusions that will be of much more validity and value than the respondents' analysis of causality.

Principle 1d: *Beware of asking respondents about solutions to complex problems.*

When decision makers are wrestling with options about how to solve problems, it may be tempting to ask survey respondents what they think. However, if a problem is complex (and most of the hard ones are), it usually is necessary to have quite a bit of information in order to have a meaningful opinion about how to solve it. Surveys do not provide a good forum for providing much information to respondents, and response options necessarily are concise (which typically means oversimplified). Occasionally, an issue has received enough public attention that many respondents do have informed opinions about how to address a problem, but it is rare. It is easy for those involved in an issue to overestimate the level of information or caring most people have about their pet problem. Most often, survey researchers will be best served by asking respondents questions to which they have answers, leaving the design of effective solutions to problems to those whose job it is to address those problems.

Principle 2. *Ask one question at a time.*

Principle 2a. *Avoid asking two questions at once.*

Example 4.4: Would you like to be rich and famous?

Example 4.5: Are you physically able to do things like run or swim without difficulty?

Comment: Both of these questions are asking two questions, the answers to which can be different. Respondents could want to be rich but not famous; they could have difficulty running but not swimming. If a question includes two questions, and both questions are important, ask two questions, one at a time.

Principle 2b: *Avoid questions that impose unwarranted assumptions.*

Example 4.6: With the economy the way it is, do you think investing in the stock market is a good idea?
Comment: Sudman and Bradburn (1982) call this a one-and-a-half-barreled question (as contrasted with a double-barreled question). In the end, only a single question is asked, but the introductory clause asks the respondent to buy into an analysis of the economy. Admittedly, the clause does not exactly specify the state of the economy. However, the implication is negative. Moreover, the question imposes a relationship between "the economy" and investing that some people might not see.

Example 4.7: Do you agree or disagree: Given the amount of crime these days, it makes sense not to walk alone at night.
Comment: The question makes respondents assume there is a lot of crime and that the assumed crime rate should affect decisions about walking alone. If a respondent does not accept these assumptions, the question is very difficult. The question about how people feel about walking alone can be asked without the introductory assumptions.

Principle 2c: *Beware of questions that include hidden contingencies.*

A major weakness of some questions as measures is that the answers reflect what is to be measured only for a subset of the population. Such questions are limited in their analytic value, because they are not meaningful measures for the whole sample.

Objective: To measure fear on the streets.
Example 4.8: In the past month, have you crossed the street from one side to another in order to avoid going near someone you thought was frightening?
Comment: Crossing the street to avoid someone who appears frightening may be an indication of when someone is fearful. However, the relevance of this particular question has at least two contingencies. First, it depends on a person having been out on the streets walking. If a person is quite fearful, he or she may avoid walking altogether. A bit more subtly, fearful people may be particularly careful when and where they walk. Their patterns may be designed to avoid situations where they might encounter people of whom they would be fearful. To the extent that they are successful, they will have avoided those situations likely to produce the occasion when they would feel compelled to cross the street.

If everyone in the sample could be assumed to have had the same degree of exposure to walking on the street, then the rate at which they reported crossing the street might be an indication of either fearfulness or the extent to which their streets contained fear-provoking people. However, the question as written provides no such opportunity to sort out people's exposures. Moreover, even if it did, the fact that the rate of this behavior would be contingent on opportunities would mean that it would be an imperfect measure for classifying all people in a sample.

Overall, a more direct rating of how fearful people perceive themselves to be walking in the streets would almost certainly be a better approach to measuring fearfulness for all individuals in the sample in a way that would be analytically useful.

Objective: To measure social activity
Example 4.9: How often did you attend religious services or participate in church-related activities during the past month?
Comment: The obvious limitation of this question as a measure of social activity is that it is contingent upon church being one of the organizations in which a person is active. For all those people who are not affiliated with or interested in churches, the answer has no meaning as a measure of social activity. In combination with other items, there is a possibility this item could be a useful part of a social activity index. However the more generally applicable the item, the better it is as a measure of social activity.

Objective: To measure limitations on physical activity resulting from health problems
Example 4.10: In the past month, has your health limited your ability to do vigorous activities, such as jogging, swimming, or biking?
Comment: For those people who do these activities, the question may provide information about the extent to which health is affecting their lives. However, for the people who do not normally do such things, their "no" answer will mean something entirely different. Instead of saying that their health is not limiting them, they essentially are saying they are not limited because they do not normally do these sorts of things. This question can provide information only for that subset of the people who normally jog, swim, or bike.

WORDING QUESTIONS

Principle 3: *A survey question should be worded so that every respondent is answering the same question.*

Principle 3a: *To the extent possible, the words in questions should be chosen so that all respondents understand their meaning, and all respondents have the same sense of what the meaning is.*

Principle 3b: *To the extent that words or terms must be used that have meanings that are likely not to be shared, definitions should be provided to all respondents.*

Principle 3b is particularly important. Occasionally, one will see a survey for which interviewers will be given definitions to provide to respondents who ask for them.

Bad Example 4.11: In the past 12 months, how many times have you seen or talked with a medical doctor about your health? (IF ASKED: Include visits to psychiatrists, ophthalmologists, and any other professional with a medical degree.)

Obviously, such a procedure breaks the principle of having all respondents answer the same question and have the same stimulus. If some respondents are given definitions that others lack, respondents are answering different questions.

Principle 3c: *The time period referred to by a question should be unambiguous. Questions about feelings or behaviors must refer to a period of time.*

Example 4.12: How often do you feel tired during the day—always, usually, sometimes, rarely, or never?
Example 4.12a: Are you able to run half a mile without stopping?
Example 4.12b: How many drinks do you usually have on days when you drink any alcoholic beverages at all?
Comment: All of these questions assume the answers are stable over time and fail to specify a reference period. In fact, it is easy to think that the answers for a short time period (yesterday, last week) might be different from the average answers over a longer period (last month, last year). An acute illness, a holiday season, or a difficult period of work are examples of recent factors that could affect answers. If respondents choose to answer about different reference periods (one chooses the past week, another chooses the past year) their answers may differ for that reason alone. It is always good practice to specify the time period about which respondents are to report.

Principle 3d: *If what is to be covered is too complex to be included in a single question, ask multiple questions.*

Principle 4: *If a survey is to be interviewer administered, wording of the questions must constitute a complete and adequate script such that, when interviewers read the question as worded, respondents will be fully prepared to answer the question.*

Wording issues are somewhat different for questions that are self-administered, where respondents read the questions themselves, than when interviewers are going to read questions. In particular, when designing an interview schedule, it is important to appreciate the fact that an interaction is going on that potentially may influence the way questions are presented. It is important to design the questions to take that reality into account (see Suchman & Jordan, 1990).

Principle 4a: *If definitions are to be given, they should be given before the question itself is asked.*

Bad Example 4.13a: How many days in the past week have you done any exercise? When you consider exercise be sure to include walking, work around the house, or work on a job, if you think they constituted exercise.

Better Example 4.13b: The next question is going to ask you about how often you've engaged in exercise. We want you to include walking, anything you may do around the house, or work you do on a job if you think they constitute exercise. So using that definition, in the last week, on how many days did you do any exercise?

Experience shows that respondents are likely to interrupt the reading of a question once they think they have heard a question. When that happens, interviewers will vary in how conscientiously they read definitions, such as those in the bad example. By putting the definitions first in a question, researchers increase the likelihood that all respondents will hear the needed definitions before they answer the question, and they will make it easier for interviewers to read the questions exactly as worded.

Principle 4b: *A question should end with the question itself. If there are response alternatives, they should constitute the final part of the question.*

Bad Example 4.14a: Would you say that you are very likely, fairly likely, or not likely to move out of this house in the next year?
Bad Example 4.14b: If the election were held today, do you think you would be more likely to vote for Governor Clinton or President Bush, considering the way you see the issues now?
Comment: In both of the above examples, respondents are very unlikely to be prepared to answer the question as read. In the first instance, experience shows that respondents will forget the response task while they are concentrating on what the question is. In the same way, when there are dangling clauses at the end of questions, respondents are likely to find they can no longer remember the terms of the question.
Better Example 4.14a: In the coming year, how likely are you to move to another home? Would you say very likely, fairly likely, or not very likely?

This question puts the response alternatives at the end. The respondent can listen to the question, knows the response task is coming up, and then hears the terms in which the question is to be answered.

One final point about questions such as the one directly above: Respondents often will interrupt the interviewer before the response alternatives are read, if it is not clear that response alternatives are going to follow. In the example, a complete question has been read before the response alternatives come into play.

The reason for trying to avoid having respondents interrupt the interviewer, before the response alternatives are read, is that interviewers are then put in an awkward position, which they handle inconsistently. Suppose a respondent jumps into the above question, saying something like, "There is very little chance that we'll be moving in the next year." By the rules of standardized measurement, the interviewer should go back and read the whole question, including all the response alternatives. However, studies show that some interviewers will try to guess what a respondent would have chosen, had the standardized question been administered. It is in the interests of the researcher to try to provide a script that maximizes the chances the interviewer will present the question exactly the same to each respondent.

Probably Better Example 4.14b: Which of these categories best describes how likely you think you are to move in the next year: very likely, fairly likely, or not likely?

Comment: Including the concept that categories are coming up in the question probably will reduce the likelihood that the respondent will interrupt the interviewer before the whole question is read.

Another Bad Example 4.15a: Please tell me whether you consider each of the following to be a big problem, a small problem, or no problem at all.

a. Pain in your bones or joints
b. Difficulty breathing
c. Any other health problem

Comment: There are numerous problems with the example above. First, the question itself is not put in a form that constitutes a script for an interviewer. In fact, there is no question. It is almost certain that if an interviewer read the words above, the respondent would be unprepared to answer a question.

Better Example 4.15b: How much of a problem do you consider (READ EACH) – big problem, some problem, or no problem at all?

In that format, it is easy to see that there is a script for an interviewer. The interviewer can read the question as worded, filling in the various health problems from the list, and prepare the respondent to answer each question.

Another common mistake is including "other health problem" in the question. Such a category is often seen in lists such as this, but in fact it does not constitute a viable question. In order to do anything at all with this question, the interviewer is forced to make up two different questions:

1. Is there any other health condition or problem that affects you?
2. Do you consider (ANSWER TO QUESTION A) to be a big problem, some problem, or no problem at all?

Even in this form, it does not make much sense. Moreover, as measurement, given the fact that only a few people will add "other problems" and there will be very little overlap among the "other problems," the analytic value of the results will be trivial. For most such series, not asking about "other problems" would probably serve the researchers best.

Principle 5: *Clearly communicate to all respondents the kind of answer that constitutes an adequate answer to a question.*

The easiest way to communicate to respondents what kind of answer to give is to provide a list of acceptable answers. Indeed, such "closed questions" constitute a major part of the survey research enterprise.

However, there are times when it is best to allow respondents to answer in their own words. In some cases, there are more response alternatives than reasonably could be provided, or the researcher may believe it is not possible to anticipate the range of possible answers. At such times, it is best to have respondents answer questions in their own words. (See also appendix C.) However, that does not mean the terms of the answer should not be clearly specified.

Example 4.16: When did you move to this community?

Possible Answers:
When I was sixteen.
Right after I was married.
In 1953.

Any of those answers constitutes an adequate answer to the question as phrased. However, they cannot be compared and analyzed. If some people answer in terms of how old they were, whereas others provide a year, there is no way to integrate the data into a single analysis.

The problem is that the question does not specify the terms in which the researcher wants the answer.

Possible Alternative Questions:
In what year did you move to this community?
How old were you when you moved to this community?

Either one of these questions communicates to all respondents the kind of answers that are acceptable and enables the researcher to easily analyze the resulting answers.

One temptation might be to ask interviewers to explain to respondents what is wanted, in the event that they do not discern it. Obviously that violates a basic principle that interviewers should be given an adequate script, and all respondents should be asked the same questions.

Another Bad Example 4.17a: Why did you go to the doctor the last time?

Possible Answers:
Because I wasn't feeling well.
Because my husband had been nagging me, and I decided it was time to go.
Because the doctor had scheduled me to come back.
To get a shot.

Once again, there is nothing in the question that specifies the kind of answer that is needed. Do we want to know what the medical condition or problem is that leads to the visit? Do we want to know what the impetus was (not feeling well, spouse was nagging) for deciding to go? Do we want to know what the patient thought or hoped was going to be done (checkups, shots, X-rays)?

The last three answers tell us nothing about the condition for which the patient was going to be treated. If we were interested in that, we should have asked:

Example 4.17b: For what kind of health condition or problem, if any, were you going to see the doctor?

We could infer that perhaps two of the answers (not feeling well, shot) were for diagnosis or treatment of a condition and not for a general checkup. The other two answers are ambiguous on that point. One approach to improving the question is to provide a list of possible answers from a single perspective.

Better Example 4.17c: Was your last visit to a doctor mainly because of a condition that you have had for some time, mainly to find out about a condition that you only recently noticed, or just for a general checkup, for no particular problem or condition?

Example 4.18: Where do you get most of your information about health?

Possible Answers:
From reading.
From newspapers.
From Ann Landers.
From the media.

In one sense, all these answers provide some information. The information is of a negative sort. The answers are *not* "from my doctor," or from "friends." However, the answers are very different. The question itself gives no clue as to how specific respondents' answers are supposed to be. When the respondent says "reading," does it matter whether the respondent is reading newspapers, magazines, or medical journals? When the respondent says, "from the media," does it matter whether it is from the television, from newspapers, or from the radio? In fact, the right answer for all the respondents giving the above answers might have been "Ann Landers." If Ann Landers was the principal source of information on health care, any one of those four answers would have been plausible, right answers.

The question itself provides no information to respondents about which level of detail is wanted. Moreover, there are no words in the question that an interviewer can use to stimulate the respondent to get to the right level of specificity. Some good, nondirective probing, such as "tell me more about that," will help to make the general answers more specific. However, to the extent that researchers can communicate to interviewers and respondents more clearly and consistently what kind of answer will meet their needs, they will have more comparable data from respondent to respondent, will make interviewing more consistent, and will have better measurement and data.

Principle 5a: *Specify the number of responses to be given to questions for which more than one answer is possible.*

Example 4.19: What was it about the brand you bought that made you buy it rather than some other brand?

Comment: Respondents will vary in the number of features they mention, and interviewers will vary in how much they probe for multiple responses. These sources of variability can be eliminated by asking:

Example 4.19a: What was the most important feature of the brand you bought that made you buy it rather than some other brand?

Comment: This form eliminates the variability in the number of answers given.

Example 4.20: Which of these forms of exercise have you done in the past 30 days?

a. Swimming
b. Jogging or running
c. Biking
d. Skiing
e. Working out on an indoor exercise equipment, such as a rower, Stair Master, or exercycle

Comment: The instruction (CHECK ALL THAT APPLY) is not consistently effective in a self-administered form; some respondents will check one box and move on. If an interviewer is involved and respondents are looking at the list of activities, this form may be all right. For self-administered forms and telephone interviews, however, a series of yes/no questions about each activity is a better question form. Interpreting a nonanswer to mean "no" is always risky and should be avoided.

FORMATTING SURVEY INSTRUMENTS

Principle 6: *Design survey instruments to make the tasks of reading questions, following instructions, and recording answers as easy as possible for interviewers and respondents.*

The job of the interviewer in a survey is intrinsically difficult. The main tasks are listening to answers, figuring out whether an adequate answer has been given and, if not, deciding what sort of follow-up probe to use to elicit an adequate answer. When designing a survey instrument, the researcher should try to make figuring out how to read the questions, which questions to read, and how to record the answers as simple as possible, so interviewers can focus on the real substance of the job.

For different reasons, it is important to make self-administered questionnaires easy. For the most part, respondents are not very motivated. In addition, it should be assumed that respondents are not facile readers. For both of those reasons, survey instruments should be designed to be as easy to go through as possible.

For an interviewer-administered instrument, some of principles enunciated above will be helpful. Providing interviewers with a good script, one that provides the needed definitions, and designing questions that communicate the kind of answers required will improve the ability of respondents to do their jobs and decrease the amount of work interviewers have to do. In addition, the simple mechanics of formatting the instrument properly can make the interviewer's job go more smoothly.

Figures 4.1 through 4.3 provide three examples of survey instruments. The questions are all the same, but the formats are somewhat different.

At least four conventions are basic to every interview schedule, and a researcher designing an interview schedule needs to attend to them in some way:

1. When question wording involves some kind of choice, such as when the interviewer has to decide on the exact words (he/she) is to read, a convention is needed. For

example, when a question asks about a (SPOUSE), a convention such as placing the word in caps can be used to designate a place where an interviewer will choose between (husband/wife) as the exact word to use. All of the examples put optional wording in parentheses. Each has a slightly different, but internally consistent, way of presenting optional wording. All of these conventions serve the purpose of alerting the interviewer that a choice is to be made, and also maintain the principle of the researcher writing the script, so words can be read exactly.
2   A clear distinction should be made between instructions to interviewers and the words that interviewers should read as part of the question. SOMETIMES INSTRUCTIONS TO INTERVIEWERS ARE WRITTEN IN CAPITAL LETTERS, and the words that interviewers are to read to respondents are put in lower case. A different convention (Figure 4.2) is to place instructions to interviewers in shaded areas. The key is to have a consistent convention, so interviewers do not

---

Figure 4.1.
Interviewer-Administered Interview, Version 1

A1. On (REFERENCE DATE) were you working at a job for pay?
1   [] YES (SKIP TO A2)
2   [] NO

A1a. Prior to (REFERENCE DATE), did you ever work at a job for pay?
1   [] YES
2   [] NO (SKIP TO A6)

A2. (On (REFERENCE DATE/ or your last job BEFORE REFERENCE DATE) what kind of business or industry did you work in?

A3. Were you self-employed or did you work for someone else?
1   [] SELF
2   [] OTHER

A4. What kind of work were you doing then?

A5. Now, some questions about your current working situation. Are you currently *working at a job for pay*, are you on *sick or disability leave from a job*, or are you *not employed now*?
1   [] CURRENTLY WORKING FOR PAY (GO TO A6)
2   [] SICK OR DISABILITY LEAVE FROM A JOB (SKIP TO A9)
3   [] NOT EMPLOYED (DO INTERVIEWER CHECK)
INTERVIEWER CHECK:
1   [] IF R'S RESPONSE TO A1a IS "NO" AND R IS NOT EMPLOYED NOW
(SKIP TO A20)
2   [] IF R'S RESPONSE TO A1a *IS NOT* "NO" AND R IS NOT EMPLOYED NOW
(SKIP TO A15)

Figure 4.2.
Interviewer-Administered Interview, Version 2

A1. On (reference date) were you working at a job for pay?

| YES GO TO A2 | NO |

A1a. Prior to (reference date), did you ever work at a job for pay?

| YES | NO —> GO TO A6, PAGE 2 |

A2. (On (reference date/ or your last job before reference date) what kind of business or industry did you work in?

A3. Were you self-employed or did you work for someone else?

| SELF | OTHER |

A4. What kind of work were you doing then?

A5. Now, some questions about your current working situation. Are you currently *working at a job for pay*, are you on *sick or disability leave from a job*, or are you *not employed now*?

> CURRENTLY WORKING FOR PAY
> ——> GO TO A6, PAGE 2

> SICK OR DISABILITY LEAVE FROM A JOB
> ——> GO TO A9, PAGE 4

> NOT EMPLOYED
> ——> GO TO INTERVIEWER CHECKPOINT

5a. INTERVIEWER CHECKPOINT

> 1 IF R'S RESPONSE TO A1a IS "NO" AND R IS NOT EMPLOYED NOW
> ↓
> GO TO A20, P.5
>
> 2 IF R'S RESPONSE TO A1a *IS NOT* "NO" AND R IS NOT EMPLOYED NOW
> ↓
> GO TO A15, P.5

have to spend time and mental energy during an interview deciding what to read to respondents and what words are instructions to them.
3.   There should be a consistent convention to help interviewers deal with skips in the interview schedule. Two of the attached examples simply use written skip instructions keyed to particular responses.

5

Figure 4.3.
Interviewer-Administered Interview, Version 3

A1. On (*reference date*) were you working at a job for pay?

YES . . . . (SKIP TO A2) 1

NO . . . . . . (ASK A1a) 2

A1a. Prior to (*reference date*), did you ever work at a job for pay?

YES 1

NO . . . (GO TO Q. A6, P.2) . . . 2

A2. On (*reference date/* or your last job *before reference date*) what kind of business or industry did you work in?

_____

(industry)

A3. Were you self-employed or did you work for someone else?

SELF 1

OTHER 2

A4. What kind of work were you doing then?

_____

(type of work)

A5. Now, some questions about your current working situation. Are you currently *working at a job for pay*, are you on *sick or disability leave from a job*, or are you *not employed now*?

CURRENTLY WORKING FOR PAY
(GO TO A6, P.2) 1

SICK OR DISABILITY LEAVE FROM A JOB
(GO TO A9, P.4) 2

NOT EMPLOYED **3**

IF R'S RESPONSE TO A1a IS "NO" AND R IS NOT EMPLOYED NOW, **GO TO Q. A20, P. 5**

IF R'S RESPONSE TO A1a *IS NOT* "NO" AND R IS NOT EMPLOYED NOW, **GO TO Q. A15, P.5**

Figure 4.4.
Self-Administered Questionnaire, Version 1

1 Since you last filled out a questionnaire have you:

A. taken any medications prescribed by a doctor to relieve your prostate symptoms?

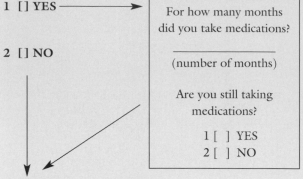

1 [ ] YES

2 [ ] NO

For how many months did you take medications?

_____

(number of months)

Are you still taking medications?

1 [ ] YES

2 [ ] NO

B. had balloon dilation of the prostate?

1   [ ] YES (How many times?) _____

2   [ ] NO

2. How much do you worry about your health because of your prostate condition?

1 [ ] A LOT

2 [ ] SOME

3 [ ] ONLY A LITTLE

4 [ ] NOT AT ALL

2a. When you worry about your health, what do you worry about?

_____

_____

SKIP TO Q3, NEXT PAGE

The other example uses boxes and arrows to make it visually evident where to go. It probably does not matter which convention is used, but being consistent throughout the interview schedule, and being clear, will make the interviewer's job easier.

4 Conventions for recording answers should be consistent. Research organizations differ in how they ask interviewers to record answers. Some have interviewers circle numbers (version 3); some have them check boxes (version 1); some have them draw x's through the chosen answer. The particular approach is less important than that the survey instrument be consistent in having interviewers do the same thing throughout an interview, without having to think about it.

The two pages after that present some examples of self-administered survey instruments (Figures 4.4 and 4.5).

1. Make it obvious to respondents which questions they are to answer and which ones they are to skip. Most designers of self-administered questionnaires try to minimize skips. However, when they are necessary, maximizing the extent to which it is visually obvious to respondents, rather than relying on reading instructions, is probably a good idea. The two examples provide several approaches to making skips visually evident.

2. Make it as obvious as possible how to answer questions. Making the response task consistent throughout a questionnaire is probably helpful. Most designers of self-administered questionnaires try to minimize or avoid altogether questions that need to be answered in narrative form.

Probably the most important point, rather than any particular solution to these problems, is that issues of ease of administration be given priority in designing survey

Figure 4.5.
Self-Administered Questionnaire, Version 2

1. Since you last filled out a questionnaire have you:

A. taken any medications prescribed by a doctor to relieve your prostate symptoms?

YES —> GO TO Aa   NO —> GO TO B

> **Aa.** For how many months did you take medications?
> _____ (number) MONTHS
>
> **Ab.** Are you still taking medications?
>
> YES   NO

> EVERYONE ANSWERS:

B. had balloon dilation of the prostate?

YES —> GO TO Bb   NO —> GO TO 2, this page

Bb. How many times? _____ (number)

> EVERYONE ANSWERS:

2. How much do you worry about your health because of your prostate condition?

A LOT   SOME   ONLY A LITTLE   NOT AT ALL
↓
GO TO Q3, NEXT PAGE

2a. When you worry about your health, what do you worry about?_____

_____

_____

instruments. That may seem self-evident, but it is not uncommon to see survey instruments in which other things, such as saving paper or putting lots of questions on pages to make an instrument look short, are given priority instead. The priority should be on making instruments that are easy to read and easy to use for interviewers and respondents.

TRAINING RESPONDENTS

Any time a standard survey process is to be carried out, there is some orientation or training of respondents that has to occur. If the purpose of the question-and-answer process is to measure intelligence, ability, or knowledge, even then there will be some training and orientation of people taking the test: what are the priorities (to answer as many questions right as possible); what are the rules of the process (how long people can take; to what extent, if any, wrong answers are discounted); what are the purposes of each section or area of a test?

Principle 7: *Measurement will be better to the extent that people answering questions are oriented to the task in a consistent way.* It is undesirable that test scores reflect differences in understanding how to take the test (as compared with differences in the knowledge the test is designed to measure). In a survey, we try to minimize differences in answers attributable to differences in the ways that respondents are oriented to the task.

There are three areas in which respondents require training:

1. The priorities or goals of the task
2. The data collection process and how to play the respondent role
3. The purposes or goals of any particular subpart of the survey

It is in the interests of researchers to try to ensure consistent training of respondents in each of these areas. In Fowler and Mangione (1990), much more detail is provided about the rationale and importance of orienting respondents to their task.

When a survey is being done by mail, researchers must rely on written instructions. We know that respondents vary in how willing they are to read detailed instructions. An information sheet, such as that found in Figure 4.6, may be a reasonably effective way to get some of this information across to respondents in a consistent way. However, one of the prices of mail surveys is that there is less ability to engage in effective respondent training.

When an interviewer is used, the potential for effective respondent training is clearly enhanced. However, some interviewers are reluctant to assume that kind of orienting role when they are asking people to volunteer to be respondents.

Interviewers need to dissociate the issue of enlisting cooperation from the issue of how the respondent is to perform the job. Researchers can help interviewers by providing standardized orienting instructions for interviewers to use.

The following is an example of an introduction that Cannell, Groves, Magilavy, Mathiowetz, and Miller (1987) have used as a way of asserting the priority of providing accurate and complete answers.

> This research is authorized by the Public Health Service Act. It's important for the Public Health Service to get exact details on every question, even on those which may seem unimportant to you. This may take extra effort. Are you willing to think carefully about each question in order to give accurate information?

If the respondent agreed, the following statement was read:

> For our part, we will keep all information you give confidential. Of course, the interview is voluntary. Should we come to any question which you do not want to answer, just let me know and we'll move on too the next one.

We also know that respondents often do not know how a standardized interview is to proceed. As a result, interviewers find it extremely helpful to read something like the following before beginning a standardized interview (Fowler & Mangione, 1990):

> Since many people have never been in an interview exactly like this, let me read you a paragraph that tells a little bit about how it works. I am going to read you a set of questions exactly as they are worded so that every respondent in the survey is answering the same questions. You'll be asked to answer two kinds of questions. In some cases, you'll be asked to answer in your own words. For those questions, I will have to write down your answers word for word. In other cases, you will be given a list of answers and asked to choose the one that fits best. If at any time during the interview you are not clear about what is wanted, be sure to ask me.

Such an instruction does two things to improve measurement. First, it teaches respondents what to expect. It makes them more likely to answer by choosing one of the categories provided or to answer slowly when they are required to provide narrative responses, so interviewers can record answers completely. Second, once interviewers have told respondents what interviewers do, it makes it easier for them to do what they are supposed to do and harder to behave in ways that are inconsistent with the way they are trained.

Finally, researchers often neglect efforts to provide respondents with an overview of the purposes of a series of questions.

Example: The next series of questions is designed to try to get a picture of all the different kinds of medical care that you have received in the last 12 months. We will be asking about doctors, going to hospitals, tests, and other things doctors may have done to diagnose or treat health conditions.

Having too many of these instructions may seem long and boring to interviewers and respondents. In particular, it is unlikely that respondents filling out self-administered forms want to read lengthy explanations for each section. On the other hand, such introductions can provide a sense of purpose and rationale to a series of questions, that otherwise might seem dispersed and redundant. More research is needed to know how to do these things best. However, almost certainly more use of orienting and explanatory introductions to sections of questions would improve the question-and-answer and measurement process.

CONCLUSION

The principles outlined in this chapter emerge largely from studies of the relationships between question characteristics and survey error. Many of the problems discussed can be identified by informed observation. Thus one approach to evaluating a survey instrument is to critically review a draft set of questions to identify those that clearly violate the principles outlined in this chapter (summarized in Figure 4.7). Some problems, such as whether or not a reference period is specified or whether questions include parenthetical clauses that should be read to everyone, can be unambiguously identified in this way. However, most of the principles enunciated pertain to how questions work for respondents and interviewers. To assess that, the opinions of members of the research team are no substitute for empirical testing. Procedures for evaluating questions prior to a survey are the topic of Chapter 5.

Figure 4.6.
Example of a Fact Sheet

MEDICARE OUTCOME STUDY:
INFORMATION SHEET

WHO IS DOING THE STUDY? The study is being done jointly by Dartmouth Medical School and the University of Massachusetts Center for Survey Research.

WHO IS SPONSORING THE STUDY? The Agency for Health Care Policy and Research, which is part of the United States Public Health Service.

WHAT IS THE PURPOSE OF THE STUDY? The purpose of the study is to get a picture of the effects of prostate radiation on a wide sample of men like yourself. It will help physicians and patients have better information about what to expect after radiation.

WHAT KINDS OF QUESTIONS WILL BE ASKED? Questions about your general health, how radiation affected you, and how you are feeling now.

HOW DID YOU GET MY NAME? Your name and address were selected from the records of the Health Care Financing Administration (HCFA), the administrators of the Medicare program. HCFA participates in important studies designed to help evaluate the effectiveness of medical care in different parts of the country.

DO I HAVE TO PARTICIPATE? Participation in the study is voluntary. In particular, you should know that participation will have no effect at all on your Medicare benefits. However, if you don't choose to participate, we will lose the benefit of your experiences and lower the accuracy of the study. If there are any questions you prefer not to answer, you can skip those questions.

HOW LONG WILL IT TAKE? The length depends somewhat on your answers. Some people have more to say than others. However, the average time to complete the questionnaire is about 20 minutes.

ARE MY ANSWERS CONFIDENTIAL? Yes. Your answers will never be used in any way that would identify you. They will be combined with answers from other respondents to make a statistical report. The ID number on the questionnaire and envelope are just so we know you returned a form.

HOW WILL THE DATA BE REPORTED? The research results will be reported in scientific journals and will provide important data for patient information materials that will be created to help patients who have prostate cancer decide how they want to be treated.

Figure 4.7.
Summary of Principles
of Good Question Design

Principle 1: The strength of survey research is asking people about their firsthand experiences: what they have done, their current situations, their feelings and perceptions.

> *Principle 1a:* Beware of asking about information that is only acquired *secondhand.*
> *Principle 1b:* Beware of hypothetical questions.
> *Principle 1c:* Beware of asking about causality.
> *Principle 1d:* Beware of asking respondents about solutions to complex problems.

Principle 2: Ask one question at a time.

> *Principle 2a:* Avoid asking two questions at once.
> *Principle 2b:* Avoid questions that impose unwarranted assumptions.
> *Principle 2c:* Beware of questions that include hidden contingencies.

Principle 3: A survey question should be worded so that every respondent is answering the same question.

> *Principle 3a:* To the extent possible, the words in questions should be chosen so that all respondents understand their meaning and all respondents have the same sense of what the meaning is.
> *Principle 3b:* To the extent that words or terms must be used that have meanings that are likely not to be shared, definitions should be provided to all respondents.

Principle 3c: The time period referred to by a question should be unambiguous.

> *Principle 3d:* If what is to be covered is too complex to be included in a single question, ask multiple questions.

Principle 4: If a survey is to be interviewer administered, wording of the questions must constitute a complete and adequate script such that, when interviewers read the question as worded, respondents will be fully prepared to answer the question.

> *Principle 4a:* If definitions are to be given, they should be given before the question itself is asked.
> *Principle 4b:* A question should end with the question itself. If there are response alternatives, they should constitute the final part of the question.

Principle 5: Clearly communicate to all respondents the kind of answer that constitutes an adequate answer to a question.

> *Principle 5a:* Specify the number of responses to be given to questions for which more than one answer is possible.

Principle 6: Design survey instruments to make the task of reading questions, following instructions, and recording answers as easy as possible for interviewers and respondents.

Principle 7: Measurement will be better to the extent that people answering questions are oriented to the task in a consistent way.

References

Abrams, D. B., Follick, M. J., Biener, L., Carey, K. B., & Hitti, J. (1987). Saliva cotinine as a measure of smoking status in field settings. *American Journal of Public Health, 77*(7), 846-848.

Anderson, B., Silver, B., & Abramson, P. (1988). The effects of race of the interviewer on measures of electoral participation by blacks. *Public Opinion Quarterly, 52*(1), 53-83.

Andrews, F. M. (1984). Construct validity and error components of survey measures: A structural modelling approach. *Public Opinion Quarterly, 48*(2), 409-422.

Andrews, F. M., & Withey, S. B. (1976). *Social indicators of well-being.* New York: Plenum.

Aquilino, W. S., & Losciuto, L. A. (1990). Effects of interview on self-reported drug use. *Public Opinion Quarterly, 54*(3), 362-391.

Belson, W. A. (1981). *The design and understanding of survey questions.* London, UK: Gower.

Benowitz, N. L. (1983). The use of biological fluid samples in assessing tobacco smoke consumption. In J. Gabrowski & C. S. Bell (Eds.), *Measurement in the analysis and treatment of smoking behavior* (NIDA Research Monograph 48). Rockville, MD: Department of Health and Human Services.

Berk, M., Horgan, C., & Meysers, S. (1982). *The reporting of stigmatizing health conditions: A comparison of proxy and self-reporting.* Hyattsville, MD: National Center for Health Services Research.

Bishop, G. F., Hippler, H.J., Schwartz, N., & Strack, F. (1988). A comparison of response effects in self-administered and telephone surveys. In R. M. Groves, P. Biemer, L. Lyberg, J. Massey, W. Nicholls, & J. Waksberg (Eds.), *Telephone survey methodology* (pp. 321-340). New York: John Wiley.

Blair, E., & Burton, S. (1987). Cognitive process used by survey respondents in answering behavioral frequency questions. *Journal of Consumer Research, 14*, 280-288.

Bradburn, N. M., Sudman, S., & associates. (1979). *Improving interview method and questionnaire design.* San Francisco: Jossey-Bass.

Cannell, C. F., Groves, R. M., Magilavy, L., Mathiowetz, N. A., & Miller, P. V. (1987). An experimental comparison of telephone and personal health interview studies. *Vital and Health Statistics* (Series 2, No. 106). Washington, DC: Government Printing Office.

Cannell, C. F., Fisher, G., & Bakker, T. (1965). Reporting of hospitalization in the Health Interview Survey. *Vital and Health Statistics* (Series 2, No. 6). Washington, DC: Government Printing Office.

Cannell, C., & Fowler, F. (1965). Comparison of hospitalization reporting in three survey procedures. *Vital and Health Statistics* (Series 2, No. 8). Washington DC: Government Printing Office.

Cannell, C. F., & Marquis, K. H. (1972). Reporting of health events in household interviews: Effects of reinforcement, question length and reinterviews. *Vital and Health Statistics* (Series 2, No. 45). Washington, DC: Government Printing Office.

Cannell, C., Marquis, K., & Laurent, A. (1977). A summary of studies. *Vital and Health Statistics* (Series 2, No. 69). Washington, DC: Government Printing Office.

Cannell, C. F., Miller, P. V., & Oksenberg, L. (1981). Research on interviewing techniques. In S. Leinhardt (Ed.), *Sociological Methodology* (pp. 389-437). San Francisco: Jossey-Bass.

Cannell, C., Oksenberg, L., & Converse, J. (1977). *Experiments in interviewing techniques: Field experiments in health reporting:* 1971-1977. Hyattsville, MD: National Center for Health Services Research.

Clarridge, B. R.. & Massagli, M. P. (1989). The use of female spouse proxies in common symptom reporting. *Medical Care, 27*(4), 352-366.

Converse, J. M., & Presser, S. (1986). *Survey questions: Handcrafting the standardized questionnaire.* Beverly Hills, CA: Sage.

Cronbach, L. (1951). Coefficient alpha and the internal structure of tests. *Psychiatrika,* 16, 297-334.

Cronbach, L., & Meehl, P. (1955). Construct validity in psychological tests. *Psychological Bulletin,* 281-302.

Densen, P., Shapiro, S., & Balamuth, E. (1963). Health interview responses compared with medical records. *Vital and Health Statistics* (Series 2, No. 7). Washington, DC: Government Printing Office.

DeVellis, R. F. (1991). *Scale development: Theory and applications.* Newbury Park, CA: Sage.

Dillman, D. A., & Tarnai, J. (1991). Mode effects of cognitively designed recall questions: A comparison of answers to telephone and mail surveys. In P. N. Biemer, R. M. Groves, L. E. Lyberg, N. A. Mathiowetz, & S. Sudman (Eds.), *Measurement errors in surveys* (pp. 367-393). New York: John Wiley.

Droitcour, L, Caspar, R. A., Hubbard, M. L., et al. (1991). The item count technique as a method of indirect questioning: A review of its development and a case study application. In P. N. Biemer, R. M. Groves, L. E. Lyberg, N. A. Mathiowetz, & S. Sudman (Eds.), *Measurement errors in surveys* (pp. 185-210). New York: John Wiley.

Eisenhower. D., Mathiowetz, N. A., & Morganstein, D. (1991). Recall error: Sources and bias reduction techniques. In P. N. Biemer, R. M. Groves, L. E. Lyberg, N. A. Mathiowetz, & S. Sudman (Eds.), *Measurement errors in surveys* (pp. 367-393). New York: John Wiley.

Forsyth, B. H., & Lessler, J. T. (1991). Cognitive laboratory methods: A taxonomy. In P. N. Biemer, R. M. Groves, L. E. Lyberg, N. A. Mathiowetz, & S. Sudman (Eds.), *Measurement errors in surveys* (pp. 393-418). New York: John Wiley.

Fowler, F. J. (1992). How unclear terms affect survey data. *Public Opinion Quarterly, 56*(2), 218-231.

Fowler, F. J, Jr. (1993). *Survey research methods* (2nd ed). Newbury Park, CA: Sage.

Fowler, F. J., & Mangione, T. W. (1990). *Standardized survey interviewing.* Newbury Park, CA: Sage.

Fox, J. A., & Tracy, P. E. (1986). *Randomized response: A method for sensitive surveys.* Newbury Park, CA: Sage.

Greenberg, B., Abdel-Latif, A., & Simmons, W. H. D. (1969). The unrelated question randomized response model: Theoretical framework. *Journal of the American Statistical Association, 64*(326), 520-539.

Groves, R. M. (1989). *Survey errors and survey costs.* New York: John Wiley.

Hauser, R. M., & Massagli, M. P. (1983). Some models of agreement and disagreement in repeated measurments of occupation. *Demography, 20(4)*, 449.

Horvitz, D., & Lessler, J. (1978). Discussion of total survey design. *Health Survey Methods: Second Biennial Conference* (DPHEW Publication No. PHS 79-3207, pp. 43-47). Hyattsville, MD: National Center for Health Services Research.

Hsiao, W., Braun, P., Dunn, D. L., Becker, E. R., Douwe, Y., Verrilli, D. K., Stamenovic, E, & Shiao-Ping, C. (1992). An overview of the development and refinement of the resource-based relative value scale. *Medical Care, 30*(11, Nov. supplement), NS1-NS12.

Jabine, T. B. (1987). Reporting chronic conditions in the National Health Interview Survey: A review of tendencies from evaluation studies and methodological test. *Vital and Health Statistics* (Series 2, No. 105, DHHS Pub. No. PHS 87-1397). Washington, DC: Government Printing Office.

Jabine, T. B., Straf, M. L., & Tanur, J. M. (1984). *Cognitive aspects of survey methodology: Building a bridge between disciplines.* Washington, DC: National Academic Press.

Kallick-Kaufmann, M. (1979). The micro and macro dimensions of gambling in the United States. *The Journal of Social Issues, 35*(3), 7-26.

Krueger, R. A. (1988). *Focus groups.* Newbury Park: Sage.

Kulka, R. A., Schlenger, W. E., Fairbank, J. A., Jordan, K., Hough, R. L., Marmar, C. R., & Weiss, D. S. (1989). Validating questions against clinical evaluations: A recent example using diagnostic interview schedule-based and other measures of Post-Traumatic Stress Disorder. In F. J. Fowler, Jr. (Ed.), *Conference Proceedings of Health Survey Research Methods* (DHHS Pub. No. PHS 89-3447, pp. 27-34). Washington, DC: National Center for Health Services Research.

Lehnen, R. G., & Skogan, W. G. (1981, December). *Current and historical perspectives.* (The National Crime Survey Working Papers, Vol I). Washington, DC: Department of Justice, Bureau of Justice Statistics.

Lessler, J., & Tourangeau, R. (1989, May). Questionnaire design in the cognitive research laboratory. *Vital and Health Statistics* (Series 6, No. 1). Washington, DC: Government Printing Office.

Lessler, J. T. (1987). *Use of laboratory methods and cognitive science for the design and testing of questionnaires.* Stockholm: Statistics Sweden.

Locander, W., Sudman, S., & Bradburn, N. (1976). An investigation of interview method, threat and response distortion. *Journal of the American Statistical Association, 71*(354), 269-275.

Loftus, E. F., Smith, K. D., Klinger, M. R., & Fiedler, J. (1991). Memory and mismemory for health events. In J. Tanur (Ed.), *Questions about questions: Inquiries into the cognitive basis of surveys* (pp. 102-137). New York: Russell Sage Foundation.

Madow, W. (1967). Interview data on chronic conditions compared with information derived from medical records. *Vital and Health Statistics* (Series 2, No. 23). Washington, DC: Government Printing Office.

Mangione, T., Hingson, R., & Barret, J. (1982). Collecting sensitive data: A comparison of three survey strategies. *Sociological Methods and Research, 10*(3), 337-346.

Mangione, T. W., Fowler, F. J., Jr., & Louis, T. A. (1992). Question characteristics and interviewer effects. *Journal of Official Statistics, 8*(3), 293-307.

Marquis, K. (1978). *Record check validity of survey responses: A reassessment of bias in reports of hospitalization.* Santa Monica, CA: RAND.

Martin, E, DeMaio, T. J, & Campanelli, P. C. (1990). Context effects for census measures of race and Hispanic origin. *Public Opinion Quarterly,* 54, 551-566.

McDowell, I, & Newell, C. (1987). *Measuring health: A guide to rating scales and questionnaires.* New York: Oxford University Press.

Moore, J. C. (1988). Self/proxy response status and survey response quality. *Journal of Official Statistics, 4*(2), 155-172.

Morgan, D. C. (1988). *Focus groups as qualitative research.* Newbury Park, CA: Sage.

Morton-Williams, J., & Sykes, W. (1984). The use of interaction coding and follow-up interviews to investigate comprehension of survey questions. *Journal of the Market Research Society, 26,* 109-127.

Neter, J., & Waksberg, J. (1964). A study of response errors in expenditure data from household interviews. *Journal of the American Statistical Association, 59,* 18-55.

Nunnally, J. C. (1978). *Psychometric theory.* New York: McGraw-Hill.

Oksenberg, L., Cannell, C. F., & Kalton, G. (1991). New strategies for testing survey questions. *Journal of Official Statistics, 7,* 349-365.

Parry, H., & Crossley, H. (1950). Validity of responses to survey questions. *Public Opinion Quarterly, 14,* 61-80.

Payne, S. (1951). *The art of asking questions.* Princeton, NJ: Princeton University Press.

Presser, S. (1989). Pretesting: A neglected aspect of survey research. In F. J. Fowler, Jr. (Ed.), *Conference Proceedings of Health Survey Research Methods* (DHHS Pub. No. PHS 89-3447, pp. 35-38). Washington, DC: National Center for Health Services Research.

Rainwater, L. (1974). *What money buys: Inequality and the social meanings of income.* New York: Basic Books.

Rasinski, K. A. (1989). The effect of question wording on public support for government spending. *Public Opinion Quarterly, 53,* 388-394.

Robinson, J. P., Rusk, J. G., & Head, K. B. (1968, September). *Measures of political attitudes* (Library of Congress # 68-65537). Ann Arbor, MI: Survey Research Center, Institute for Social Research.

Robinson, J. P., & Shaver, P. R. (1973). *Measures of social psychological attitudes* (Rev. ed.). Ann Arbor, MI: Survey Research Center, Institute for Social Research.

Robinson, J. P., Shaver, P. R., & Wrightsman, L. S. (Eds.). (1991). *Measures of personality and social psychological attitudes* (Vol. 1). San Diego, CA: Academic Press.

Rodgers, W. L., & Herzog, A. R. (1989). The consequences of accepting proxy respondents on total survey error for elderly populations. In F. J. Fowler, Jr. (Ed.), *Conference Proceedings of Health Survey Research Methods* (DHHS Pub. No. PHS 89-3447, pp. 139-146). Washington, DC: National Center for Health Services Research.

Royston, P. N. (1989). Using intensive interviews to evaluate questions. In F. J. Fowler, Jr. (Ed.), *Conference Proceedings of Health Survey Research Methods* (DHHS Pub. No. PHS 89-3447, pp. 3-8). Washington DC: National Center for Health Services Research.

Schaeffer, N. C. (1991). Interview: Conversation with a purpose or conversation? In P. N. Biemer, R. M. Groves, L. E. Lyberg, N. A. Mathiowetz, & S. Sudman (Eds.), *Measurement errors in surveys* (pp. 367-393). New York: John Wiley.

Schaeffer, N. C., & Bradburn, N. M. (1989). Respondent behavior in magnitude estimation. *Journal of the American Statistical Association, 84*(406), 402-413.

Schuman, H. H., & Presser, S. (1981). *Questions and answers in attitude surveys.* New York: Academic Press.

Schwartz, N., & Hippler, H. (1991). Response alternatives: The impact of their choice and presentation order. In P. N. Biemer, R. M. Groves, L. E. Lyberg, N. A. Mathiowetz, & S. Sudman (Eds.), *Measurement errors in surveys* (pp. 41-56). New York: John Wiley.

Schwarz, N., Knauper, B., Hippler, H.-J., Noelle-Neumann, E., & Clark, L. (1991). Rating scales: Numeric values may change the meaning of scale labels. *Public Opinion Quarterly, 55,* 570-582.

Sieber, J. (1992). *Planning ethically responsible research: Developing an effective protocol.* Newbury Park, CA: Sage.

Smith, A. F. (1991). Cognitive processes in long-term dietary recall. *Vital and Health Statistics* (Series 6, No. 4, Public Health Services). Washington, DC: Government Printing Office.

Smith. T. W. (1991). Context effects in the general social survey. In P. N. Biemer, R. M. Groves, L. E. Lyberg, N. A. Mathiowetz, & S. Sudman (Eds.), *Measurement errors in surveys* (pp. 367-393). New York: John Wiley.

Stewart, A. L., & Ware, J. E., Jr. (Eds.). (1992). *Measuring functioning and well-being: The medical outcomes study approach.* Durham, NC: Duke University Press.

Stewart, D. W., & Shamdasani, P. N. (1990). *Focus groups.* Newbury Park, CA: Sage.

Suchman, L., & Jordan, B. (1990). Interactional troubles in face-to-face survey interviews. *Journal of the American Statistical Association, 85,* 232-241.

Sudman, S., & Bradburn, N. (1974). *Response effects in surveys.* Chicago: Aldine.

Sudman, S., & Bradburn, N. (1982). *Asking questions.* San Francisco: Jossey-Bass.

Sudman, S., & Ferber, R. (1971). A comparison of alternative procedures for collecting consumer expenditure data for frequently purchased items. *Journal of Marketing Research, 11,* 128-135.

Sudman, S., Finn, A., & Lannon, L. (1984). The use of bounded recall procedures in single interviews. *Public Opinion Quarterly, 48,* 520-524.

Tanur, J. (Ed.). (1991). *Questions about questions: Inquiries into the cognitive bases of surveys.* New York: Russell Sage Foundation.

Turner, C. F., Lessler, J. T., & Gfroerer, J. C. (1992). *Survey measurement of drug use: Methodological studies.* Washington, DC: National Institute on Drug Abuse, Department of Health and Human Services.

Turner, C. F., & Martin, E. (Eds.). (1984). *Surveying subjective phenomena.* New York: Russell Sage.

Ware, J. (1987). Standards for validating health measures: Definition and content. *Journal of Chronic Diseases, 40,* 473-480.

Willis, G. B., Royston, P., & Bercini, D. (1989). Problems with survey questions revealed by cognitively-based interviews. *Proceedings, 5th Annual Research Conference* (pp. 345-360). Washington, DC: Bureau of the Census.

5

This article was first published in the Survey Methods Centre Newsletter and is reproduced by permission of the Survey Methods Centre

Survey Methods Centre Newsletter Volume 16 No. 1

DESIGNING RESPONDENT-FRIENDLY SELF-COMPLETION QUESTIONNAIRES

Cleo Jenkins

The talk given by Cleo Jenkins drew heavily from a chapter written with Don Dillman for the forthcoming book, "Survey Measurement and Process Quality".

Cleo began with a quote from John Dewey's "Human Problem Solving":

> *"We must recall that language includes much more than aural and written speech. Gestures, pictures, monuments, visual images, finger movements, anything consciously employed as a sign is logically language."*

This quote summed up the main message of the paper, that writing good questions is necessary but not sufficient in the construction of self administered questionnaires. The visual presentation of the information is every bit as important. The paper therefore discussed visual perception, and then presented a working model and principles for guiding the questionnaire design process. Finally, the issues were brought together using the census short form as a case study.

PATTERN RECOGNITION

To make sense of the information presented on a questionnaire, respondents must be able to see patterns. Pattern recognition is a perceptual process that involves identifying a complex arrangement of sensory stimuli. It is accomplished through two complementary sub processes, bottom-up and top-down processing. In bottom-up processing, pattern recognition begins with the arrival of stimulus. In contrast, top down processing

FIGURE 1 Example of pattern recognition using bottom-up processing.

FIGURE 2 Example of pattern recognition Using top-down processing.

FIGURE 3 Illustration of figure and Ground.

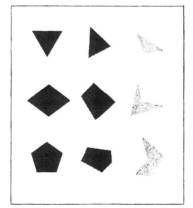

FIGURE 4 Illustration of the Law of Pragnanz.

FIGURE 5 The Law of Proximity.

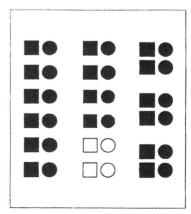

FIGURE 6 Illustration of the Gestalt Grouping Laws in operation.

emphasises the role of context and expectations in identifying a pattern. That is, our knowledge about how the world is organised helps us to identify pattern.

If in figure 1 you see a "c" on the left and a "b" on the right, you have just engaged in pattern recognition and you have probably used bottom-up processing. But in figure 2 you would be likely to use top-down processing to decipher the words, by placing well-founded expectations on the middle letter. When respondents fill out a questionnaire, they apply both bottom-up and top-down processing. The top-down processing comes from common experiences such as reading and looking at objects. One would expect, however, that the very act of filling out the questionnaire would begin to influence the top-down processing so that as respondents move along they begin to associate particular visual information with particular requests. This argues for a consistent application of visual information.

ATTENTION AND PRE-ATTENTIVE PROCESSING

Although the world extends 360° around us, our field of vision spans only about 210°, and we can only see with any real acuity within 2°. That is a very small area and translates into about nine characters of text. So when we are presented with simultaneous tasks, like the need to perceive a 210° field, we must focus our attention on one task at a time. In stationary visual perception this corresponds to choosing a place to look first and moving our eyes to a second place and soon. In contrast, pre-attentive processing involves the automatic registration of features at a global or holistic level and occurs when individuals survey an entire visual field, instantaneously recognising features well enough to make sense of a scene. These processes imply that we must pay attention to how visual information is presented at both the macro and micro levels on a questionnaire. Respondents should be able to glance at a questionnaire and as a result of pre-attentive processing be able to quickly understand where to start and generally where to go. And then the path should continue to be unambiguous as respondents begin to attend to the details of the questionnaire.

EYE MOVEMENTS

Humans have preferred eye movements. In 1945 Brandt constructed a card with squares symmetrically located about a locus, so the quadrants were of equal visual interest. He discovered that people's eyes tended to fall in the upper left quadrant, closer to the centre of the page than the extreme corner, and then their eyes would move left and upwards and fall by clockwise motion around the locus. The least preferred space was the lower right hand quadrant. Questionnaire designers can take advantage of these tendencies.

However, most scenes are not of equal visual interest. In that case, people will focus on physically informative areas like height contrast areas or areas of ecological significance. For example, when looking at a face, people tend to focus on the eyes and mouth. How we look at pictures is important, but is not all we need to know to design questionnaires. We must also understand how we read. Contrary to what we might think, we do not read text smoothly. Our eyes fixate every eight to nine letters, corresponding to our 2° of sharp vision. This area is known as the foveal region. Generally our eyes are fixated about 90% of the time and the rest of the time they are rapidly moving between fixations in what are known as saccades. Immediately to the right of the foveal region is the para-foveal region, which plays an important role in our ability to recognise words during reading. Previewing the initial letters of the next word helps us to recognise that word more quickly when we come to fixate on it. Questionnaires deprive readers of the ability to engage in this normal and optimal reading behaviour when they present conceptually connected information at separate locations.

VISUAL ELEMENTS

The eyes and their movements are the mechanism by which we take in our surroundings, but what we take in are visual elements. Visual elements are best described in terms of brightness, colour, shape and location. A simple line drawing is a picture based primarily on the visual element of shape, whereas other sorts of pictures may rely more heavily on colour or contrast. Bringing together the visual elements leads to an important outcome – we are able to distinguish between figure and ground. Distinguishing figure from background depends on contrast, but can also be ambiguous. Is figure 3 a candlestick or two profiles?

According to Gestalt psychologists, a number of perceptual principles guide our understanding and interpretation of figures. The law of Pragnanz states that simple shapes, like those on the left of figure 4, will be more easily perceived and remembered than the irregularly shaped polygons on the right. The law of proximity states that when similar figures are located in close proximity to each other we tend to see them as belonging to the same group. Do the dots in figure 5 suggest horizontal lines or vertical lines? Figure 6 illustrates the grouping laws. The left-hand side of the figure, viewed in isolation, may appear to be a column of squares and a column of triangles. That is because according to the law of similarity we tend to see similar shapes as belonging together. In the middle, we see three groups of different contrasts. And on the right we see the same three groups, but now they are differentiated by the law of proximity.

Paying close attention to how information is displayed on a page is clearly important, as respondents will extract meaning from how the information is shaded, shaped and grouped. The challenge to survey researchers is to learn how to visually communicate our intentions.

Cleo Jenkins discussed a working model that she and Don Dillman have been developing to guide researchers in this process. The model had two components, 1) providing navigational guides, and 2) achieving good information organisation. Navigational guides aim to motivate and guide respondents through a questionnaire in the absence of an interviewer. Information organisation concerns what a respondent would hear if she or he were being interviewed. The model contained five major principles of questionnaire design, two related to navigation and three related to information organisation. Cleo Jenkins concentrated her discussion on two of those principles, one from each area.

Principle 1: Use the visual elements of brightness, colour, shape and location in a consistent manner to define desired navigational paths for respondents to follow.

A copy of the questionnaire for the 1993 National Survey of College Graduates was presented to the audience, and Cleo Jenkins went through the questionnaire describing why she thought it did a good job of successfully manipulating the visual presentation of information.

The questions, answer categories and the other information on the page appeared in dark blue on a very pale blue background. This made them stand out clearly as figures, distinct from the background. An important attribute of the questionnaire was that question numbers were prominently displayed. They stood out because they were located on the left hand side, which is a highly visible area, and because they were set apart somewhat from the questions (law of proximity).

Another important attribute was that the beginning of the questionnaire was clearly marked "A1". The questionnaire did not place information before the "A1', that might confuse respondents about where to begin. Contrast was also used to advantage. Question numbers and questions were in bold type to help them stand out, and there was effective contrast between the shaded background and white answer spaces. Answer boxes were equally sized, simple shapes that were vertically aligned, all of which is in keeping with the Gestalt grouping laws. As a result, the elements of shape, brightness and location gave rise to a well-defined regular pattern on the questionnaire that is immediately evident at the pre-attentive level and can be used to guide respondents through the form at the attentive level.

Another good feature of the questionnaire was that codes needed for data processing were a slightly deeper shade of blue than the background. The subtle contrast should have helped make the codes less visible to respondents, while still being easily read by processing personnel. A minor visual flaw was the use of dotted lines beneath the writing spaces. Since the law of closure states that respondents will connect these lines anyway, they might as well have been solid from the start.

Next, the audience were shown a questionnaire from the 1992 US Census of Agriculture. This was used as an example of poor design[1]. The front page provided conflicting information about where to begin. The areas of highest contrast, to which the eye is likely to be drawn, included some "office use only" boxes which were in bold. One of the answer boxes also appeared in bold, thus attracting undue attention. An alternative point to which the eye might have been drawn was the question number "1". This was some way down the page, below certain instructions to respondents. Anyone beginning to read at that point would have missed important information. The lesson for questionnaire designers is to avoid giving respondents the impression that information is not important, by making sure that visual clues are consistent. Otherwise, respondents are likely to get confused about which messages to follow and in what order.

Cleo Jenkins then presented some examples of lessons learnt about questionnaire design through cognitive research. The examples were based upon a teacher questionnaire that had been tested using the concurrent think-aloud technique.

The first example illustrated a situation where the questionnaire designer needs to be aware of respondents' tendency to use top-down processing. The questionnaire included a couple of questions which asked the respondent to enter an answer in a box in a certain way, followed by a question which had a similar-looking box, which was in fact labelled for office use only. Not surprisingly, the initial reaction of respondents was to assume that they were required to write an answer in the box.

Another example demonstrated the gestalt grouping laws. Alternative answer categories to a question were listed vertically. Each consisted of a tick box with a label, apart from one, about half way down, which included a long box for a write-in answer. The effect of the long box was to visually divide the other answer categories into two groups. Consequently, respondents might initially consider only the first half of the list, while expecting the rest of the list to constitute a separate question. Cleo Jenkins played an interesting tape recording of a respondent thinking through his approach to answering this question. The respondent answered the question correctly, but only after considerable thought and effort. It was therefore suggested that questionnaire designers should be concerned not only with obtaining "correct" responses, but also with treating respondents sensitively and minimising processing time and effort.

This thought led to the next principle of questionnaire design:

Principle 2: Present information in a manner that does not require respondents to connect information from separate locations in order to comprehend it.

The Census of Agriculture questionnaire was used as an example of failure to follow this principle. A question asked, "Were any of the following crops harvested from this place in 1992?" There followed a vertical listing of 12 crops, with three answer boxes to the right of each. These three columns were headed, "acres harvested", "quantity harvested", and "acres irrigated". The question requires a yes or no response, whereas the column headings suggest that respondents are really being asked to report numerical data. Only by making the effort to perceive and integrate each separate part can the meaning of the question be deciphered. Presenting conceptually connected information in a physically disconnected way is problematic for three reasons. First, it requires greater effort on behalf of respondents to perceive information that is out of their foveal and para-foveal view. Second, it leads to an increase in processing times as respondents will not have the chance to preview the information in para-foveal view. Finally, it requires respondents to store the separate pieces of information in short term memory long enough to integrate them. This is likely to burden short term memory more than if the pieces were already consolidated.

A way of simplifying the respondents' task is to ask a comprehensive question, which logically and visually consolidates the information. For example, the question referred to might be re-worded along the lines of, "For each of the following crops, how many acres and bushels were harvested from this place in 1992? In addition, please indicate how many of the acres for each crop were irrigated." (There are arguments for re-structuring this question into three separate questions to further simplify the respondents' task. But that involves another principle.)

READING STRUCTURE

Cleo Jenkins then discussed the way respondents read a questionnaire page. She believed respondents could be broadly divided into two camps – "readers" and "skimmers". Readers read all or most of the material presented. Skimmers, on the other hand, read only as much as they think they need to.

Using a real questionnaire cover page as an example, the way in which it was read was demonstrated. The page contained two columns of instructions, plus an address label attached at 90° to the text. The readers would tend to read diligently down the first column, turning the page sideways to read the label at the point where they were instructed to do so. However, many of them failed to then read the second column, thinking they had finished with the page when they reached the bottom. The skimmers generally did not read the page at all – they glanced at it, and turned the page. By drawing the path which the eye had to follow in order to read the page as intended, it was demonstrated that the reading structure of the page was very challenging, with unexpected moves across, up, and down the page. The overcomplicated structure had led to respondents, particularly skimmers, making some important response errors, as they had not read relevant instructions. These errors had caused major problems for the survey.

The cover page had subsequently been redesigned to incorporate a much more natural reading structure, flowing smoothly from left to right and from top to bottom of the page. Cleo Jenkins felt that the importance of a simple reading structure really could not be over-stressed.

AN EXAMPLE

An experiment used to examine the questionnaire design model was briefly described. The "simplified questionnaire test" was designed to test alternative versions of the US decennial census short form against the form actually used in 1990[2]. The audience were shown both the 1990 form, and one redesigned alternative version.

The 1990 form was a single very large page in matrix format with questions running down the left side and person names across the top. The form clearly contradicted a number of the design principles that had been set out. It had a complicated reading structure, poor instructions, poor use of contrast and colour, and too many lines.

The redesigned version of the questionnaire used an "individual space format", where all the questions relating to one individual appeared together, within a clearly defined space. The visual element of location was used effectively to guide respondents through the form, instructions were clear and wellplaced, and contrast and colour were used effectively to demarcate questions, answer spaces, and background. The one factor which may have worked against the redesigned questionnaire was that it appeared longer, occupying an eight page booklet (with standard 82 by 11 inch pages), whereas the original form had been a single sheet, albeit extremely large (102 by 28 inches).

The redesigned questionnaire achieved a completion rate of 66.8% versus 63.4% for the original 1990 questionnaire.

CONCLUSION

Cleo Jenkins hoped she had convinced the audience that there was a need to graduate beyond reliance on convention and common sense to design self-administered questionnaires. She believed it was necessary to work towards the development of a set of scientifically derived and experimentally proven design principles which would help in the quest to improve response rates, processing times and accuracy of responses. Her work with Don Dillman was clearly a step in that direction, but much remained to be tested, considered and re-tested.

References and Notes

[1]   Copies of pages from the questionnaires used during this talk are available from the author.

[2]   See also Dillman, DA, Clark J, and Sinclair, MD (1993). The 1992 simplified questionnaire test: effects of questionnaire length, respondent friendly design, and request for social rates. Paper presented to US Census Bureau Annual Research Conference.

This chapter was first published by Sage Publications and is reproduced by permission of Sage Publications

Mail Surveys. CA: Sage (1995)

Thomas W. Mangione

CHAPTER 6
THE BASICS OF AVOIDING NONRESPONSE ERRORS

NONRESPONSE ERROR

Just because you draw a large, random sample does not mean that your data are perfectly valid. Another potential source of error beyond sampling error is nonresponse error. This error is caused by failing to get a return from 100% of your sample and the fact that there are differences between those who respond to your survey and those who do not. The size of this error is dependent, therefore, on how big the nonresponse is and how different the nonresponders are from the responders (Armstrong & Overton, 1977; Barnette, 1950; Baur, 1947; Bishop, Hippler, Schwartz, & Stack, 1988; Blair, 1964; Blumberg, Fuller, & Hare, 1974; Brennan & Hoek, 1992; Campbell, 1949; Champion & Sear, 1969; Clausen & Ford, 1947; Cox, Anderson, & Fulcher, 1974; Daniel, 1975; Dillman, 1978; Donald, 1960; Eichner & Habermehl, 1981; Filion, 1975; Gannon, Northern, & Carrol, 1971; Gough & Hall, 1977; Jones & Lang, 1980; Larson & Catton, 1959; Newman, 1962; Ognibene, 1970; Reuss, 1943; Suchman & McCandless, 1940).

Nonresponse error is the single biggest impediment to any survey study, but it is particularly a risk for mail surveys. Unfortunately, in many studies very little is known about the nonresponders and therefore we are left with uncertainty about the quality of the data. The solution to this concern is to do everything in your power to conduct a study that has a very high response rate. By obtaining a very high response rate, it is very unlikely that the nonresponders will have an impact on the validity of your population estimates even if the nonresponders were different.

What is considered a high response rate? Certainly a response rate in excess of 85% is viewed as an excellent rate of return. It would need a peculiar set of circumstances to throw off your results by very much. Response rates in the 70% to 85% range are viewed as very good. Responses in the 60% to 70% range are considered acceptable, but you begin to be uneasy about the characteristics of nonresponders. Response rates between 50% and 60% are barely acceptable and really need some additional information that contributes to confidence about the quality of your data. Response rates below 50% really are not scientifically acceptable. After all, a majority of the sample is not represented in your results.

Besides ensuring high response rates, it is always a useful effort to try to obtain information about the nonresponders so that you can compare them to responders. Sometimes this information is available from the list that you originally sampled. For instance, city lists that are used to confirm eligibility for voter registration have the person's age, gender (you can usually figure it out from first names), occupation in broad categories, precinct or voting district, whether the person is registered to vote or not, and, if registered, party affiliation. By keeping track of who has and has not responded from your original sample, you can compare the characteristics of those who did respond with those who did not respond.

Sometimes you can obtain small amounts of information from nonresponders as a supplement to the original data collection effort. You have to limit yourself to a few indicators, and you have to make it very easy for the person to respond. You may even need to include some type of incentive. In choosing which indicators to try to collect information about, you want to select questions that are easy to answer and make a big difference in your results. It is very important to include questions that describe the demographic characteristics of your sample *as well* as some key questions about the central issue you are studying. This allows you to compare directly nonresponders and responders on the key concepts as well as to compare indirectly on any question that is correlated with demographic characteristics. On a study of alcohol use, we asked nonresponders to tell us their age, gender, marital status, education, current frequency of drinking (in broad categories), and whether they had ever had a drinking problem. We sent the one-page questionnaire along with $2, and we received a 50% return from among those people who had not responded to our survey.

Based on our study and others (Baur, 1947; Campbell, 1949; Gannon et al., 1971; Gelb, 1975; Goodstadt, Chung, Kronitz, & Cook, 1977; Ognibene, 1970; Peterson, 1975; Robins, 1963; Suchman, 1962), we can get a picture of the usual type of nonresponder. They tend to be less educated, or elderly, or unmarried, or male, or to have some characteristic that makes them seem less relevant to the study (e.g., abstainers for a drinking study, nondrivers for a traffic safety study, or lower-income people on a study about mortgages).

The reason that these types tend to be nonresponders are commonsensical. The less educated may be intimidated by the survey process or have less appreciation for the value of research. The elderly may have trouble filling out the questionnaire, and on average they have less education than the rest of the population. They also may be more suspicious of the purposes of the research. Unmarrieds and males may feel like they have less time to fill out a questionnaire, and males perhaps are somewhat less cooperative as a group than are females. People who have characteristics that seem to make the study less relevant to them may feel that their participation is less important, or they may be less interested in the issues.

Nonresponse errors create problems for your study in two ways. First, if people who do not respond hold different views or behave differently from the majority of people, your study will incorrectly report the population average. It will also drastically underreport the number of people who feel as the nonresponders do. The basic problem is that nonresponders make your picture of the population wrong. How far off the mark you are depends on the pattern of nonresponse, but in any event your findings will not be accurate.

Even if nonresponders are not that different from responders, low response rates give the appearance of a poor quality study and shake the consumer's confidence in the results of the study. The study becomes less useful or less influential because it does not have the trappings of quality.

As we said above, nonresponse error is a major problem with mail surveys. The major reason that mail surveys are vulnerable to nonresponse error is that it is *very* easy for a person not to respond to a mail survey. It is not like you have to close a door in someone's face, or even hang up the phone on a persistent interviewer; all you have to do is throw it in the waste basket. In addition, you can also become a nonresponder just because you never got around to filling out that questionnaire.

All levels of response rates are reported in the literature. It is safe to assume that some of the worst response rates never see the light of an academic journal. If the only thing you did was to put a questionnaire in an envelope and ask people to fill it out, it would be common to see response rates in the 20% range, and it would not be surprising to see them in the 5% range. This is a long way from the 75% or so response rates that inspire confidence in data. How do you get better response rates? Is it just luck, or is there some magic formula that produces success? It turns out that there are some very specific things that you can, and must, do to achieve good response rates.

HOW TO GET GOOD RESPONSE RATES
There are a variety of procedures that all mail surveys should use to ensure that they obtain good response rates. We will describe each of these in this chapter. In the following chapter, we will describe other mechanisms that you can use to increase your response rates even further.

A Good Respondent Letter
Because most mail surveys arrive in the mail without any prior contact, the respondent letter has to do all the work of explaining the study and the general procedures, as well as motivating the respondent to participate (Andreasen, 1970; Champion & Sear, 1969; Hornik, 1981; Houston & Nevin, 1977; Simon, 1967). It is critical that you produce a respondent letter that is "just right." There are several elements that need to be included in the letter, and there are several things that you want to make sure you say.

1. The letter should not be too long. Keep it to one page.

2. Use professionally produced letterhead that makes it clear who is sending out the survey and who the supporting institution is. Do not just refer to a study name (e.g., The Healthy Family Study). Instead, include the name of the university or research institution as well.

3. Make it clear how people can get in touch with you if they have questions. You need a name of a contact person. You need a phone number, perhaps even an "800" number or the instruction to "call collect."

4. You need to have a "grabber" as your first sentence, something that encourages the respondent to read the rest of the letter. In a study of police officers concerning gambling enforcement policies, we started with: "We'd like the benefit of your professional experience and ten minutes of your time!" For a corporate study of alcohol policies we started with: "Many people are concerned about alcohol abuse in the workplace."

5. You need to tell the respondent why this study is important and how this information may be used. Respondents want to participate only in things that they think are important and useful and that they feel relate to their lives in some specific way.

6. You need to explain who is being asked to participate in the survey and how you got their name and address.

7. You need to explain whether this is a confidential survey or an anonymous survey (they are not the same thing), and you need to explain how you are achieving confidentiality or anonymity.

8. You need to mention that participation in the study is voluntary, but also you should emphasize the importance of participation.

9. You need to make it clear how to get the questionnaire back to you.

10. You want to make sure that your letter is easy to read in terms of type size, layout, reproduction quality, and language level.

By following these suggestions for respondent letters, you should get your study off on the right foot.

Return Postage
It almost goes without saying that to get a good return rate you have to supply the respondent with a return envelope, already addressed to you, and return postage. (See Armstrong & Lusk, 1987; Brook, 1978; Gullahorn & Gullahorn, 1963; Harris & Guffey, 1978; Kernan, 1971; Kimball, 1961; McCrohan & Lowe, 1981;

7

Peterson, 1975; Vocino, 1977; Yammarino, Skinner, & Childers, 1991) You have two options for return postage. You can place a postage stamp on the return envelope or you can use a business reply envelope. Placing the postage stamp on the envelope puts subtle pressure on the respondent to send back the questionnaire so that the "stamp will not go to waste." The risk you run is that if they do not return the questionnaires, you have "wasted" the money on the unused stamps.

Business reply envelopes are efficient to use. You only get charged by the post office for the questionnaires that come back. You do have to set up an account with the post office first, and there are strict rules about how the envelope should be laid out, but business reply envelopes make the mailing process simple for the respondent.

In the next chapter we will discuss how different types of postage make an impact on your return rate.

Confidentiality/Anonymity

Respondents are generally more likely to respond if they feel that their answers are kept confidential instead of being attributed to them directly (Boek & Lade, 1963; Bradt, 1955; Childers & Skinner, 1985; Cox *et al.*, 1974; Fuller, 1974; Futrell & Hise, 1982; Futrell & Swan, 1977; Kerin & Peterson, 1977; McDaniel & Jackson, 1981; Pearlin, 1961; Rosen, 1960; Wildman, 1977). There are some fairly direct methods for maintaining confidentiality. First, you do not put any names or addresses directly on the questionnaires themselves. Instead, put some kind of code number on the survey. The list of names and addresses with the corresponding code numbers can be kept separately and out of view of people who are not on the research team.

Second, when the questionnaires come back, do not leave them lying around for curious eyes to read. Instead, keep them in file cabinets, preferably locked when you are not around, and lock your office when you are not there.

Third, do not tell colleagues, friends, or family the answers from individual questionnaires.

Fourth, do not present data in reports or papers that allow readers to figure out who people are. Sometimes this means describing individuals with characteristics somewhat different from those they really have, or it sometimes means not presenting information on very small groups of people. For example, in a company report you would not present data on the group of three vice-presidents by saying "two thirds of the senior management group reported thinking about changing jobs in the next year." Data being presented for groups such as companies, schools, or hospitals should be presented without the groups being named unless there was a prior specific agreement that this would be done.

Maintaining anonymity is distinctly different from maintaining confidentiality. For confidentiality *you* know who filled out which questionnaire, but you promise not to divulge that information to anyone outside the research team. For anonymity, even you do not know which

questionnaire belongs to which person. This is achieved by not putting any code number on the questionnaire before it is sent out. This way there is no link between the questionnaire and any sample list you have.

It seems logical that studies that could offer true anonymity (no identification numbers on the questionnaires) versus those that offer only confidentiality (a promise of no disclosure) would produce better response rates. Studies have not clearly proved such advantages (Andreasen, 1970; Boek & Lade, 1963; Bradt, 1955; Mason, Dressel, & Bain, 1961; Pearlin, 1961; Rosen, 1960; Scott, 1961). Perhaps this is too technical a distinction for respondents to understand. Perhaps they assume because you knew how to mail the questionnaire to them, you can somehow find them again if you want to. There is also the cynical interpretation that says "they could figure out who I am by putting together several demographic characteristics, so their promise of anonymity is really not much more than a promise of confidentiality." Finally, many surveys are rather innocuous, and respondents would not care if people knew what they thought on these topics. It is probably best to provide anonymity if you can because no one has shown that promising anonymity produces worse response rates. Even when the data are anonymous, you still must follow the other procedures described above in which you do not leave questionnaires lying around for idle eyes to view and in which you do not report data for small groups of respondents.

Reminders

Probably the single most important technique to use to produce high response rates is to send out reminders (Denton, Tsai, & Chevrette, 1988; Dillman, Carpenter, Christenson, & Brooks, 1974; Eckland, 1965; Etzel & Walker, 1974; Filion, 1976; Ford & Zeisel, 1949; Furse, Stewart, & Rados, 1981; House, Gerber, & McMichael, 1977; Jones & Lang, 1980; Kanuk & Berenson, 1975; Kephart & Bressler, 1958; Linsky, 1975; Yammarino *et al.*, 1991). Even under the best of circumstances you will not achieve acceptable levels of returns if you do not send out any reminders. Actually, it is important to send out several reminders, and it is important to pay attention to the timing of the reminders.

If you carefully keep track of the daily returns that you get, an interesting pattern unfolds. For the first few days after you mail out the questionnaires you get nothing back. This makes sense because it takes time for a survey to be delivered, it takes a short period to fill it out, and then a day or two to get it back to you in the mail (actually this can be a day or two longer if you use business reply returns). About 5 to 7 days after you send out the initial mailing you begin to get a few back; then in the next few days you get a lot more back, with more coming in each day than the day before. Around the 10th day after your mailing, the returns start to level off, and then around the 14th day they start dropping off precipitously.

This drop-off in returns is a signal that whatever motivational influence your initial letter had is now fading. Respondents who have not returned

Returns

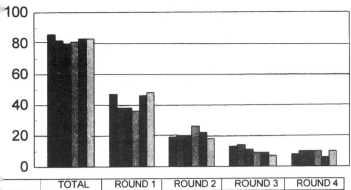

	TOTAL	ROUND 1	ROUND 2	ROUND 3	ROUND 4
Company	86	47	19	13	8
Company	82	38	20	14	10
Company	80	38	20	11	10
Company	81	36	26	9	10
Company	83	46	22	9	6
Company	83	48	18	7	10

Figure 6.1. Proportion Returned by Rounds of Mailings for Six Companies

questionnaires by now are going to begin to forget doing it, or they are going to misplace the survey under a pile of things on their desk. You want to plan your first reminder to arrive at the respondents' addresses just at this point in the return pattern, at about the 14th day.

After sending out a reminder, we then see the same pattern repeating itself: A few days of no impact, then a burst of returns with more coming in each day, and then a precipitous decline at about 14 days after the second mailing (the 1st reminder).

The other interesting feature about this return pattern is that whatever return rate you got in the first wave (e.g., 40%), you will get about half that amount in the second wave (e.g., 20%). Figure 6.1 shows this pattern very clearly. These were the return rates for six different companies to which we sent mail questionnaires to managers asking their opinions about work-related alcohol policies and problems at their worksites. As you can see, the overall response rates were very good (exceeding 80% for each company), and in each round of reminders we received back about half the amount that we had received from the previous round.

Therefore, because I recommend shooting for at least a 75% return rate, you should plan on at least four mailings—the initial mailing and then three reminders. Each of these mailings should be spaced about two weeks apart. This should give you approximately the following pattern of returns: 40% + 20% + 10% + 5% = 75%. This means that your total mailing period will take about 8 to 9 weeks because you have to leave time after your last reminder for the returns to come in. Sending reminders out sooner than two weeks does not speed up the returns. All it does is send reminders to people who were going to do it anyway.

Spreading two or three reminders out over a longer time (to save money on postage) is not as effective in producing a good return rate. You do not keep building momentum among the nonresponders with your

reminders because the gap in time is so long that they have forgotten about the survey. Each reminder has to start all over again in getting people to decide to participate.

What is also interesting about this pattern is that the rate of returns and the number of reminders have nothing to do with the total size of your sample. You follow the same procedures whether your sample size is 200 or 20,000. The only impact on size is that you have to have a bigger staff of people to help you get out the mailings each round.

What should you put in each mailing? Is each mailing just a repeat of the first mailing? No. I recommend sending a complete package (respondent letter, questionnaire, return envelope) in the first and third mailings. In the second and fourth mailings I believe you can limit yourself to a postcard or letter reminder.

In each of the four mailings, the letter addressed to the respondent should focus on slightly different issues. For the first mailing you want to be the most thorough, covering all the bases. In the second mailing you want to be gentle and friendly. "Just a reminder in case you haven't yet sent in your questionnaire. We would really like to hear from you." In the third mailing you want to emphasize the confidentiality of responses and the importance of getting a good return so that all points of view are represented. You should also note that you are including another copy of the questionnaire in case they misplaced the first one you sent. The fourth mailing should be a last call." Set a specific deadline and encourage people to send in their questionnaire so that their points of view can be represented.

If you are using a procedure that promises confidentiality, then you can keep track of the questionnaires being returned by placing a code number on the survey form and then sending out reminders only to people from whom you have not yet received questionnaires. This saves you money on postage, printing, and supplies and keeps respondents from being annoyed (or confused) by receiving reminders after they have already sent in their surveys.

If you want a procedure that gives the respondents anonymity, then the steps to follow are a little more complicated. Because you do not know who has sent back their questionnaire and who has not, you have two alternate strategies for producing reminders. The first method is to send reminders to everybody and always include a line that says "If you've already sent in your questionnaire, thank you very much." You probably also want to say, "Because your returns are anonymous we don't know which of you have sent in your questionnaires and which of you have not, so that is why we are sending this reminder to everyone." I personally do not like to use this strategy because (a) it is wasteful of postage, supplies, and resources; (b) it irritates respondents to get reminders when they have returned their questionnaires; (c) it confuses them and sometimes leads to respondents worrying that their survey got lost in the mail, so that they fill out a second one that you do not want but cannot remove from the pile because

7

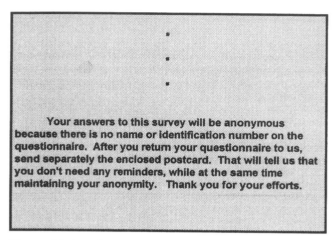

Figure 6.2. Sample of Postcard and Associated Paragraph in Respondent Letter

you do not know if it is someone's second questionnaire; and (d) it dilutes your reminder letters because some of the verbiage is apologizing to people who have already returned their questionnaires and not just focusing on those who have yet to return them.

I prefer a second strategy that I call the "reminder postcard strategy." This strategy enables you to accomplish two things at once: It maintains complete anonymity for the respondents' returned questionnaires while also letting you know who has and has not returned the questionnaire. This lets you send reminders only to those who have yet to respond. The way to accomplish this is to enclose a postage-paid, return postcard that *does* have either an identification code or the person's name (or both) on it. The instructions tell the respondent explicitly that returning this postcard tells us that they do not need any reminders. You also instruct them to mail the postcard back *separately* from the questionnaire. By using this procedure you know who has returned the questionnaire without having to put any identifying information on the questionnaire itself. Figure 6.2 shows an example of this type of postcard.

The first thing researchers worry about is "what if the respondent just sends back the postcard and not the questionnaire." That would be a problem, but it turns out that it is not the case. You usually get more questionnaires back than postcards. Some respondents forget to mail their postcards, some lose them, and some purposely do not send them back as a way of

ensuring their anonymity. These latter folks are willing to put up with getting reminders they do not need to guarantee their anonymity. Thankfully there are only a few who take this route (e.g., 5% or so), or else the method would not achieve its intended purpose of providing you information about who has responded while maintaining anonymity.

What If You Cannot Afford to Do Follow-Ups?
Many times researchers choose to do mail surveys because they are on a very limited budget, and therefore the suggestion to do four mailings conflicts with budgetary constraints. Also, researchers may be under time pressure to get the survey results quickly and therefore feel that they cannot afford the time that it takes to do four mailings.

Researchers in this bind sometimes fall into the trap of creating a survey design that provides for a large sample that gets only one mailing without any reminders, and settling for the 30% to 40% return rate. They still wind up with enough surveys to analyze because of the large sample. These researchers draw comfort from having 1000 questionnaires returned because the sampling error formula says that the amount of sampling error for a sample of 1000 is relatively small. The fallacy in this thinking is that somehow a bigger number of questionnaires that represents a 30% return rate is more valid than a smaller number of questionnaires that represents a 30% return rate. Unfortunately both circumstances produce flawed surveys because we can never be certain that the 30% who responded accurately represent the whole population.

So how does the researcher who has budgetary and time constraints deal with these conflicting pressures? As a fall-back method I recommend sending follow-ups to a random subset of your overall sample. What does this accomplish? It provides a way of testing to what extent your low response rate returners are different from a "true" random subset on *all* of the variables measured in your study while at the same time not costing as much as sending reminders to everyone.

To set up this mechanism you need to divide your original sample into two groups: One group (presumably the larger of the two) will be designated to get fewer reminders (in order to save money and time) and the other group (the smaller) will get the full arsenal of techniques.

You need to distinguish the two groups in your code numbers so that you can (a) keep track of the different return rates and (b) analyze the data separately for the two groups.

When you are ready to begin your analyses, you compare the lower responding group to the higher responding group's answers. You hope to find no differences, or only a few unimportant differences, in the two groups. If this is so, you can present the data from your low responding group with the full confidence that it is "representative" of the whole sample even though you obtained a low response rate.

7

In other words, the choice of whether to respond or not was not correlated with the answers to your questions. The nonresponders looked just like the responders.

Things get a little bit more complicated if there are differences. How you deal with the situation depends on the extent of the differences. If there are a few sharp differences between the low responding sample and the high responding sample, then the easiest thing to do is to report the findings on these few characteristics based only on the high responding group. For instance, if there were differences in the proportion of males who were included in the high and low responding groups, you would describe the gender distribution of your population based on the findings from the high response group.

If, however, you find out that the group that is underrepresented also gives different answers to the rest of the questions, then additional corrections must be made. One strategy is to present your findings on these other answers separately for the over- and underrepresented groups (for example by males and females). Another strategy is to force your data to mirror the "correct" proportion of males and females (and hence also represent the correct mix of male and female answers to the rest of your questions). You do this by weighting your data in such a way that the underrepresented group is restored to its proper proportion of the overall sample. This procedure "assumes" that the males who did respond were like the males who did not respond, and the only thing you need to adjust is the proportion of males in the total sample.

Because you have complete information on a small subset, you are actually in a good position to test out this assumption by comparing the answers of males in the low responding group to the answers of the males in the high responding group. If they are similar, then the assumption holds.

If the answers between the low responding subsample and the high responding subsample are different on a variety of indicators, then you are stuck. You have clearly shown that your responding sample is not a representative group. You may have to relent and try to scrape together enough extra resources to send reminders to the rest of the nonresponding sample. In the worst case you would try to publish your report with a lot of caveats about the nonrepresentativeness of the returns.

Length of the Questionnaire

It almost goes without saying that you are likely to get a better response rate with a shorter questionnaire than with a longer one. Within this general recommendation, the real world is a little more complicated. It turns out that there are no clear demarcation points. It is not like a 12-page questionnaire will get a decent response rate but a 13-page questionnaire will not. There has been a fair amount of research on this issue, but the results are muddled because of several confounding factors (Berdie, 1973; Burchell & Marsh, 1992; Champion & Sear, 1969; Childers & Ferrell, 1979; Lockhart, 1991; Mason et al., 1961; Roscoe, Lang, & Sheth, 1975; Scott, 1961).

Part of the confusion has to do with how we measure the length of the questionnaire. Are we talking about the number of questions, are we referring to the number of pages, or are we talking about some combination of the two? (Thirty questions on 3 pages may seem different from 30 questions on 6 pages.) Another confounder is that different length questionnaires may be perceived differently in terms of interest levels or in terms of importance. Longer questionnaires may actually be seen as more interesting or more important because they can get a fuller picture of a topic than a more cursory version. Even within one methodological study to test the effects of varying questionnaire length, it is hard to "hold constant" such other factors that may play a role in response rates. Many studies that try hard to control these issues wind up comparing different length questionnaires that are actually not that different. For example, a study by Adams and Gale (1982) made comparisons of surveys with 1 versus 3 pages versus 5 pages. They found no difference in response rates between one and three pages but did find a lower response rate for 5 pages.

In addition, drawing conclusions from findings on a series of studies is difficult because they each have differences in topics covered, sample, reminder procedures, and so on. An ambitious review by Heberlein and Baumgartner (1978) that covered 98 methodological studies was unable to document any zero order correlation between length measures and overall responses.

The message to take away from this is that length by itself is not the sole determining factor that decides response rates. No matter what the length, other design factors can influence whether a good response rate is obtained or not. Within a specific design, however, I believe shorter questionnaires will on average do better than substantially longer versions.

From my experience, I think the real issue for the researcher is to design a questionnaire that *efficiently* asks about all the elements that are important to the study. You want to avoid series of questions that seem off the topic; you want to avoid questions that are redundant; you want to avoid unnecessarily long sequences of questions that try to measure very minor differences in issues (e.g., asking about the actual length of time you had to wait in a doctor's waiting room, plus how long you had to wait in the examining room before the doctor came in, plus asking overall how long of a wait you had, plus asking how satisfied you were with the waiting time). There are also important issues of presentation and layout that can affect the perceived length of the questionnaire. These will be described in the next chapter.

Clarity of Instructions

Another factor that contributes to perceived respondent burden and that in turn affects response rates is the clarity of the instructions that are part of the questionnaire. It is not surprising to find that forms that have complicated or confusing or wrong instructions create frustration for respondents and that the result of this frustration is a failure to return the questionnaire.

7

Instructions should be precise, short, and clearly visible. In addition, various format aids such as boldface type or boxing or arrows to supplement written directions help the respondent to comply with instructions. Figure 6.3 shows an example of trying to make instructions clear. The purpose is stated at the top of the page; the skip instructions are listed in all capital letters for categories #9 and #10 of question #1; and the definition of a "drink" is put in a box at question #2. In addition, it helps to use someone who has a graphical perspective to review the layout of your questionnaire. We will discuss these issues in more detail in Chapter 8.

Respondent Motivation

In discussing the techniques to produce higher response rates in this chapter, we have alluded to various respondent motivations. It is useful, however, to be more specific about these motivational patterns so that as you choose among your techniques you can do so with an eye toward procedures that will help respondents decide to participate.

People do not want to spend their time doing things that are not useful, not interesting, or painful. If people think that participating in a study will accomplish something useful, then they are motivated to follow through and complete the survey. The primary mechanism to create the sense of usefulness is the respondent letter. Usually one or two paragraphs are all you devote to this part of the letter, so you can see how important it is that these paragraphs are well written. To the extent that you can articulate how this survey will directly affect the respondents' lives, you will go a long way toward convincing the respondent that completing the questionnaire is a useful process.

Making your questionnaire interesting has a lot to do with the topics you choose to ask about, but it also depends on how the questions are put together, including formatting and sequencing. Pretesting and literature reviews will help you to focus on those questions that provide the information you need and also are easy for respondents to relate to. Pretesting will also give you feedback on questions for which the formatting causes problems or confusion. You want to alter the question format in any way necessary to make it easy for respondents to use the questionnaire. The flow of the questionnaire can make it seem more interesting to the extent that the questions are ordered in logical sequences and relevant groupings of issues. There is no one way to do this; taking a crack at it and then making improvements in response to feedback is the best way to accomplish this goal.

It also is common sense that respondents will not want to fill out a questionnaire if it is painful-either immediately in the sense that it is an ordeal to fill out or delayed in the sense that they fear something bad will happen to them because they filled out the questionnaire. Again clarity and logical flow go a long way toward solving the immediate pain issue. Using grammatically correct and unambiguous terms reduces immediate pain.

SECTION H

Individual Background Characteristics

These questions are being asked only so that we can compare answers of differe groups of managers/supervisors. No data will be released to anyone that would ever allo identification of an individual.

1. Considering all of your drinking behavior in the past 30 days, about how often did you have any beer, wine, or liquor to drink?

1 Three or more times a day
2 Twice a day
3 Once a day
4 Nearly every day (five or six days a week)
5 Two to four days a week
6 Once a week
7 Three days a month
8 One or two days a month
9 Not at all in past month, but I do drink (SKIP TO Q5)
10 Not at all, because I don't drink (SKIP TO Q5)

2. In the past 30 days, on a typical day that you drank, about how much did you have to drink in a day?

One "drink" means:
a 12-ounce can or bottle of beer or
a 4-ounce glass of wine or
a 12-ounce wine cooler or
a 1-ounce shot glass of liquor or spirits, alone or in a mixed drink.

1 One drink
2 Two drinks
3 Three drinks
4 Four drinks
5 Five drinks
6 Six drinks
7 Seven drinks
8 Eight or more drinks

3. In the past 30 days, what was the most you had to drink on any one day?

1 One drink
2 Two drinks
3 Three drinks
4 Four drinks
5 Five drinks
6 Six drinks
7 Seven drinks
8 Eight drinks
9 Nine drinks
10 Ten or more drinks

4. How many days in the past 30 days did you drink that much?

1 One day
2 Two or three days
3 Four to seven days
4 Eight to thirteen days
5 Fourteen to twenty days
6 More than twenty days

5. How do your drinking patterns during the last three years compare to what they were previously?

1 Drinking more now
2 Drinking less now
3 No change

12

Figure 6.3. Example of Formatting for instructions: Alcohol Sequence in Policy Questionnaire

Staying true to your promises of confidentiality or anonymity is the primary mechanism to protect respondents from any delayed pain. You also need to be careful in how the data are analyzed and reported to ensure that no harm comes to respondents. Primarily this means presenting data for large groups of people and being careful to mask institutional affiliations. For instance, you would not say: "Respondents who joined the health club after January 1 were unanimous in denouncing the management of the club." By reporting this finding in that way, you have broken the shield of confidentiality that you promised respondents.

The final issue to keep in mind about respondents participating in a mail survey is that the action needed from the respondents is not that high on their list of priorities. There are lots of things in people's lives that may seem more important or pressing than getting around to completing your questionnaire. That is why it is so important to plan a process that includes reminders and that the timing of reminders keeps the momentum up as the respondent finally reaches the action point of finishing the questionnaire and putting it in the mail to you.

This chapter was first published by Sage Publications and is reproduced by permission of Sage Publications

Mail Surveys. CA: Sage (1995)
Thomas W. Mangione

CHAPTER 7

ADDITIONAL WAYS TO REDUCE NONRESPONSE ERRORS

In this chapter we want to discuss additional strategies that you can use to reduce the nonresponse rate in your surveys. There are a variety of mechanisms that you can use, and using as many of them as feasible should be your goal. We will also discuss some ideas that in some situations have proven beneficial but other times have not shown themselves to be effective. Obviously, you will want to assess whether you believe these strategies will help in your particular situation.

INCENTIVES

Other than follow-up reminders, there is no technique more likely to improve your response rate than incentives. It turns out, however, that the research findings hold some surprises as we consider various options in providing incentives to respondents. The logic of an incentive is simple: Raise the stakes explicitly for the respondents by giving them something in return for filling out the questionnaire. The differences come in when we try to figure out what to give to the respondents and when to give it to them.

Logically one would assume that you would send the respondents a reward after they returned the questionnaire, and you would let the respondents know in the respondent letter that this was the deal. More respondents would be motivated to participate because of the promise of this reward. Obviously, the respondent would have to value whatever it was that you were offering, or else it would not have any motivational value. One disadvantage with this mechanism is that respondents receive a delayed reward; they get their reward several weeks (probably) after their "good" behavior.

Another possibility would be to offer the reward in advance, including it with the mailing in anticipation of the respondents' participation. The advantage here is that the impact is immediate; the respondent gets the benefit right away. We should not underestimate the motivational power of the implied contract: "They gave me this reward, so I had better do my part by filling out the questionnaire or else I wouldn't be living up to my end of the bargain." The disadvantage here (both financially and morally) is that some people get the reward but do not deserve it because they do not return the surveys anyway. Because of this problem, one goal in using this technique is to figure out the least value of the reward that you need to give in order to achieve the effects that you want.

Monetary Rewards

The simplest and most direct reward is to give people money. There have been a variety of studies and reviews of the literature that show that if you offer monetary incentives, your response rate will be improved (Armstrong, 1975; Brennan, Hoek, & Astridge, 1991; Church, 1993; Dommeyer, 1988; Duncan, 1979; Fox, Crask, & Kim, 1988; Friedman & San Augustine, 1979; Heberlein & Baumgartner, 1978; Hopkins & Gullickson, 1992; Huck & Gleason, 1974; Kanuk & Berenson, 1975; Linsky, 1975; Scott, 1961; Yammarino, Skinner, & Childers, 1991; Yu & Cooper, 1983). What is also clear from this research is that prepaid monetary incentives are more effective than promised monetary rewards (Blumberg, Fuller, & Hare, 1974; Cox, 1976; Hancock, 1940; O'Keefe & Homer, 1987; Schewe & Cournoyer, 1976; Wotruba, 1966). There have been contradictory conclusions drawn about the impact of promised monetary rewards compared to no rewards, but there are examples of studies that have shown benefits for promised rewards although they are not as great as prepaid rewards (Yu & Cooper, 1983).

What is surprising about these research results is that it does not seem to take a very big reward to stimulate an improved response rate. Many studies are reported in the literature that show the benefits of $.25 and $.50! However, many of these studies were done 15 to 20 years ago. It seems important to extrapolate the findings from these studies to the "current" value of the dollar. The review by Hopkins and Gullickson (1992) equated these values to 1990 dollars and still showed improvements for values less than $.50.

The question about whether there are increasing benefits for increasing dollar amounts is harder to answer definitively. It turns out that much of the experimentation that has been done to test alternate amounts have not tended to use dollar amounts more than $1, therefore, the number of studies we have available to make generalizations about larger sized incentives is relatively few. The review by Hopkins and Gullickson (1992) did show an increasing percentage of improvement over "no incentive" control methods for greater incentive values, but the top group was designated as $2 or more and included only eight studies.

Another point that speaks to the issue of whether larger rewards (e.g., $5) or smaller rewards (e.g., $1) are better has to do with our understanding of the meaning

8

of the reward to the respondent. With small amounts of money people clearly do *not* interpret the reward as a fair market exchange for their time. Even a $1 reward for filling out a 20 minute questionnaire works out to only a $3 per hour rate of pay. Therefore, people must view the reward in another light; one idea is that it represents to the respondent a token of good faith or a "trust builder" (Dillman, 1978). The respondent feels that the research staff is nice to show their appreciation by giving the incentive and therefore feels motivated to reciprocate by filling out the questionnaire.

According to this perspective, then, the problem with giving a larger reward such as $5 is that now the amount does approach fair market value for people's time. For instance, $5 for filling out a 20-minute questionnaire is equivalent to $15 an hour. Now the reward looks like a real job (even if a short-lived one), and the respondent thinks, "I'm being offered this job, do I want to do it? Maybe not." So in a funny way, the larger the reward, the more the respondent is free to view it as a job offer and feel free to decline the job.

There is another psychological theory called cognitive dissonance theory that gives a slightly different interpretation about why larger amounts may not be better than smaller amounts. According to this theory, the respondent might conclude that there is something wrong with the study if the researchers have to pay someone so much money to fill it out. If that is their viewpoint, then they would be justified in not participating even if they kept the money. The smaller amounts of money used as a reward work in the opposite fashion and therefore support the notion that this is an important study (Hackler & Bourgette, 1973).

Just to give this theorizing a touch of reality, there have been a few studies that do report providing larger sized rewards, and it looks like response rates for larger rewards tend to be higher than for those with smaller rewards (Hopkins & Gullickson, 1992; James & Bolstein, 1992; Yu & Cooper, 1983). In particular, higher incentive amounts are reported in the literature when conducting surveys of persons in professional occupations, particularly doctors. Incentive amounts from $20 to $25 to $50 have been used (Godwin, 1979). In these circumstances, higher response rates are obtained with higher rewards (Berry & Kanouse, 1987). In addition, my own experience with our recent nonexperimental study dealing with alcohol use and work had one worksite in which we used a $5 upfront incentive. The resulting response rate was 82%.

One final point about monetary incentives and their desired effects is that the key to effectiveness seems to be creating a climate in which the prepaid incentive is seen as a feel-good thing rather than as a manipulative technique to coerce the respondent into participation.

Another variation on the idea of monetary rewards is using a "lottery" prize structure. This technique falls within the "promised reward" category, but with a twist. Respondents are offered a "chance" at a "big" prize, although they also have, of course, a chance of getting nothing. Again, research on this variation is limited, so

that definitive generalizations about its effectiveness are not possible (Hopkins & Gullickson, 1992; Gajraj, Faria, & Dickinson, 1990; Lorenzi, Friedmann, & Paolillo, 1988). The logic behind this idea is that the chance of hitting big will be such an inducement that respondents will fill out their surveys to qualify. This technique also works well if you are trying to encourage respondents to mail in their surveys by a particular deadline.

The other issue that must be dealt with if you want to use this technique is anonymity, or rather the lack of it. In order to have a drawing and give out prizes, you need to know the name and address associated with each returned survey. This lack of anonymity may be counterproductive in some circumstances. The "postcard" mechanism that we discussed in the previous chapter provides a solution to this dilemma. The surveys themselves are returned anonymously, but the postcards have the respondents' names and addresses on them. To be eligible for the lottery, the postcard would need to be returned.

It seems like enterprising respondents would realize that all they really have to do to be eligible for the lottery is to turn in their postcard. You would not really be able to tell whether they actually sent in their questionnaires. It seems that the more attractive the "prize," the more motivation there would be to cheat. However, respondents do not seem to do that. My recent experience with this technique in 12 different worksites across the county showed that we never received more postcards back than we did questionnaires, even though we were offering three $250 lottery prizes at each worksite.

Nonmonetary Rewards

Of course it is possible to reward respondents with other things besides money (Brennan, 1958; Furse & Stewart. 1982; Hansen, 1980; Nederhof, 1983). All sorts of things have been, and can be, used—ball point pens, cups, movie tickets, and so on. The logic of giving a "gift" is similar to that for giving a token amount of money. The idea is to express to the respondent that you are appreciative of their efforts and want to thank them for their participation. Again, like money rewards it is possible to think about the gift being given as a "prepaid" gift or as a "promised" gift that is sent after the survey is returned (Brennan, 1958; Pucel, Nelson, & Wheeler, 1971).

There has not been as much research on the differences between prepaid versus promised gifts but one would assume that the effectiveness would follow the same pattern as with monetary rewards—prepaid gifts would probably have a better effect. Also, there has not been much research done on the "value" of the gift to see what the trends are with more valuable gifts. To some extent the concept of value is less obvious with many types of gifts. Also, it is possible that the gift's perceived value exceeds the actual cost of the gift itself. This could arise because respondents may not have a good sense about how much such a gift costs, or it may be because by buying in bulk you can get a discount. Movie passes are great in this regard because they cost you only about $4 although they are good at movies that cost about $7 normally.

Other Incentives

Sometimes respondents can be offered other incentives that encourage them to respond (Dommeyer, 1985; Hubbard & Little, 1988). These alternate devices will provide improvements in response rates to the extent that the offer is viewed as valuable by respondents. I recently had occasion to be part of a survey study in which respondents were asked to fill out a short questionnaire concerning their nutritional intake. The researchers also needed respondents to include a clipping from their toenails! As an incentive, respondents were told that when they returned the survey they would receive a detailed nutritional analysis of their own diet based on their report and their toenail clippings. Returns were over 70% with only one reminder.

Another interesting incentive is to offer a contribution to a charity in the respondents' names if surveys are returned (Robertson & Bellenger, 1978). Obviously the perceived value of the charity might have some impact on its effectiveness. This technique can be used on an individual basis or group basis. The individual strategy would be to contribute a certain amount (say $5) to a charity for each survey returned. Specific charities can be designated, or you can allow respondents to check off among a few offerings, or you can ask them to write in their own suggestions. The group strategy would provide a significant payment to a charity if the sample as a whole provided a certain number or percentage of returns (e.g., a 70% return rate). My recent worksite study included two sites in which we used the group strategy, a $750 contribution to charity, and wound up with response rates of 68% and 78%.

Incentives Versus Reminders

Now that we have extolled the virtues of incentives as well as reminders, a legitimate question is whether incentives should be used instead of reminders. The question can be answered from the perspective of final response rates, cost effectiveness, and quickness of returns. A study by James and Bolstein (1990) gives some information on this issue. They ran an experiment using different amounts of incentives (none, $.25, $.50, $1, and $2) and kept track of the response rates at the end of each of the four mailings using a four-page questionnaire. The highest rates of returns were provided by using both methods in combination—four mailings and a $2 prepaid incentive. This strategy is also the most expensive. Good return rates (although a little lower than the combination method) were also obtained by using two mailings and a $2 incentive or four mailings and no incentive. The no incentive strategy was slightly less expensive than the incentive strategy but of course it took more time for the additional waves of mailings to be administered. If time rather than money is the limiting factor, then using incentives may allow you to save some time; if money is the limiting factor then planning for multiple mailings with no incentives may be the best. If a high response rate is the major goal, then multiple mailings and incentives should be used together.

OTHER TECHNIQUES

There are other techniques beyond reminders and incentives that have been shown to improve response rates. Some techniques show consistent improvements; some have shown improvements in only some circumstances.

Prenotification

One interesting variation of the reminder mechanism is to prenotify respondents before they receive the survey. In a sense this is a reminder done ahead of time. Basically it is a contact by mail or phone that "warns" the respondent that they have been selected to be in a survey and to keep an eye open for its arrival in the mail a week or two in the future. The impact of the prenotification is generally equivalent to one reminder (Allen, Schewe, & Wijt, 1980; Brunner & Carroll, 1969; Ford, 1967; Furse, Stewart, & Rados, 1981; Heaton, 1965; Jolson, 1977; Kerin & Peterson, 1977; Myers & Haug, 1969; Parsons & Medford, 1972; Schegelmilch & Diamantopoulos, 1991; Stafford, 1966; Walker & Burdick, 1977; Wynn & McDaniel, 1985; Yammarino et al., 1991).

This procedure provides one way to shorten the interval from the first mailing of the survey until the last reminder. You can "gain" 2 weeks on your return schedule by mailing out the prenotification letter a couple of weeks before you send out the questionnaire. You would send it out about the same time that the questionnaire goes off to the printer.

Return Postage

It almost goes without saying that paying for the return postage will increase response rates. Maybe because this is such an obvious procedure, there have not been all that many studies that explicitly test this assertion. The few that have been done certainly confirm this point (Armstrong & Lusk, 1987; Blumberg et al., 1974; Ferris, 1951; Harris & Guffey, 1978; McCrohan & Lowe, 1981; Price, 1950; Yammarino et al., 1991).

There has been more research on the type of postage put on the return envelope. The alternatives are to use some kind of business reply franking or to put a stamp on the return envelope. The advantage of the business reply is that you get charged only for questionnaires that are actually returned. By the way, the post office does charge a little extra for this service, something on the order of magnitude of $.07 per returned questionnaire. This "extra" cost needs to be factored in when comparing the costs of alternate postage mechanisms. The disadvantage of this choice is that it gives more of the appearance of impersonality.

The alternate procedure of putting a stamp on the return envelope seems to produce a small increase in return rates (Brook, 1978; Jones & Linda, 1978; Kimball, 1961; Watson, 1965). The reason for this is that respondents do not want to "waste" the stamp by

8

not returning the questionnaire and yet are not crass enough to peel it off and use it for their own purposes. We are using the value put on avoiding wastefulness to induce a better response rate. There have also been some studies that show using pretty commemorative type stamps has a slight advantage over regular stamps (Henley, 1976; Jones & Linda, 1978; Martin & McConnell, 1970). The disadvantage of this approach is its cost. Not only do you "pay" for stamps that ultimately never get used but it also costs time and money to get the stamps, lick them (the post office now offers self-stick stamps in some denominations), and stick them on all the envelopes.

Outgoing Postage

The usual alternatives for types of outgoing postage are stamps or metered mail using a postage meter. There have been a few studies done that show a slight advantage for stamps, particular commemorative stamps, on outgoing envelopes (Blumenfeld, 1973; Dillman, 1972; Hopkins & Podolak, 1983; Kernan, 1971; McCrohan & Lowe, 1981; Peterson, 1975; Vocino, 1977). The explanation for this difference is that respondents are less likely to assume the mailing is "junk mail" if there is a stamp on the envelope and therefore actually open the envelope. The only disadvantage for stamps again is the extra cost of sticking them on the envelopes.

There is a third postage option. It is called a first class indicia. It is like the business reply except that it is used for outgoing first class mail. You print your account number and a first class designation on your outgoing envelopes. The post office keeps track of your mailings and deducts the postage amounts from a prepaid account that you have set up with them. This is the least labor intensive method of sending out your questionnaires, but it probably suffers somewhat from the same problem as metered mail in that it may be confused with "junk mail."

There has also been some research on the value of using premium postage for mailings such as special delivery or next day delivery services. The research shows there to be some advantage for this type of postage, but the costs are so substantial that many consider this prohibitive (Clausen & Ford, 1947; Kephart & Bressler, 1958). When special postage is used, it is most often used for the final reminders. At least you are mailing to only part of your sample at this stage.

Study Sponsorship

Respondents are more likely to respond to surveys that they consider important or prestigious (Doob, Freedman, & Carlsmith, 1973; Houston & Nevin, 1977; Jones & Lang, 1980; Jones & Linda, 1978; Peterson, 1975; Roeher, 1963; Watson, 1965). Therefore they are more likely to respond to surveys that are sponsored by government agencies or well-known universities (Houston & Nevin, 1977; Jones &

Lang, 1980; Jones & Linda, 1978; Peterson, 1975). Also, perhaps they are less concerned that the survey is a ploy to sell them real estate or insurance if it comes on university or government agency letterhead.

Color of the Questionnaire

There have been a few studies that show that the color of the questionnaire cover affects return rates (Gullahorn & Gullahorn, 1963; Pressley & Tullar, 1977; Pucel et al., 1971). The explanation for this effect is that a color other than white might stand out more on the respondent's desk so the respondent is less apt to misplace it or to forget to deal with it. Green versus white are the colors that have been tested most often; the relative values of colors other than green have not been tested to any large extent.

ADDITIONAL TECHNIQUES TO CONSIDER

There are a variety of other techniques that have not consistently shown improvements in response rates but that have from time to time shown an impact. Unfortunately it is hard to know when these might have a positive effect and when they might not. Using them is riskier, therefore, at least in terms of ensuring positive results. On the other hand, for most, using it will not hurt.

Types of Appeal

When you write your cover letter and you come to the paragraph that speaks to why the respondent should participate, there are several different approaches that could be taken. You can use the scientific approach—"our sample won't be valid unless everyone responds." You can use the egoistic approach—"this is how participating will benefit you." You can use the social utility approach—"this study is important and worthwhile." None of these approaches has consistently proved better than the others (Bachman, 1987; Childers, Pride, & Ferrell, 1980; Hendrick, Borden, Giesen, Murray, & Seyfried, 1972; Houston & Nevin, 1977; Yammarino et al., 1991; Yu & Cooper, 1983).

Personalization

A closely related technique is personalization, either through the salutation to the respondent by using a name as opposed to a more anonymous greeting such as "dear Boston resident," or by personally signed letters. Neither procedure has consistently shown benefits for response rates (Andreasen, 1970; Carpenter, 1975; Dillman & Frey, 1974; Frazier & Bird, 1958; Houston & Jefferson, 1975; Kawash & Aleamoni, 1971; Kerin & Peterson, 1977; Kimball, 1961; Rucker, Hughes, Thompson, Harrison, & Vanderlip, 1984; Simon, 1967; Weilbacher & Walsh, 1952). Some authors have commented that by personalizing the letters you may have just the opposite effect by calling attention to the fact that you know the respondent's name.

8

Deadlines

Providing the respondents with a deadline for responding has a nice appeal to it. The presumption is that respondents would try harder to return the questionnaire by the deadline, rather than putting it aside for a while and then forgetting it. The use of a deadline gets a little complicated when you are also using reminders. You do not want to say that 2 weeks from now is the deadline for responding, and then send the respondent a reminder at that time saying "please respond, we're giving you 2 more weeks." On the other hand, you do not want to give a deadline of 8 weeks in the future, because that hardly serves any motivating purposes.

What research has been done on the use of deadlines does not show any particular advantage in final response rates. What it does show is that the returns come in a little faster (Futrell & Hise, 1982; Henley, 1976; Kanuk & Berenson, 1975; Linsky, 1975; Nevin & Ford, 1976, Roberts, McCrory, & Forthofer, 1978; Vocino, 1977). My suggestion is to use soft deadlines that also incorporate the information about subsequent reminders, such as "Please try to respond within the next week, so we won't have to send you any reminders."

8

This article was first published in the Survey Methods Centre Newsletter and is reproduced by permission of the Survey Methods Centre

Survey Methods Centre Newsletter, Volume 18 No.2 (1998). London: SMC

THE USE OF RESPONDENT INCENTIVES IN SURVEYS
Gerry Nicolaas and Peter Lynn

INTRODUCTION

Recent years have seen growing concern about survey response rates, both in the UK and elsewhere (ONS 1997, de Heer and Israels 1992). Although the reported decline in response rates does not appear very large, it is claimed that this relative stability has been achieved by increasing the input of survey resources (Foster and Bushnell, 1993, Groves and Couper 1996).

A wide variety of tools and strategies are used to improve survey response rates, such as sending advance letters, reducing the length of the questionnaire/interview and improving interviewer training strategies. One tool which has consistently been shown to improve response rates is the provision of incentives to respondents.

This article documents our thoughts on the use of incentives in social surveys from a British perspective. It was stimulated by the perception that the time may now be ripe for a reappraisal of the role of incentives in surveys in Britain.

We first describe recent and current practice with respect to the use of incentives in Britain. We then propose a framework for considering the use of incentives. This describes a number of important dimensions. We then provide a brief overview of published research which addresses some of the areas of concern, and comment on likely applicability to the British situation. Finally, we make some tentative predictions about the ways in which incentives might be used in Britain in the future, and we make some suggestions for further research.

CURRENT PRACTICE

General policy at SCPR is not to provide incentives to survey respondents. This is true of mail surveys, as well as interview surveys. Exceptions are made when an unusual burden is placed on respondents, such as diary keeping or panel membership. Also, payments are made to those taking part in qualitative research. Similar policies are held by government research organisations in this country and elsewhere; e.g. Social Survey Division at ONS, Bureau of the Census in the USA, Statistics Netherlands, Statistics Sweden, Danmarks Statistik, INSÉE in France, Australian Bureau of Statistics (Luppes and Barnes, 1994).

Nevertheless, there is an ongoing debate within and between research organisations about the possibility of extending the use of incentives to improve response rates. In the USA the Council of Professional Associations on Federal Statistics hosted a symposium on the provision of incentives to survey respondents in 1991. The use of incentives is a recurring theme at the International Workshops on Household Survey Non-Response.

In market research the use of incentives is much more common. Mail surveys are often sent to respondents with pens enclosed. The value of cash incentives varies from less than £1 to £20 or more.

IMPORTANT DIMENSIONS

There are many aspects of the use of incentives on surveys which may affect conclusions about utility, appropriateness, cost and so on. In any discussion of the use of incentives, it is important to consider these aspects explicitly. Some of the important aspects are the following:

Mode of data collection.

The effect of an incentive can be very different for face-to-face, telephone, mail and other surveys. This may be partly because response patterns in the absence of incentives differ by mode, so the *potential* for incentive effects is different; it may also be partly because the mode affects the method and timing of the introduction and administration of the incentive, which in turn affects the *impact* of the incentive on an individual.

Type of incentive.

Incentives can take many forms, including cash, cash-equivalents (postage stamps, telephone cards, shopping vouchers), gifts, lotteries, donations to charity. These may affect sample members in different ways.

Timing of incentive.

The incentive may be introduced either in advance of the request for co-operation with the survey (e.g. in an advance letter) or at the same time (e.g. on the doorstep or with a mailed questionnaire). Furthermore, the incentive may either be supplied at that time or merely promised (a further variant is that the promise can be conditional on response or unconditional).

Nature of survey population.

Clearly, any incentive may have a different impact on different sorts of people, so the effect of an incentive could well depend on the nature of the sample (e.g. young people, older people, workers, mothers, etc.)

Nature of survey task.

We have already mentioned that current practice at SCPR is to use incentives only on surveys believed to impose a heavy respondent burden. This partly reflects a belief that reluctance to respond will correlate with burden.

Nature of effect.

There are many aspects of survey quality that can be affected by incentives. Response rate is a crude proxy for one important component of survey error – non-response bias. But there are also other important components, particularly response error (validity and reliability).

Conduit of effect.

On interviewer-administered surveys, we need to be aware that any effect of an incentive may be either directly upon the respondent or indirectly *via* an effect upon the interviewer. The impact of incentives on interviewers is an important consideration.

Other aspects of survey design.

The tone of the advance letter, the call-back/follow-up strategy, etc, may interact with the incentive effect.

PREVIOUS RESEARCH

A review of the published literature reveals that most experiments with incentives are based on mail surveys, mainly carried out in the USA. One reason why researchers have focused on mail surveys is that these have always been plagued by lower response rates than face-to-face surveys. Hence, there has always been concern about the possibility of non-response bias on mail surveys.

MAIL SURVEY RESPONSE RATES

Many experiments have tested the effect of incentives on the response rates of mail surveys. Overall, the literature consistently shows that incentives improve response rates. Church (1993) conducted a meta-analysis of 38 experimental or quasi-experimental studies (74 observations) on the use of incentives in mail surveys. Almost 90% of these observations showed that incentives produced an improvement in response rates. An average increase in response rates of 13.2% was reported. However, this average conceals a wide range of effect sizes from a decrease of 1% to an increase of 22.5%.

Church also looked at variables which may serve as "incentive effect moderators", and found that the type of incentive (monetary or nonmonetary) and the time at which the incentive is offered (prepaid versus promised) explained some of the variation in effect sizes. His meta-analysis showed average increases in response rates of 19.1% for prepaid monetary incentives, 4.5% for promised monetary incentives, 7.9% for advance nonmonetary incentives and 1.2% for promised nonmonetary incentives.

Another meta-analysis, carried out by Hopkins and Gullickson (1992), also found an average increase in response rates of 19% for prepaid incentives in mail surveys (N=73 comparisons). They also concluded that a single mailing with a prepaid incentive could result in better response than two mailings without an incentive.

Further qualitative analysis revealed that the studies with the smaller effect sizes were not well designed (e.g. bad timing for data collection period) compared to those with larger effect sizes (Hopkins and Gullickson 1992).

Another variable which has been shown to influence the effect of monetary incentives is the value of the incentive. However, the reported effects are not consistent. Some researchers have reported a positive linear relationship between response rates and value of the incentive (Yu and Cooper 1983, Hopkins and Gullickson 1992). Others have claimed that the relationship between response rates and value of the incentive fits a model of diminishing returns (Armstrong 1975, Fox et al 1988). James and Bolstein (1992) concluded that the optimum value would increase as a function of the length and difficulty of the questionnaire. There is also a suggestion that a large incentive may be counterproductive with some people as it undermines their sense of social responsibility (Brehm 1994).

There is contradictory evidence about the effectiveness of charitable donations and lotteries. Some studies have shown that charitable donations can improve response rates (Robertson and Bellenger 1978, Faria and Dickenson 1992) while others showed no improvement (Furse and Stewart 1982, Hubbard and Little 1988, Warriner et al 1996). Similar contradictory results have been found for lotteries (Hubbard and Little 1988, Warriner et al 1996).

Hopkins and Gullickson (1992) compared the effect sizes between experiments conducted in the USA and those conducted elsewhere (only 7 out of 73 comparisons) and did not find a significant difference.

In conclusion, on mail surveys, incentives increase response rates, monetary incentives work better than nonmonetary incentives, prepaid incentives are more effective than promised incentives and the effect of incentives increases with the value of the incentive (possibly with diminishing returns).

Personal interview survey response rates

In recent years, increasing numbers of interviewer-mediated surveys have used incentives, possibly under the assumption that the effects on response rates would be similar to those for mail surveys. However, only a few experiments testing the use of incentives in interviewer-mediated surveys have been published. Again almost all of these have been conducted in the USA or Canada.

Goyder (1994) tested the use of cash incentives in a face-to-face survey in Canada. He split his sample into four groups: (1) no incentive (the control group), (2) $1.00 enclosed in the advance letter, (3) $1.00 promised on completion of the interview, and (4) $10 promised on completion of the interview. He only found a significant increase in response rates for group 2 relative to the control group – 59.8% compared to 47.6%.

Willimack et al (1995) tested the use of a pen as an incentive. Interviewers were unaware to which of the two groups the sampled addresses belonged. The refusal rate for those who received the pen was only 12.4%, compared with 16.1% for the control group ($P = 0.029$). They also showed that this decrease in refusal rates could not be achieved by increasing the number of follow-up visits.

9

Eleanor Singer and colleagues managed to find 37 experimental studies which tested the effectiveness of incentives in face-to-face and telephone surveys. (Singer *et al*, forthcoming). The results of their meta-analysis showed similar results to those found for mail surveys: the use of incentives increases response rates, prepaid incentives tend to produce higher response rates than promised incentives, monetary incentives are more effective than nonmonetary incentives, and there is a positive linear relationship between the amount of the incentive and response rate.

Recently, two experiments with incentives on interview surveys have been carried out in the UK by the SCPR Survey Methods Centre. The first was based on a time use survey (Lynn and Sturgis 1997). At a random half of addresses, an incentive of £10 was promised to each member of the household conditional on the household completing all components of the survey (which included interviews and diaries). This conditional incentive slightly improved response rate to the interviews, but dramatically improved completion rates for the diaries. The incentive appeared to be especially effective in improving response rates among those aged 55 or over, who tend to be underrepresented in surveys (Barnes 1992). The effect of the incentive was further enhanced when combined with another experimentally-manipulated factor, interviewer call-backs.

The other incentives experiment carried out by the Survey Methods Centre (Lynn et al 1997) was attached to wave 7 (telephone interview) and wave 8 (face-to-face interview) of the British Election Panel Study (Brook and Taylor 1996). Overall the conclusion of this experiment was that a £5 prepaid monetary incentive had a strong positive effect on response rates, independent of other experimental factors. The researchers inferred that if incentives produce higher response rates at the later stages of a panel study, the effect could be even greater at the earlier stages of a panel study.

The effect of advance incentives was also studied by Brehm (1994) on a two-wave study. The first wave was face-to-face and the second was carried out by telephone. The experiment, carried out at wave 2, involved four treatment groups: no advance letter nor incentive, advance letter only, advance letter with pen, advance letter with one dollar. The response rates were 71%, 75%, 81% and 78% respectively, so it was concluded that incentives improved response rates.

Brehm was able to look at the effect of incentives by the attitude of the respondent towards the first wave survey. Among those who were neither negative about the interview (e.g. who thought the interview was too long or too boring) nor negative about themselves (e.g. expressed doubts about their own suitability for the survey), response rates were improved with the advance letter, the pen and the dollar. Among those who were negative about the interview, the prepaid monetary incentive was effective whereas the advance letter and pen were not. Among those who were negative about themselves, the results were almost the opposite: the advance letter proved

effective whereas the pen and the dollar did not. Brehm concluded that these variations correspond to different decision-making processes for taking part in a survey: cost-benefit calculations among those who are negative about the survey versus an appeal to reciprocity.

DATA QUALITY

Only a few studies have examined the effect of incentives on data quality. Most of these focus on item non-response and reported detail. Some researchers were concerned that the provision of incentives should not alter the answers given by individual respondents. Surprisingly, very few studies made any reference to non-response bias. However, to reduce non-response bias, incentives must improve response rates substantially.

Overall, it would appear that monetary incentives tend to reduce item non-response and generate more comments at open-ended questions. However, this is not always the case. James and Bolstein (1990) did not find any difference in item non-response between those who had received monetary incentives and those who had not. Similarly, Goyder (1994) found that a prepayment of $1 had no effect on item non-response but there was some indication that postpayments of $1 and $10 <u>in</u>creased item non-response. A reduction in item non-response and an increase in the number of events recorded in a diary were reported by Lynn and Sturgis (1997) but only when monetary incentives were combined with call-backs.

LIMITATIONS OF THE PREVIOUS RESEARCH

Though some clear generalisations emerge from the literature, it remains difficult to predict the impact of incentives on any particular survey. In meta-analyses it is not possible to take into account all the variables which may interact with the effect of incentives because these variables are not consistently reported. Variables such as the survey sponsor, quality of questionnaires and advance letters, training of interviewers and so on also affect response rates, and the effects will interact with those of incentives. For example, in a situation where a wide variety of techniques are already employed to maximise response rates, it seems unlikely that incentives could improve response by anything like the 19% quoted above.

DRAWBACKS TO THE USE OF INCENTIVES

Although incentives may improve response rates (and may possibly therefore reduce non-response bias), there are also negative aspects to their use, above and beyond the monetary cost.

Expectation effects.

A concern of many researchers is that the use of an incentive, particularly if monetary, may lead to expectations of similar payments on future surveys. If a future survey does not pay an incentive, co-operation rates may reduce. However, initial (limited) research has found no evidence of such an effect. Two studies have been carried out on panel surveys, one in the UK and one in the USA (Lynn et al 1997, Singer et al 1998) where a split-run experiment was carried out on one wave (incentive vs. none), followed by a wave at which no incentives were offered. In both cases response rate at the latter wave was no lower amongst those who received an incentive at the earlier wave than amongst those who had not. But it could be argued that the earlier payment may create a residual obligation effect at the next round of a panel. To address this issue, Singer and her colleagues carried out a further experiment (personal communication) where a split-sample (incentive vs. none) was subsequently re-contacted a year later by a different research organisation requesting an interview on a very different topic. Again, response rates did not differ between the two groups.

It must be recognised, though, that even if these findings are generalisable currently, the situation could change if and when incentive payments become normative.

Response quality.

Another valid concern is that incentives may cause a shift from intrinsic to extrinsic motivation to take part in surveys, producing a decline in response quality. Again, however, little evidence of this has been found. As described above, the studies that have addressed this issue have mostly found <u>higher</u> quality responses (as measured by item non-response rates, level of detail in responses, length of verbatim answers etc.) when an incentive is paid.

LIMITATIONS OF THE BRITISH CONTEXT

A specific issue in Britain is the way that the administration of an incentive interacts with the sampling frame most commonly used for general population surveys.

The literature shows clearly that incentives are most effective when paid unconditionally in advance of the request for participation. However, the sampling frame used for most general population surveys in Britain is a list of postal addresses, with no information to indicate whether an address is residential, or who lives there. In practice, about 12% of listed addresses are non-residential. So, to mail an incentive in advance would involve mailing

to many ineligible addresses, a use of public money that would be difficult to defend, and that would also cause accounting problems. This issue is described further in Lynn *et al* (1998). The upshot is that the mode of administration likely to be most effective is ruled out for face-to-face surveys in Britain, and sub-optimal alternatives have to be considered instead.

THE WAY FORWARD

We believe that incentive payments will soon become commonplace on social surveys in Britain. However, more research is needed in order to establish the optimum mode of administration and the optimum form and value of the incentive, particularly for the most reluctant respondents.

A recent small-scale experiment at SCPR (unpublished) has suggested that a small (£1) conditional promised donation to charity can produce a significant increase in response rate. This approach warrants further investigation as it is relatively cheap and easy to administer this form of incentive.

Other experiments have compared different values of an incentive (Lynn *et al*, 1998) and it is not yet clear what level of payment is most cost effective.

It would also be highly desirable for further research to address the issue of whether the response rate improvements brought about by incentives actually appear to reduce non-response bias. If this could be combined with comparisons of other aspects of data quality, then some systematic comparisons of survey error may become possible, enabling estimation of the cost-effectiveness of incentive payments.

Virtually all the previous research on incentives has not only concentrated on response rates, but has concentrated on the marginal impact of incentives in addition to other response-inducing aspects of the survey design. An area worth exploring might be the extent to which incentives could constitute a cost-effective <u>substitute</u> for other techniques.

A final important issue is the effect(s) of incentives on interviewers. There has been little research in this area and what there is has been inconclusive. There is clearly potential for incentives to have serious negative impacts on interviewers, and this needs to be addressed.

References

Armstrong SJ (1975) Monetary incentives in mail surveys. *Public Opinion Quarterly*, 39: 111-116.

Barnes B (1992) Studies of non-respondents in OPCS household surveys, using Census data: past studies and future plans. *Survey Methodology Bulletin*, 30: 21-25.

Brehm J (1994) Stubbing toes for a foot in the door? Prior contact, incentives and survey response. *International Journal of Public Opinion* 6(1): 45-63.

Brook L, Taylor B (1996) *The British Election Panel Survey (BEPS), 1992-1995: Interim Technical Notes.* CREST Working Paper no. 41. London and Oxford: CREST.

Church AH (1993) Estimating the effect of incentives on mail survey response rates – a meta-analysis. *Public Opinion Quarterly* 57(1): 62-79.

Faria AJ, Dickenson JR (1992) Mail survey response, speed, and cost. *Industrial Marketing Management*, 21: 51-60.

Foster K, Bushnell D (1993) Non-response bias on government surveys in Great Britain. Paper prepared for the 5th International Workshop on Household Survey Non-Response, Ottawa, Canada, September 1994.

Fox RJ, Crask MR, Kim J (1988) Mail survey response rate: a meta-analysis of selected techniques for inducing response. *Public Opinion Quarterly* 52(4): 467-491.

Furse DH, Stewart DW (1982) Monetary incentives versus promised contribution to charity: new evidence on mail survey response. *Journal of Marketing Research*, 19: 375-380.

Goyder J (1994) An experiment with cash incentives on a personal interview survey. *Journal of the Market Research Society* 36(4): 360-366.

Groves RM, Couper MP (1996) Household-Level Determinants of Survey Nonresponse. In: *Advances in Survey Research, New Directions for Evaluation*, No. 70, edited by Braverman MT and Slater JK. San Francisco: Jossey-Bass.

de Heer WF, Israels AZ (1992) Nonresponse trends in Europe. Paper presented at the Joint Statistical Meetings of the American Statistical Association, Boston.

Hopkins KD, Gullickson AR (1992) Response rates in survey research: a meta-analysis of the effects of monetary gratuities. *Journal of Experimental Education*, 61(1): 52-62

Hubbard R, Little EL (1988) Promised contributions to charity and mail survey responses. *Public Opinion Quarterly*, 52: 223-230.

James JM, Bolstein R (1992) Response Rates with Large Monetary Incentives. *Public Opinion Quarterly*, 56(4): 442-453.

Luppes M, Barnes B (1994) On the use of incentives: an overview of policies in several countries. Paper presented at the 5th International Workshop on Household Survey Non-Response, Ottawa, Canada.

Lynn P, Taylor B, Brook L (1997) Incentives, information and number of contacts: Testing the effects of these factors on response to a panel survey. *Survey Methods Centre Newsletter*, 17(3): 7-12.

Lynn P, Thomson K, Brook L (1998) An experiment with incentives on the British Social Attitudes survey. *Survey Methods Centre Newsletter*, 18(2): 12-14.

Lynn P, Sturgis P (1997) Boosting survey response through a monetary incentive and fieldwork procedures: an experiment. *Survey Methods Centre Newsletter*, 17(3): 18-22.

ONS (1997) *Living in Britain: results from the 1995 General Household Survey.* London: The Stationery Office.

Robertson DH, Bellenger DN (1978) A new method of increasing mail survey responses: contributions to charity. *Journal of Marketing Research*, 15: 632-633.

Singer E, Van Hoewyk J, Maher M (1998) Does the payment of incentives create expectation effects? *Public Opinion Quarterly*, 62: 152-164.

Singer E, N Gebler, T Raghunathan, J Van Hoewyk, and K McGonagle (forthcoming). The Effects of Incentives on Response Rates in Face-to-Face and Telephone Surveys. *Journal of Official Statistics.*

Warriner K, Goyder J, Gjertsen H, Hohner P, McSpurren K (1996) Charities, No; Lotteries, No; Cash, Yes: Main effects and interactions in a Canadian Incentives Experiment. *Public Opinion Quarterly* 60(4): 542-562.

Willimack DK, Schuman H, Pennell BE, Lepkowski JM (1995) Effects of a prepaid nonmonetary incentive on response rates and response quality in a face-to-face survey. *Public Opinion Quarterly*, 59(1): 78-92

Yu J, Cooper H. (1983) A quantitative review of research design effects on response rates to questionnaires. *Journal of Market Research*, 20: 73-78.

9

This article was first published in the Survey Methods Centre Newsletter and is reproduced by permission of the Survey Methods Centre

Survey Methods Centre Newsletter Volume 16 No. 1

ORGANISATION AND MANAGEMENT OF POSTAL SURVEYS

Regina Dengler

Regina Dengler discussed the practical issues involved in carrying out a postal survey. The paper assumed that a clear research objective had already been defined, that it had been decided that the most appropriate methodology was to carry out a postal survey, and that a well designed questionnaire had been produced. It was also assumed that any necessary ethical approval or other clearance had already been obtained, that the survey is covered by the Data Protection Act, that there exists an appropriate budget to carry out the survey, and that the necessary sample details exist.

Regina Dengler's talk was illustrated with examples from the Trent Health Lifestyle Survey (THLS).

THE SAMPLE

The first important practical consideration is the form in which the sample details are received, and the time that it might take to obtain them. For example, some THLS samples from FHSA registers took between one and four months to obtain. It then takes a few more weeks to manipulate the samples and get the names and addresses into a suitable format for printing on to labels. If a sample arrives as printed lists time and effort will be required to enter them on to the computer.

IMPROVING RESPONSE

Response rates were the next topic of Regina Dengler's talk. Peter Lynn had already emphasised the importance of getting a high response rate; Regina Dengler discussed the practical steps to achieving that. Generally, measures which are likely to improve response cost money.

Reminder mailings are the most important influence on response[1,2]. If no reminders are sent, response will be poor. Often the questionnaire is followed by one, two or three reminders – two or three are common. It is best to send reminders only to sample members who have not yet responded, although there will always be some people who get a reminder because their questionnaire crosses the reminder in the post. To minimise such occurrences, one needs to consider the interval between reminders, and bear in mind that it can take four or five days to actually mail out a reminder once labels have been produced. Regina Dengler suggested that about three weeks between mailings might be optimal, as the rush of responses to the previous mailing would be beginning to subside by then. It was also suggested that if there was only to be one reminder, it should include another copy of the questionnaire and another return envelope, whereas if there were to be two or more reminders, the first could be a postcard, which saves money without affecting response[3].

The second most important thing is that sample members should not have to pay to respond. In other words, a postage-paid return envelope must be included (eg. business reply). Also, it helps if the research seems to be relevant, and if the sponsor is credible. One study had achieved an 84% response rate with an FHSA as sponsor, but only 66% when coming from a research institute[4]. It may also be helpful to use a very local sponsor, for example a GP in a survey of patients. It may also help – but perhaps not much – if letters are personalised and/or contain a handwritten signature. However, that may not be practical if the sample size runs to thousands! Another positive factor appears to be to use stamps instead of a business reply envelope, and the larger and prettier the stamps the better[5]. The timing of the survey is also important. August is generally not a good period, as many people are not at home. It may also help if the sponsor is known personally to the respondents, for example a GP carrying out a survey of his or her patients[5]. However, recontacting respondents may adversely affect response,. For example, the THLS had found that in some areas of Nottingham response rates are very poor. This is partly due to the fact that these are deprived areas, but also partly because they are *City Challenge* areas, where many surveys have been carried out.

There are some practical decisions which may or may not affect response – there is conflicting evidence. One is the day of the week on which the survey is posted. Another is the issue of offering guarantees of anonymity and confidentiality. These issues may need further research. Financial incentives seem to help, but the effectiveness of other incentives is less clear[6].

Improving Response

- Reminders
- Business reply envelope
- Research relevant
- Sponsor credible
- Personalised letter
- Hand written signature
- Stamps instead of business reply
- Mailing outside holiday period
- Personal prior contact

SAVING MONEY

There are some practical considerations which do not affect response but might save money. These include the choice of first or second class postage[6], whether to use recycled paper, and the colour of the envelopes.

DOCUMENT DESIGN

Regina Dengler then discussed practical issues in the design of survey documents, showing examples from the THLS. The initial covering letter may be incorporated in the questionnaire itself, in order to reduce printing and collation effort. The letter should follow good design principles, perhaps with a personalised signature (printed). The example letter shown did not include a telephone number where sample members could contact the researchers with queries. The reason for this was that in the first year the survey was carried out (1992) the researchers were inundated with calls, and had to employ somebody just to answer the telephone! They reasoned that anyone strongly motivated to do so would either write or look up the telephone number.

The design of the outward envelope is also important. The envelope used on the THLS displayed the survey logo in the top left-hand corner, to give the mailing a more "friendly" appearance, and included a return address at the bottom. It is important to encourage the return of undelivered questionnaires in order to interpret response rates to postal surveys. The THLS generally receives about 6% post office returns.

ENVELOPE STUFFING

Envelope stuffing is an extremely important part of the postal survey process – not least because it can require an awful lot of time and effort. It is unlikely to be possible to stuff more than 200 envelopes per hour – in many cases it is not possible to exceed 50 per hour. With small surveys, researchers often stuff the envelopes themselves, but if there are 1,000 envelopes to stuff, say, at 50 per hour this will take three solid days of researcher time. Envelope stuffing can be a boring and demoralising task, and those doing it will also be prone to paper cuts. This must be considered at the planning stage. A better option might be to use a mailing house, which should cost in the region of £40 per 1,000 packets.

If the job is being done in-house, however, it is important to use self-sealing envelopes, as it is quicker and less likely to cause injury. Envelope stuffing is also important in terms of survey error. Careful control must be exercised to ensure that the identifier (serial number) on the questionnaire corresponds with the addressee.

Another consideration with postal surveys is a strategy for dealing with mailings to inappropriate people, for example people who have died recently. The survey control system must ensure that such people do not receive any reminders or further mailings, and the researcher must consider whether they are going to write a letter of apology.

MAIL SORT

Regina Dengler then described a system called Mail Sort, which is a service of the Royal Mail that can save money for postal surveys. It saves money in two ways. First, the sender pays a rate based on the exact weight rather than a range. For example, for a 28g packet one would normally have to pay the postage for 20g to 50g, which is 28p. But using Mail Sort one pays the rate for 28g, which is 24p. Second, there is an overall discount which, in this example, would bring the unit price down to 21p. To obtain these savings, the sender has to undertake to sort the packets by postal district, all addresses must include postcodes, and at least 1,000 packets must be mailed simultaneously. But because the savings in postage can be considerable, it can be possible to use a mailing house to do the sorting and still make a net saving.

IDENTIFICATION NUMBERS

The use of identifiers (serial numbers) is another important practical issue. The THLS uses an identifier on the top-left corner of the front of the questionnaire. Being located on the left, by the spine of the document, makes it easier to flick through piles of questionnaires in order to locate a particular number. Some researchers would argue that the identifier should be "hidden" in the middle or at the back, or that it should be printed using ultra violet ink to make it invisible, but the experience of the THLS was that people generally accept an obvious identifier. Some may question its purpose, but an explanation of its use to generate reminders is usually accepted, and only a tiny handful of respondents return a questionnaire with the identifier removed or obliterated. Each sample member must of course have a unique identifier, so that it can be used to generate reminders, and to query responses if necessary. Hand written numbers are best avoided due to risk of transcription errors and illegibility.

SUB-CONTRACTING

For any aspects of the survey that are being subcontracted it is important to get several quotes and to be clear what the quote covers. For example, if data entry is to be sub-contracted, the level of accuracy and validation should be specified. An apparently more expensive quote could be due to the fact that it is the only one to include automatic verification. The prior experience and capabilities of potential sub-contractors should also be considered. The THLS rejected one data entry company whose office seemed far too small to hold the questionnaires! Transport of survey documents also requires planning. How are the questionnaires going to get from the printers to the mailing house, and from the research team to the data entry company and back again?

When sub-contractors are involved, security and confidentiality become particularly important issues, especially if one company is doing both the mailing and the data entry. It must be ensured that names and

10

addresses and data are kept separate. Also subcontractors must be able to work to specified deadlines. And it is important to have one key contact at the sub-contractor's office who maintains overall control and takes responsibility for liaison with the researchers.

OTHER ISSUES

Publicity can be used to raise the public profile of a survey, and may consequently boost response. Feedback should also be considered. It seems only fair to offer some sort of feedback in return for co-operation with the survey. This may be done via general media dissemination of results or by sending a summary findings sheet direct to sample members. Another option is to offer sample members some relevant information. On a survey on a sensitive subject, the THLS team had enclosed a card with emergency

telephone numbers; on a diet survey, respondents were offered the option of ticking a box to receive more information on diet. Such options increase the survey administration workload and cost, of course.

Storage of questionnaires is something not to be taken lightly. If the sample size is large, a lot of room is required. The questionnaires must be stored in a comprehensible and accessible way, to allow resolution of edit queries and so on.

Finally, it must be remembered that the completion of field work is not the end of the story. It remains to check, edit, and analyse the data, write reports and papers, disseminate the findings and so on. It is also particularly important to document and evaluate all relevant aspects of the survey methodology, in order to provide guidance for future surveys, as well as to aid interpretation of the data from this particular survey.

References

1 Cartwright, A (1983) *Health Surveys in Practice and Potential*. London: Kings Fund.
2 Scott, C (1961) Research on mail surveys. *Journal of the Royal Statistical Society Series A*, vol. 124: 143-205.
3 Roberts, H, Pearson, J C G, and Dengler, R (1993) The impact of a postcard against a questionnaire as a first reminder in a postal lifestyle survey. *Health Education Research*, vol.47: 334-335.
4 Jacoby, A (1990) Possible factors affecting response to postal questionnaires: findings from a study of general practitioner services. *JPHM*, vol. 12: 131-135.
5 Choi, B C, Pak, A W, and Purdham, J T (1990) Effects of mailing strategies on response rate, response time, and cost in a questionnaire study among nurses. *Epidemiology*, vol. 1: 72-74.
6 Harvey, L (1987) Factors affecting response rates to mailed questionnaires: a comprehensive literature review. *Journal of the Market Research Society*, vol. 29: 341-353.
7 Goyder, J (1986) Survey response behaviour: motives and attitudes. *SCPR Survey Methods Newsletter*, Autumn: 4-5.